Student Study Guide to Accompany

EDUCATIONAL PSYCHOLOGY:

DEVELOPING LEARNERS

Third Edition

Jeanne Ellis Ormrod

University of Northern Colorado
University of New Hampshire

Merrill,
an imprint of Prentice Hall

Upper Saddle River, New Jersey   *Columbus, Ohio*

©2000 by Prentice-Hall, Inc.
Pearson Education
Upper Saddle River, New Jersey 07458

Printed in the United States of America

10 9 8 7 6 5 4 3 2

ISBN: 0-13-013977-7

PREFACE

As I wrote the third edition of *Educational Psychology: Developing Learners*, I had two primary goals in mind. First, I wanted to share many of the things that psychologists have discovered about school-age children and adolescents—how they change as they grow older, how they learn most effectively, what things motivate them, and so on—and to do it in a way that my readers would find informative, enjoyable, and at times perhaps even fascinating. Second, I wanted to give future teachers a toolbox full of ideas about how they can best help students with diverse backgrounds and abilities achieve academic, personal, and social success at school.

I hope that you learn a great deal from reading *Educational Psychology*. I have done several things in the book itself to help you learn and remember what you read more effectively. I've been selective about what I've included in the book, focusing on the concepts and principles that I think are most important for teachers to know and making sure that I explain those concepts and principles in an understandable fashion. I've included two classroom case studies in each chapter and incorporated numerous other examples of students and teachers in action throughout the text and in "Into the Classroom" boxes. Using "Thinking About What You Know" questions, I've asked you to consider some of your own personal experiences that may be directly relevant to topics under discussion. I've included many "Experiencing Firsthand" exercises that illustrate important principles of thinking, learning, and behavior by showing you how *you* think, learn, and behave. And I've used the margins of the book both to highlight classroom applications and to encourage you to think more deeply about some of the ideas I present.

This *Student Study Guide* provides additional ways of helping you learn and remember what you read in *Educational Psychology*. It presents a brief overview of each chapter. It describes common misconceptions that students have when they begin reading about a particular topic—misconceptions that often interfere with their ability to understand and interpret the material accurately. It lists a number of "Focus Questions" that you should be able to answer once you've read each chapter. It provides many "Application Exercises" through which you can practice applying the concepts and principles you're studying to classroom situations. It answers some of the questions that appear in the margins of the textbook. It includes examples of the types of questions you may find on any tests that your instructor may give you. Finally, it includes three supplementary readings that your instructor may assign.

A Companion Website accompanies the textbook as well; this site can give you additional assistance as you read and study the textbook. In addition to presenting some of the same features you see here in the *Student Study Guide*, the site also provides a "Message Board" where you can communicate with your instructor and classmates, as well as a list of other Internet sites related to course content. You can find the Companion Website on the Internet at www.prenhall.com/ormrod.

Our knowledge of how children and adolescents learn and develop increases rapidly with each passing year. As a result, I will be writing fourth editions of both *Educational Psychology* and the *Student Study Guide* sometime within the next few years. I am always eager to hear from my readers. Please send your comments and suggestions to either of my two e-mail addresses: jormrod@ttlc.net or jormrod@bentley.unco.edu.

Enjoy the book!

J.E.O.

CONTENTS

USING THE STUDENT STUDY GUIDE

Chapters 1 through 16 of this study guide include several features that should help you learn, remember, and apply the material presented in Chapters 1 through 16 of *Educational Psychology*. Let me tell you a little bit about each one of these features.

Chapter Overview

At the beginning of each chapter in this study guide, I give a brief overview of the topics that its corresponding chapter in the textbook addresses. As you will discover when you read textbook Chapter 13, such an overview is called an *advance organizer*. Numerous research studies have shown that students can more effectively remember the things that they read when they have a general idea ahead of time of what they will be reading about.

Common Student Beliefs and Misconceptions Related to Chapter Content

Research tells us that when students have erroneous beliefs about a topic they are studying, they often misinterpret the new information they receive and so learn it incorrectly. Here in the study guide, I alert you to some of the beliefs and misconceptions I have observed in my own students over the years—prior "knowledge" that has occasionally wreaked havoc with their ability to learn successfully in my classroom. If you recognize any of these beliefs and misconceptions in yourself, I urge you to read the textbook with the mind-set that you will encounter information that contradicts what you now believe.

Chapter Outline and Focus Questions

Each chapter includes a two-column table that lists headings for each section, along with "focus questions" that you should be able to answer once you've finished reading that section. Use these questions to test yourself on what you've learned from your reading. Use them again when you study for any exams that your instructor might give you. (The Companion Website at www.prenhall.com/ormrod provides more general "Key Questions" that can guide your studying as well.)

Chapter Glossary

The chapter glossary presents definitions of all the key concepts that are introduced in boldface print in the chapter and then listed at the end of the chapter. (This glossary is also available on the book's Companion Website at www.prenhall.com/ormrod.)

Application Exercises

In the textbook itself, I've included numerous applications of the concepts and principles that I've described. Here in the study guide, I give *you* the opportunity to apply many of these same concepts and principles. Each application exercise includes a number of situations for you to analyze and interpret using the ideas that a particular chapter presents. As you do these exercises, I encourage you to proceed in the following manner:

1. First see if you can interpret each situation using only your *memory* of the ideas you have read in the textbook.
2. If you are unable to carry out Step 1 successfully, reread the relevant sections of the textbook and once again try to interpret the situation.
3. As a last resort, refer to the answers that follow each application exercise. Don't look at these answers until after you've made a concerted effort to apply the material on your own.

Keep in mind that the answers I provide are *my* interpretations of the situations, based on the concepts and principles presented in a particular chapter. If you disagree with, or perhaps don't understand, any of my analyses, you may want to consult your instructor for his or her opinion.

Answers to Selected Margin Notes

I've used the margins of the textbook to pose many questions that will, I hope, encourage you to think about and make sense of the things you are reading. Some of the questions might be answered very differently, yet equally correctly, by different students. But others have clear right and wrong answers. I answer the latter set of questions here in the study guide.

Sample Test Questions

Ask your instructor if he or she will be using the test bank that accompanies *Educational Psychology* when constructing tests for your class. If so, you can find examples of the kinds of test questions your instructor will be asking you here in the study guide. Some questions have a number one (**1**) to their left; these items assess *lower-level skills* and ask you about the information actually presented in the textbook. Other questions have a number two (**2**) to their left; these items assess *higher-level skills* and ask you to apply, analyze, or synthesize concepts, principles, theories, and research findings. You may want to use both kinds of sample test questions to spot-check yourself on what you have learned. (These test questions also appear on the Companion Website at www.prenhall.com/ormrod. The website provides hints about where in the textbook you can find information relevant to each question, and it gives immediate feedback about your answers to the questions.)

USING THE COMPACT DISK

Included with the third edition of *Educational Psychology: Developing Learners* is a compact disk (CD) called "Simulations in Educational Psychology." This CD contains four activities that resemble actual research studies in educational psychology:

- The Pendulum Experiment (to be used with either Chapter 2 or Chapter 9)
- Assessing Moral Reasoning (to be used with Chapter 3)
- Bartlett's Ghosts (to be used with Chapter 7)
- Intuitive Physics (to be used with Chapter 7, Chapter 8, or Chapter 9)

You will participate in these activities in much the same way that students in the original research studies participated. Each activity will ask you to make certain responses, after which you will receive feedback about your responses. Following the activity, you will discover some possible implications that the study has for educational practice.

To use the CD, simply place it in the appropriate disk drive in your computer. Instructions on the CD itself will guide you from there.

STUDY TIPS

As both a teacher and an educational researcher, I have discovered that many college students simply do not know how to study. Following are a number of suggestions for reading and studying textbooks more effectively. Many of them are from my 1989 book, *Using Your Head: An Owner's Manual*.

- **Determine your best learning times and use them wisely.** Are you a "morning person"? Are you a "night owl"? Identify the times that you read and concentrate most effectively, and leave the dirty dishes, campus errands, and favorite television programs (use a VCR to record them!) for times when you're relatively brain dead.

- **Be realistic about how much you can learn in one sitting.** As you will discover when you read Chapter 6, you can think about and learn only a limited amount of information in a limited amount of time. Don't try to do too much too fast. And certainly don't leave everything until the last minute!

- **Minimize distractions.** Find a quiet place to study where you will have few things competing for your attention. Turn the radio and CD player off, or play soft background music that you will barely notice. And definitely turn off that television set!

- **Mark up the book.** Underline or highlight the main ideas of each paragraph and section. Mark essential details that support the main ideas. Put brackets or stars beside examples that you find especially helpful.

- **Pay attention as you read.** Don't let your eyes wander mindlessly down the pages. Keep your mind actively attuned to the things you are reading.

- **Relate what you read to things you already know.** Think about how the ideas I present are consistent with personal experiences you've had or with things you've learned in other classes.

- **Elaborate on what you read, going beyond it and adding to it.** Draw inferences from the general statements I make. Generate your own examples of the concepts and principles I describe. Derive implications for your own teaching practice from the theories I present.

- **Use the tables to help you organize and summarize the material.** Use the "Compare/Contrast" tables to find similarities and differences among various positions and perspectives. Use the "Principles/Assumptions" tables to focus in on key ideas.

- **Use the pictures, photographs, and cartoons to help you remember the ideas they represent.** For most students, visual images provide one highly effective means of remembering information.

- **Use mnemonics to help you remember hard-to-learn information.** Use memory tricks that make difficult ideas more memorable. For examples of strategies you might use, see the section "Using Mnemonics in the Absence of Relevant Prior Knowledge" in Chapter 6 of your textbook.

✏ **Periodically check yourself to make sure you understand and remember what you've read.** Try to summarize each section as soon as you've read it. Ask yourself questions similar to the focus questions in each chapter of this study guide, or have a classmate ask you such questions. Try to explain a difficult concept to someone who doesn't yet understand it.

✏ **Answer the questions in the margins.** These questions encourage you to do some of the things I've just suggested, such as relating new ideas to your prior experiences, drawing inferences, and periodically checking yourself.

✏ **Know when to quit.** If you're tired or having a hard time concentrating, close your book for the time being. Pick it up again when you're more rested and less distracted.

✏ **Review.** Research is clear on this point: Periodic review of previously learned material definitely helps students remember it more effectively and accurately.

✏ **Reward yourself for your accomplishments.** Give yourself a break or a treat when you've finished a section or a chapter. Get a bite to eat. Call a friend on the telephone. Go to the mall, the movies, or the park.

As you read the textbook, you will learn even more about how you can learn most effectively. In fact, I urge you to skim Chapters 6, 7, and 8 (even before your instructor assigns them!) to get some ideas.

Chapter Study Guides

Chapter 1

EDUCATIONAL PSYCHOLOGY AND TEACHER DECISION MAKING

Chapter Overview

This chapter gives you a taste of what educational psychology is all about. You will begin the chapter by taking the OOPS Test, a pretest that may alert you to certain misconceptions you have about learning, development, motivation, or classroom assessment. You will discover why educational psychologists rely heavily on psychological and educational research for the conclusions they draw; you will also see how those conclusions evolve into principles and theories that can guide you in your efforts to promote students' learning and development. You will find several strategies through which you can also promote your *own* learning and development as a teacher. At the end of the chapter, you will look ahead to the rest of the book, examining seven themes that run throughout it and learning three general principles that can help you study educational psychology more effectively.

Common Student Beliefs and Misconceptions Related to Chapter Content

Below are several misconceptions that college students sometimes have when they first enroll in an educational psychology course. As you read Chapter 1, be on the lookout for evidence that contradicts these common misconceptions:

1. Sometimes students erroneously believe that the field of educational psychology deals primarily with counseling techniques or psychotherapy in the classroom.

2. Some students believe that good teaching decisions rest solely on "common sense" and that educational and psychological research findings have little relevance to classroom practice.

3. Students often infer cause-effect relationships from correlational data. In fact, only experimental studies allow us to draw conclusions about cause-effect relationships.

4. Many students have misconceptions about effective study strategies. For example, some believe that they can learn course material through sheer exposure to it, even when they are not paying attention or otherwise thinking about it in any way.

CHAPTER OUTLINE	FOCUS QUESTIONS
OOPS—A PRETEST Answer Key for the OOPS	• Do you have possible misconceptions about some of the topics discussed in the book?

DRAWING CONCLUSIONS FROM PSYCHOLOGICAL AND EDUCATIONAL RESEARCH
 	
    Descriptive Studies
 	
    Correlational Studies
 	
    Experimental Studies
 	
    An Example: Research on Visual-Spatial Thinking
 	
    Drawing Conclusions from Research: A Cautionary Note
	• Can you describe the three types of research studies in your own words? What kinds of questions can each type of study answer?
	
	• Why is it important for teachers to be aware of cause-effect relationships whenever possible?
	
	• Why can we draw conclusions about cause-effect relationships only from experimental studies? What essential condition is absent in descriptive and correlational studies?

DERIVING PRINCIPLES AND THEORIES	• How are principles and theories different? Can you think of additional examples of both principles and theories?
USING PRINCIPLES AND THEORIES TO MAKE CLASSROOM DECISIONS	• What role do principles and theories play in teacher decision making?
DEVELOPING AS A TEACHER	• In what way does the job of teaching become easier as time goes on? • How can you continue to grow as a teacher?
LOOKING AHEAD TO THE FOLLOWING CHAPTERS	• What topics will you learn more about as you read the book?
THE BIG PICTURE: COMMON THEMES THROUGHOUT THE BOOK Considering Student Diversity	• What seven themes will you see throughout the book? Make some predictions about the chapters in which you will encounter each one. • What do we mean by the term *students with special needs*? What implication does the practice of *inclusion* have for classroom teachers?
STUDYING EDUCATIONAL PSYCHOLOGY MORE EFFECTIVELY	• What three strategies does the book suggest you use as you read and study?

Supplementary Reading

Your instructor may assign Appendix B, "Describing Relationships with Correlation Coefficients," as supplementary reading; you can find it at the end of your textbook.

Chapter Glossary

Control group. A group of people in a research study who are given either no treatment or a presumably ineffective (placebo) treatment. The subsequent performance of this group is compared to the performance of one or more treatment groups.

Correlation. The extent to which two variables are related to each other, such that when one variable increases, the other either increases or decreases in a somewhat predictable fashion.

Correlational study. A research study that explores relationships among variables. Such a study enables researchers to predict one variable on the basis of their knowledge of another but not to draw a conclusion about a cause-effect relationship.

Descriptive study. A research study that describes situations. Such a study enables researchers to draw conclusions about the current state of affairs but not about correlational or cause-effect relationships.

Elaboration. A cognitive process in which learners expand on new information based on what they already know.

Experimental study (experiment). A research study that involves the manipulation of one variable to determine its possible effect on another variable. It enables researchers to draw conclusions about cause-effect relationships.

Inclusion. The practice of educating all students, even those with severe and multiple disabilities, in neighborhood schools and general education classrooms.

Pedagogical content knowledge. Knowledge about effective methods of teaching a specific content area.

Principle. A description of how one variable influences another variable. It evolves when similar research studies yield similar results time after time.

Students with special needs. Students who are different enough from their peers that they require specially adapted instructional materials and practices.

Theory. An organized body of concepts and principles related to a particular phenomenon; a description of possible underlying mechanisms to explain why certain principles are true.

Treatment group. A group of people in a research study who are given a particular experimental treatment (e.g., a particular method of instruction).

Visual-spatial thinking. The ability to imagine and mentally manipulate two- and three-dimensional figures in one's mind.

Here is an additional glossary item if your instructor has assigned Appendix B:

Correlation coefficient. A statistic that indicates the nature of the relationship between two variables.

Application Exercise #1: Drawing Conclusions from Research Studies

From which of the following research studies can we draw conclusions about cause-effect relationships?

1. A biology teacher is teaching her students the hierarchy that biologists use to classify living things: kingdom, phylum, class, order, family, genus, and species. She wants to find out if the sentence "King Philip comes over for good spaghetti"—a sentence with words that begin with the same letters as the words in the hierarchy (K P C O F G S)—will help her students remember the hierarchy. She makes two handouts describing the classification hierarchy; both handouts are the same, except that one includes the "King Philip" sentence and one does not. She shuffles the two handouts together in a pile and distributes one handout to each student in her class. The following day, she finds that students who have been given the "King Philip" sentence remember the hierarchy more accurately.

2. Many of the boys in the town of Greenwood play soccer in the local recreational soccer program. Greenwood has no equivalent program for girls' soccer. The physical education teacher at Greenwood Elementary School believes that the boys' soccer skills are superior to those of the girls and suspects that the boys' greater experience playing soccer has made the difference. To test his hypothesis, he develops a test of soccer skills that he can score objectively, and he finds that, yes, the boys do have better soccer skills.

3. A junior high social studies teacher finds that some of her students can easily remember the ideas she presents, yet others have trouble remembering anything from one day to the next. She suspects that the students who have better memories for class material are those who are taking more complete notes in class. She collects students' notebooks one day and finds that students who are doing well in class take twice as many notes as students who are doing poorly.

4. Thirty fifth graders are learning how to add, subtract, multiply, and divide fractions by means of instructional computer software. The students are each given a computer disk that enables them to load the software on a personal computer in the school's computer lab; they then progress at their own pace through the computer program. The program gives them many practice problems that they can solve directly on the computer; it also provides immediate feedback as to whether or not they have solved each problem correctly. Unbeknownst to anyone, some of the students have received faulty software: rather than receiving feedback after every problem they solve, they get feedback after every third problem. These students learn how to work with fractions more slowly than do students who get feedback about every problem they solve.

5. Ms. Santos notices that some of her students get exceptionally tense when they take tests in her class, and these students tend to do more poorly on her tests. With the assistance of a local college professor, she has each student take a mock classroom test while being hooked up to a biofeedback machine. She finds that students who get low test scores show signs of greater physiological stress than students who get high scores.

6. Ms. Randall's class has fifteen copies each of the first and second editions of the same geography textbook. In the second edition, the main idea in each paragraph is emphasized with italics; otherwise, the second edition is exactly the same as the first. To distribute the textbooks as fairly as possible, Ms. Randall chooses the students who will receive each edition by drawing names out of a hat. She doesn't tell her students that some of them will have an advantage over others, however. Two weeks later, she finds that students reading the second edition perform better on their first geography quiz.

7. Children from low-income families who participate in a Headstart preschool program before they begin kindergarten do better in school than children who have not participated in Headstart.

8. An educational psychologist videotapes 20 high school history teachers in action for a period of four weeks. He then codes each teacher statement into one of three categories: presenting new information, asking a question, or giving instructions. He finds that when teachers ask more questions in class, students are more likely to do well on the districtwide history achievement test given later that year.

9. Mr. Hughes's students are packed into his tiny classroom like sardines. He wants to discourage cheating in such tight quarters, so when he develops his first multiple-choice test, he constructs two different forms of the test. Both forms have the same test items. However, on one form of the test, the easiest items are at the beginning; on the other form, the most difficult items appear first. Mr. Hughes distributes the two forms of the test to his students in a random fashion. As he is scoring the test papers that night, he discovers that students who had the easiest items at the beginning have done better on the test overall than students who had the most difficult items first.

10. As part of a districtwide evaluation for merit pay, a school principal observes each of her teachers in action for an entire school day, then writes an evaluation of his or her classroom performance. In looking over the completed evaluations, she discovers that she has evaluated teachers with a Master of Arts degree more highly than teachers with only a Bachelor of Arts degree.

Answers to Application Exercise #1

1. Cause-effect. We can conclude that knowledge of the sentence influenced memory for the hierarchy. The teacher is manipulating students' access or nonaccess to the "King Philip" sentence. The handouts are the same in every way *except* for the sentence. And by shuffling the two handouts before she distributes them, she is able to assign students to the treatment and control groups in an essentially random fashion.

2. No cause-effect. We cannot conclude that the soccer program causes the difference between boys and girls. Girls and boys are likely to have other background differences as well; furthermore, we have not ruled out possible genetic differences between boys and girls. To determine the actual effect of the soccer program, we would have to have both boys and girls involved in the program and would also have to select the participants on a random basis—conditions that are probably not possible in this situation.

3. No cause-effect. We cannot conclude that note taking leads to better memory for class material. The two groups of students are likely to be different in other ways besides note taking; for example, the higher-achieving students may be more interested in the subject matter than their classmates, or they may be more motivated to get good grades.

4. Cause-effect. We can conclude that more frequent feedback leads to faster learning. The two versions of software are identical except for the amount of feedback they give. The computer disks appear to have been distributed in a random fashion, so that those students receiving the faulty software are similar, on average, to those receiving error-free software.

5. No cause-effect. We cannot conclude that tension influences test performance. The high scorers and low scorers may be different in additional ways; for example, the high scorers might know the material better and be less tense during the test as a result.

6. Cause-effect. We can conclude that having the main ideas emphasized in the textbook facilitates learning. The textbooks are identical in every way except for the italics, and the two groups of students have been chosen randomly. (Now that Ms. Randall knows there is a difference, she underlines the main ideas in each copy of the first edition so that all her students have equivalent instructional materials.)

7. No cause-effect. The study does not necessarily lead to the conclusion that Headstart promotes later school achievement. The Headstart participants might be different from nonparticipants in a number of ways; for example, they may have parents who are more concerned about their school achievement.

8. No cause-effect. We cannot conclude that asking questions promotes achievement in history. The teachers may be different in other ways besides their question-asking; for example, those who ask more questions may be more enthusiastic instructors or have higher expectations for student performance.

9. Cause-effect. We can conclude that placing easier items at the beginning of the test facilitates test performance. Everything about the tests is the same except for the order of the items, and students receiving each form of the test have been selected randomly.

10. No cause-effect. We cannot conclude that an advanced degree leads to better performance in the classroom. The teachers with an M.A. are likely to be different from those with a B.A. in several ways. For example, they will probably be older and more experienced than their less educated colleagues. They may also be more motivated to improve their teaching.

Answer to Margin Note

Note: Some of the margin notes in every chapter of the textbook pose questions that ask you to elaborate on what you're learning. When the questions have definite right answers, I will provide the answers here in the *Student Study Guide*.

- Page 14: *Which of these italicized statements propose an internal mechanism to explain human performance? In other words, which ones are theories rather than principles?*
Explanations of behavior based on internal mechanisms are most evident in the first, third, and fifth statements, which propose that *prior knowledge, attention,* and a *reason to learn* (three things that are "inside" an individual) are important factors influencing learning. The second statement talks about thinking, but there is no attempt to explain *why* abstract thought emerges later than concrete thought; therefore, this statement reflects a principle rather than a theory. The fourth statement describes the effects of consequences on behavior without any reference to internal mechanisms at all, so it is also a principle rather than a theory.

Sample Test Questions

Items marked with a "1)" on the left-hand side are lower-level questions that assess your general knowledge and understanding of the material. Items marked with a "2)" on the left-hand side are higher-level questions that assess your ability to apply what you have learned to a new situation.

Multiple-Choice

1) 1. Considering research findings described in the textbook, identify the only *true* statement among the statements below.
    a. In most cases, students quickly change their erroneous beliefs about the world once they hear more accurate explanations.
    b. As early as second grade, boys begin to demonstrate noticeably higher achievement in mathematics than girls.
    c. Students are most likely to learn when they are quite anxious about their classroom performance.
    d. Students who take notes on class material are more likely to remember it later on.

2) 2. Which one of the following conclusions can be drawn only from an *experimental* study?
    a. Teachers can help students understand classroom material better when they occasionally stop to ask questions that students must answer.
    b. Students who elaborate on classroom material remember it better than those who don't.
    c. Teachers who have higher expectations for their students have students who actually do achieve at higher levels.
    d. Older children think more logically than younger children.

2)   3.   Three of the following are principles of learning. Which one is a *theory* rather than a principle?
  a. Students learn more quickly when they get consistent feedback about right and wrong answers.
  b. Visual aids are effective instructional tools because they help students form visual images of classroom material.
  c. Cooperative learning activities help students form friendships with classmates of different cultural backgrounds.
  d. Students who study for one hour each day for five days remember more than students who study for five hours all at once.

2)   4.   The textbook describes how you are likely to develop as a teacher. Which one of the following common sayings best summarizes the textbook's description of teacher development?
  a. Beauty is in the eye of the beholder.
  b. A rolling stone gathers no moss.
  c. Turn the other cheek.
  d. Practice makes perfect.

2)   5.   Which one of the following best illustrates *inclusion* as educators use the term?
  a. Ashley, who has a severe and highly contagious case of hepatitis, is home-schooled by a special tutor provided by the school district.
  b. Brian, a sixth grader who has exceptionally poor reading skills, is in a class especially designed for students with learning disabilities.
  c. Carol, who is blind, is in the regular classroom all day long; she has her reading materials tape-recorded or printed in braille.
  d. Darren, a ten-year-old with mental retardation, spends most of each day with a special education teacher, but he joins a regular second-grade class for art and music.

Essay

1)   6.   Explain how descriptive studies, correlational studies, and experimental studies are different from one another, and give a concrete example of a research question that each type of study might address.

2)   7.   A researcher finds that students who are physically aggressive at school are more likely to have abusive parents than students who are not aggressive. The researcher concludes that child abuse causes aggressive behavior. Is this conclusion warranted? Why or why not?

Answers to Sample Test Questions

1. d—Only this alternative is consistent with research findings presented in the textbook's discussion of the OOPS test. (See the answers to items 2, 4, 6, and 9 of the OOPS.)

2. a—A cause-effect relationship is implied here: Teacher questions promote greater student learning. The other three alternatives describe relationships among two variables but do not propose that one variable causes another. (See the discussion of correlational and experimental studies on textbook pages 8-9.)

3. b—A visual image is an internal, mental phenomenon used to explain the effectiveness of visual aids. (See the discussion of theories on textbook pages 12-14.)

4. d—Development of teaching expertise is most likely to come with practice and further education (see textbook pages 15-16).

5. c—Inclusion is the practice of educating all students, even those with special educational needs, within a general education setting for most or all of the school day (see textbook page 20).

6. The three types of studies are described on textbook pages 8-9. Table 1-1 presents several examples of research questions that can be answered by each type of study; you can use three of these questions in your response, or you can use your own new examples.

7. The conclusion is *not* warranted. The researcher has conducted a correlational study, rather than an experimental study, and therefore has not ruled out other possible explanations for the differences in aggressiveness. (For example, perhaps impoverished living conditions are the cause of both child abuse and aggression.) See the discussion of "Drawing Conclusions from Research: A Cautionary Note" on textbook pages 11-12.

Chapter 2

COGNITIVE AND LINGUISTIC DEVELOPMENT

Chapter Overview

This chapter presents several prominent views of how thinking, learning, and language capabilities change throughout childhood and adolescence. After considering general principles of development, you will explore Jean Piaget's classic theory of cognitive development—a theory that describes four discrete stages of increasingly more complex and logical thinking processes. You will then examine two perspectives of cognitive development that are prominent at the present time: (1) Lev Vygotsky's theory, which proposes that children acquire more sophisticated thinking processes through their interactions with adults and other more advanced individuals, and (2) information processing theory, which focuses on how specific cognitive processes and learning strategies evolve during childhood and adolescence. As you turn to linguistic development later in the chapter, you will find that children's language skills continue to develop throughout the elementary and secondary school years. Finally, you will discover how your students are likely to show considerable diversity in their cognitive and linguistic abilities.

Included in the chapter are numerous suggestions for classroom practice. For example, you will see how Piaget's concepts of *assimilation* and *accommodation* and Vygotsky's concept of *internalization* have clear implications for instruction. And you will look at current research findings regarding how students most easily learn a second language. Some of the chapter's suggestions will show you how to match instructional strategies to the age level of your students. Many others will show you how, as a teacher, you can help maximize your students' cognitive and linguistic growth during the time that you have them.

Common Student Beliefs and Misconceptions Related to Chapter Content

Listed below are a number of commonly held beliefs that may interfere with an accurate understanding of cognitive and linguistic development. As you read Chapter 2, be on the lookout for evidence that contradicts these ideas:

1. Some future teachers believe that they only need to know the developmental characteristics of the particular age group at which they will be teaching. In reality, effective teachers know how learners develop *throughout* the K-12 school years and use that knowledge to promote their own students' development.

2. Most people typically use the word *maturation* in a different sense than developmentalists use the term (see textbook page 28 for developmentalists' meaning of the word).

3. Many students who have previously studied Piaget's theory believe that his four stages of cognitive development are accurate descriptions of how children think and behave at various ages.

4. Most people typically use the word *egocentrism* to mean "self-centeredness"—a meaning very different from Piaget's meanings of the term (see textbook pages 33 and 39).

CHAPTER OUTLINE	FOCUS QUESTIONS
BASIC PRINCIPLES OF HUMAN DEVELOPMENT Role of the Brain in Development	• What general principles are common across many aspects of child and adolescent development? • What do all stage theories have in common? • What do developmentalists mean by *maturation*? • How have various theorists interpreted current findings in neurological research?

PIAGET'S THEORY OF COGNITIVE DEVELOPMENT
  Piaget's Basic Assumptions
  Piaget's Stages of Cognitive Development
  Current Perspectives on Piaget's Theory
	• What assumptions underlie Piaget's theory of cognitive development? What roles do *assimilation, accommodation,* and *equilibration* play in development? What implications do Piaget's assumptions have for classroom practice?
	
	• What characteristics are associated with each of Piaget's four stages? What strengths and weaknesses do children have at each stage?
	
	• What form does *egocentrism* take during the preoperational stage? What form does it take during the formal operational stage?
	
	• Which characteristics of the concrete operational and formal operational stages are especially relevant to mathematics and science instruction?
	
	• What forms of reasoning are you likely to see in students at the grade level you will be teaching? What implications do these reasoning capabilities have for your own teaching?
	
	• What does recent research tell us about the strengths and weaknesses of Piaget's theory?

CHAPTER OUTLINE	FOCUS QUESTIONS

VYGOTSKY'S THEORY OF COGNITIVE DEVELOPMENT
 	
  Vygotsky's Basic Assumptions
 	
  Contemporary Applications of Vygotsky's Ideas
	• What assumptions underlie Vygotsky's theory of cognitive development? What role does *internalization* play in development? What implications do Vygotsky's assumptions have for classroom practice?
	
	• In what ways do thought and language become interdependent? From Vygotsky's perspective, what function do self-talk and inner speech play?
	
	• Describe Vygotsky's *zone of proximal development (ZPD)* in your own words. Can you think of some tasks that are likely to be in the ZPD of the students you will be teaching?
	
	• What do contemporary theorists mean by *guided participation* and *apprenticeships*?
	
	• What is a *cognitive apprenticeship*? In what specific way is it "cognitive"?
	
	• What is *scaffolding*? How does it change over time? Can you think of a new example of this concept?

AN INFORMATION PROCESSING VIEW OF COGNITIVE DEVELOPMENT
 	
  Attention
 	
  Learning Strategies
 	
  Knowledge Base
 	
  Metacognition
	• How is information processing theorists' notion of *trends* in cognitive development different from Piaget's notion of discrete stages?
	
	• As children develop, what changes do we see in attention, learning strategies, knowledge, and metacognition? What implications do these developmental changes have for teaching children of different ages?
	
	• From the perspective of information processing theory, what strengths and weaknesses are students likely to have at the grade level you will be teaching?

COMPARING PIAGET, VYGOTSKY, AND INFORMATION PROCESSING THEORY	• What ideas do the perspectives of Piaget, Vygotsky, and information processing theorists have in common?

CHAPTER OUTLINE	FOCUS QUESTIONS

LINGUISTIC DEVELOPMENT
    Theoretical Perspectives on Language Development
    Trends in Language Development
    Learning a Second Language
	• Why do theorists believe that both heredity and environment play roles in language development?
	
	• In what ways do students' receptive and expressive language capabilities change during the school years? What abilities are students likely to have at the grade level you will be teaching?
	
	• What are *undergeneralization, overgeneralization,* and *overregularization*? Can you think of a new example of each of these phenomena?
	
	• What can teachers do to promote students' language development? How can they promote *metalinguistic awareness*?
	
	• What are the advantages of learning a second language? When is immersion more effective? When is bilingual education more effective?

CONSIDERING DIVERSITY IN COGNITIVE AND LINGUISTIC DEVELOPMENT Accommodating Students with Special Needs	• How are your students likely to differ from one another in terms of cognitive and linguistic development? • How can teachers adapt instruction to promote the cognitive and linguistic development of students with special needs?
THE BIG PICTURE: RECURRING THEMES IN COGNITIVE AND LINGUISTIC DEVELOPMENT	• What common themes do we see in both cognitive and linguistic development?

Using the Compact Disk

"The Pendulum Experiment" on the *Simulations in Educational Psychology* CD is a hands-on activity similar to the "Pendulum Problem" Experiencing Firsthand exercise presented in the textbook.

Chapter Glossary

Accommodation. In Piaget's theory, dealing with a new event by either modifying an existing scheme or forming a new one.

Actual developmental level. In Vygotsky's theory, the extent to which one can successfully perform a task independently.

Apprenticeship. A situation in which a learner works intensively with an expert to learn how to accomplish complex tasks.

Assimilation. In Piaget's theory, dealing with a new event in a way that is consistent with an existing scheme.

Bilingual education. An approach to second-language instruction in which students are instructed in academic subject areas in their native language while simultaneously being taught to speak and write in the second language. The amount of instruction delivered in the native language decreases as students become more proficient in the second language.

Cognitive apprenticeship. A mentorship in which a teacher and a student work together to accomplish a challenging task or solve a difficult problem; in the process, the teacher provides guidance about how to think about the task or problem.

Cognitive processes. The ways in which one thinks about (processes) information.

Concrete operations stage. Piaget's third stage of cognitive development, in which adultlike logic appears but is limited to concrete reality.

Conservation. The realization that if nothing is added or taken away, amount stays the same regardless of any alterations in shape or arrangement.

Constructivism. A theoretical perspective that proposes that learners construct a body of knowledge from their experiences—knowledge that may or may not be an accurate representation of external reality.

Deductive reasoning. Drawing a logical inference about something that must be true, given other information that has already been presented as true.

Developmental milestone. The appearance of a new, developmentally more advanced behavior.

Dialect. A form of English characteristic of a particular region or ethnic group.

Disequilibrium. The state of being *un*able to explain new events in terms of existing schemes.

Egocentric speech. Speaking without taking the perspective and knowledge of the listener into account.

Elaboration. A cognitive process in which learners expand on new information based on what they already know.

Equilibration. The movement from equilibrium to disequilibrium and back to equilibrium—a process that promotes the development of more complex forms of thought and knowledge.

Equilibrium. A state of being able to explain new events in terms of existing schemes.

Expressive language. The ability to communicate effectively through speaking and writing.

Formal operational egocentrism. The inability of individuals in Piaget's formal operations stage to separate abstract logical thinking from practical considerations and the unpredictability of human behavior.

Formal operations stage. Piaget's fourth and final stage of cognitive development, in which logical reasoning processes are applied to abstract ideas as well as to concrete objects.

Guided participation. Giving a child the necessary guidance and support to perform an activity in the adult world.

Immersion. An approach to second-language instruction in which students hear and speak that language almost exclusively within the classroom.

Inner speech. "Talking" to oneself mentally rather than aloud.

Internalization. In Vygotsky's theory, the process through which social activities evolve into mental activities.

Irreversibility. An inability to recognize that certain processes can be undone, or reversed.

Knowledge base. One's knowledge about specific topics and the world in general.

Learning strategy. One or more cognitive processes used intentionally for a particular learning task.

Level of potential development. In Vygotsky's theory, the extent to which one can successfully execute a task with the assistance of a more competent individual.

Limited English proficiency (LEP). A limited ability to understand and communicate in oral or written English, usually because English is not one's native language.

Maturation. The unfolding of genetically controlled changes as a child develops.

Metacognition. One's knowledge and beliefs regarding one's own cognitive processes, and one's resulting attempts to regulate those cognitive processes to maximize learning and memory.

Metalinguistic awareness. The extent to which one is able to think about the nature of language.

Multiple classification. The recognition that objects may belong to several categories simultaneously.

Object permanence. The realization that objects continue to exist even after they are removed from view.

Operation. In Piaget's theory, an organized and integrated system of thought processes.

Organization. A cognitive process in which learners find connections (e.g., forming categories, identifying hierarchical relationships) among the various pieces of information they need to learn.

Overgeneralization. Having too broad a meaning for a word, applying the word in situations where it's not appropriate.

Overregularization. Applying syntactical rules in situations where those rules don't apply.

Pragmatics. Knowledge about the culture-specific social conventions guiding verbal interactions.

Preoperational egocentrism. In Piaget's theory, the inability of children in the preoperational stage to view situations from another person's perspective.

Preoperational stage. Piaget's second stage of cognitive development, in which children can think about objects beyond their immediate view but do not yet reason in logical, adultlike ways.

Proportional thought. The ability to understand proportions (e.g., fractions, decimals, ratios) and use them effectively in mathematical problem solving.

Receptive language. The ability to understand the language that one hears or reads.

Rehearsal. A cognitive process in which information is repeated over and over as a possible way of learning and remembering it.

Reversibility. The ability to recognize that certain processes can be undone, or reversed.

Scaffolding. A support mechanism, provided by a more competent individual, that helps a learner successfully perform a task within his or her zone of proximal development.

Scheme. In Piaget's theory, an organized group of similar actions or thoughts.

Self-talk. Talking to oneself as a way of guiding oneself through a task; also known as *private speech*.

Semantics. The meanings of words and word combinations.

Sensitive period. An age range during which a certain aspect of a child's development is especially susceptible to environmental conditions.

Sensorimotor stage. Piaget's first stage of cognitive development, in which schemes are based on behaviors and perceptions.

Separation and control of variables. The ability to test one variable at a time while holding all other variables constant.

Single classification. The ability to classify objects in only one way at any given point in time.

Sociocultural perspective. A theoretical perspective that emphasizes the importance of society and culture for promoting cognitive development.

Stage. A period in a child's development characterized by certain behaviors and/or reasoning skills. The nature and sequence of different stages of development are believed by stage theorists to be relatively consistent from one child to another.

Stage theory. A theory that depicts development as a series of stages, with relatively slow growth within each stage and more rapid growth during the transition from one stage to another.

Symbolic thinking. The ability to represent and think about external objects and events in one's head.

Syntax. The set of rules that one uses (often unconsciously) to put words together into sentences.

Transductive reasoning. Making a mental leap from one specific thing to another, such as identifying one event as the cause of another simply because the two events occur close together in time.

Undergeneralization. An overly restricted meaning for a word, excluding some situations to which the word does, in fact, apply.

Universals. In development, the similar patterns we see in how children change over time regardless of the specific environment in which they are raised.

Zone of proximal development (ZPD). In Vygotsky's theory, the range of tasks between one's actual developmental level and one's level of potential development—that is, the range of tasks that one cannot yet perform independently but *can* perform with the help and guidance of others.

Application Exercise #2: Recognizing a Student's Zone of Proximal Development

Which of the following students are working within their *zone of proximal development*? Defend your choices.

1. An elementary physical education teacher is teaching her second graders the basics of soccer. She describes the different positions that team members might play and explains the specific roles that players in each position have. She breaks the class into two teams of eleven players each and assigns each student a specific position on the field. Yet once the ball is in motion, everyone on the field immediately flocks to it, resulting in a game of "magnet" ball.

2. Selena is learning how to play the trumpet. She still has trouble with some of the high notes but does better when her teacher reminds her what she needs to do.

3. When Mr. Marino asks his fifth graders to write a short story, they seem to be at a loss for ideas. But when he suggests that they write a "Just So" story explaining why the elephant has such a big trunk or why the giraffe has such a long neck, they are each able to write a story with a main character, plot, conflict, and resolution.

4. Julian can locate virtually any place on the globe if he knows its latitude and longitude.

5. An art teacher demonstrates how to paint with watercolors and then walks around the room to watch his students work. He offers guidance when he sees someone having trouble creating new colors or keeping different colors from running together on the paper.

6. Regina is quite adept at algebra problems. While her classmates are solving for x on paper, she arrives at the correct answer in her head.

7. A fourth-grade teacher asks his students to read an article in a recent issue of *Time* magazine. He describes the main point of the article before his students begin reading it, and he gives them several questions that they should try to answer as they read. Even so, his students are unable to understand what they are reading.

8. In her unit on genetics, a high school science teacher has students working with fruit flies. Because the students are initially confused about what they are supposed to do, she writes specific instructions on the chalkboard, then circulates around the room and assists students who are having trouble identifying males and females correctly.

Answers to Application Exercise #2

1. No. Even with assistance, the students are unable to play their respective positions.

2. Yes. Selena plays the high notes successfully only with her teacher's assistance.

3. Yes. The students can write a short story successfully only when Mr. Marino structures the task for them and gives them some ideas about characters and plots.

4. No. Using latitude and longitude is obviously an easy task for Julian, because he needs no help from anyone else.

5. Yes. The students are sometimes having trouble with watercolor technique and therefore benefit from their teacher's assistance.

6. No. Regina is solving the problems quickly and easily, without help from anyone else.

7. No. Even with their teacher's assistance, they are unable to comprehend the article.

8. Yes. The students are able to proceed only with their teacher's instructions, and some of them are having difficulty sex-typing the flies without her assistance.

Application Exercise #3: Identifying Typical and Atypical Behaviors

In the following scenarios, which students are exhibiting behaviors typical for their age-group, and which ones are not? Justify your choices on the basis of Piaget's theory, information processing theory, or research findings related to language development.

1. When a fourth-grade teacher describes decimals, her students are totally confused. She tries several different ways of teaching the concept *decimal*, but without success.

2. A high school freshman is very distractible in class. Any little noise seems to draw her attention away from what she is supposed to be doing.

3. A first grader asserts that a lobster can't possibly be an animal because it doesn't have fur.

4. A second grader living in an inner-city ghetto comes to school upset about a neighbor who was killed in a drive-by shooting the night before. "The world would be a much better place if it didn't have guns," she says despondently.

5. In a high school physics lab, students are instructed to design and conduct an experiment to determine whether or not *weight* affects the speed at which something falls. As the students compare the speed with which objects of different weights fall, they are careful to use objects that are similar in size and shape, and they make sure that they drop all of them from the same height at exactly the same time.

6. A group of kindergartners sit quietly and politely as the school principal describes the procedure they should follow during a fire drill, but many of them are unable to describe the procedure themselves after the principal leaves the room.

7. A second-grade class is learning about Columbus's first trip across the Atlantic Ocean. Although the teacher has said nothing about what Columbus and his crew must have been thinking and feeling after weeks on the open sea, Ophelia raises her hand and asks, "Weren't they all really scared that they might never see land again?"

8. A seventh-grade teacher gives her students a five-page reading assignment in their social studies textbook; the following day, she gives them a quiz over what they have read. She is pleased at her students' excellent performance on the quiz and asks them what they did when they read and studied the assignment. The strategies they describe are similar to things she did when she studied as a college student.

9. Six-year-old Marianne sees a mother rabbit run into its hole and thinks that, because the mother no longer exists, her babies must now be orphans with no one to take care of them.

10. A fifth grader studies his spelling words by repeating the letters of each word over and over again.

11. The Sudbury High School and Pine Grove High School ice hockey teams are playing for the regional championship. When Sudbury's star player is sent to the penalty box for five minutes, the Pine Grove coach shouts, "All right, men! Let's make hay while the sun shines!" The team members realize that the coach's statement has nothing to do with making hay, that instead it means that they should try to score a goal while they have the advantage.

12. Five-year-old Ethan watches his teacher pour poster paint from a tall, thin jar into a short, wide aluminum cup so that Ethan can dip his brush into the paint more easily. The teacher asks if there is the same amount of paint in the cup as there had been in the jar. Ethan says yes, although he cannot explain why he thinks so.

13. When a teacher asks his seventh-grade class why the sun doesn't fall down from the sky, Elliott replies in all seriousness, "Because it's yellow."

14. Five preschoolers are working on an art project at the same table; they have only two pairs of scissors and one bottle of glue to share among them. Martin wants to keep the glue and one pair of scissors to himself; he doesn't understand why he must let the other children use them as well.

15. A fourth-grade class is studying different denominations of money and has learned what pennies, nickels, dimes, and quarters are worth. As the students watch, the teacher places ten nickels in a stack and spreads another ten nickels all around on the floor. "Which set of nickels would you rather have—the ten nickels stacked up or the ten nickels spread apart?" Louise says she would rather have the ten nickels stacked up because there are more of them.

16. Fifteen-year-old Nancy asserts that if the United Nations took a strong stand on dealing with world hunger, no child would ever go hungry again.

17. Maria is surprised to discover that her kindergarten teacher has children of his own. "You can't be a daddy, " she says. "You're a teacher."

18. Ten-year-old Kevin doesn't understand how $54 \div 6 = 9$ is the opposite of $9 \times 6 = 54$.

19. A ninth grader studies three hours for her geography test and thinks she knows the material well. Her low test score the following day indicates that she doesn't understand it at all.

20. A first-grade teacher places fifteen different objects on his desk and asks his students to look at them carefully. He says, "I'm going to cover these up in just a few seconds. How many things do you think you will be able to remember a few minutes from now?" His students confidently agree that they will be able to remember almost all of the objects. As it turns out, they can remember an average of only seven objects apiece.

21. When a second grader hears her teacher say, "The soldier was shot by the old woman," she thinks that the soldier did the shooting.

22. In his history class, a high school senior writes, "Cortez took a great deal of gold from the Aztecs, although he was exceptionally greedy." He does not understand that he is using the word *although* incorrectly here.

23. On Monday morning, five-year-old Susan tells her teacher what she did over the weekend. "We drove to the McAllisters' farm and rode Betsy." When her teacher explains that she doesn't know the McAllisters and wonders what kind of animal Betsy is, Susan becomes annoyed at her teacher's ignorance about these things.

24. An eighth grader writes, "John Wesley Powell *goed* down the Grand Canyon in a canoe."

Answers to Application Exercise #3

1. Typical. Decimals are proportions. From Piaget's perspective, proportional thinking doesn't appear until formal operations, when children are, on average, about eleven or twelve.

2. Not typical. Information processing research tells us that, although children are easily distracted during the early elementary years, they become increasingly able to focus their attention as they grow older.

3. Typical. Young children often have too restricted a meaning of the word *animal*—an instance of undergeneralization.

4. Not typical. From Piaget's perspective, reasoning about contrary-to-fact ideas does not appear until the formal operations stage.

5. Typical. The students are demonstrating separation and control of variables, a characteristic of Piaget's formal operational stage.

6. Typical. Young children often think that being a "good listener" merely means sitting still and being quiet; they do not necessarily realize that listening also involves understanding and remembering what the speaker says.

7. Not typical. Ophelia is demonstrating elaboration—she is going beyond the information her teacher has actually presented. Elaboration, at least when used intentionally as a learning strategy, is rare before early adolescence.

8. Not typical. Students become increasingly knowledgeable about effective study strategies throughout the high school years. Seventh graders use relatively ineffective strategies compared to those that high school and college students are likely to use.

9. Not typical. Object permanence—recognizing that things continue to exist even when they disappear from sight—develops before the age of two, during Piaget's sensorimotor stage.

10. Typical. Rehearsal is a commonly used learning strategy during the later elementary school years.

11. Typical. Most high school students can look beyond the literal meanings of spoken messages and understand the figurative nature of common expressions and proverbs.

12. Typical. Children in the later years of Piaget's preoperational stage can sometimes think logically, but they are often unable to explain their reasoning.

13. Not typical. Thinking that the sun's color is responsible for its continuing presence in the sky is an example of transductive reasoning, which is common only during Piaget's preoperational stage.

14. Typical. Egocentrism, the inability to view the world from another person's perspective, is common during Piaget's preoperational stage.

15. Not typical. Conservation of number appears in early concrete operations, sometime around six or seven years of age.

16. Typical. Idealism is common among adolescents in Piaget's formal operations stage, but their idealistic beliefs may not be realistically accomplishable.

17. Typical. Children in Piaget's preoperational stage often have difficulty classifying things as belonging to two or more categories at the same time.

18. Not typical. Reversibility appears early in Piaget's concrete operations stage, sometime around six or seven years of age.

19. Typical. Many students overestimate what they have learned, even at the high school level.

20. Typical. Children in the early elementary grades tend to be overly optimistic about how much they will be able to remember.

21. Typical. Children in the early elementary grades often have difficulty interpreting passive sentences correctly.

22. Not typical. Children as old as twelve have trouble using connectives such as *although* correctly, but a high school senior should not have such difficulty.

23. Typical. Egocentric speech—speaking as if other people already know the things you're talking about—is common during Piaget's preoperational stage.

24. Not typical. Applying the *-ed* rule to irregular verbs—an instance of overregularization—is common in the early elementary years but unusual in adolescence.

Application Exercise #4: Identifying Developmentally Appropriate Teaching Practices

Which of the following teaching practices are appropriate for the age level of the students, and which are not? Defend your choices.

1. Nathan temporarily forgets the answer to 9 – 6, so his third-grade teacher gives him a hint by saying, "Three plus six equal nine, so nine minus six must equal. . . ."

2. In an attempt to foster her students' creativity, a first-grade teacher divides her class into five groups and gives each one a creative activity to pursue (writing a play, making an invention, composing a song, and so on). She allots a two-hour period for this activity, then pulls the class back together to find out what everyone has accomplished.

3. A high school physical education teacher describes the steps that students should take when they execute a difficult dismount from the parallel bars. As students begin practicing the dismount, the teacher encourages them to repeat the steps to themselves as they proceed.

4. A middle school offers a class in introductory Russian that sixth and seventh graders may take as an elective.

5. An eleventh-grade mathematics teacher asks students to solve for x in problems such as this:
$$3/7 = 12/x$$

6. A third-grade teacher asks students to consider what might have happened if Columbus had not sailed to the New World in 1492.

7. When giving his high school students their evening's reading assignment, Mr. Rodriguez provides a list of questions that they should be able to answer when they have finished.

8. An eighth-grade science teacher describes how biologists divide forms of animal life into two main categories: vertebrates and invertebrates.

9. A music teacher has her second-grade students performing in a Halloween play tomorrow. Marnie plays the lead character—an absentminded ghost—but still doesn't know most of her lines. "Don't worry, Ms. Jackson, I'll have my dad read them to me once tonight, so I'll be sure to remember them tomorrow." Ms. Jackson calls Marnie's father to make sure that he *will* read Marnie her lines at least once.

10. A high school science teacher asks students in a chemistry lab to find out whether water boils faster when more heat is applied. He gives them the equipment they need and shows them how to use it safely, but he provides no additional guidance about how to approach the task.

11. Ms. James explains what her first-grade students should do at each of the four learning centers around the classroom this morning. Even though she thinks she has explained the procedures clearly, she encourages students to ask questions if they are unsure about what to do next.

12. A fourth-grade teacher gives a short lecture explaining how the Rocky Mountains were formed by forces pushing upward from within the earth.

13. A middle school language arts teacher encourages students to study their new vocabulary words by repeating the definitions over and over to themselves.

Answers to Application Exercise #4

1. Appropriate. Within the framework of Piaget's theory, a third grader should be in the concrete operations stage and so should be capable of reversibility.

2. Not appropriate. Young children are easily distracted and therefore have trouble focusing their attention on any one thing for very long. Students in each group will inevitably be distracted by the things that other groups are saying and doing.

3. Appropriate. According to Vygotsky, self-talk is not limited to young children; it is common for people of any age when they are performing a difficult task for the first time.

4. Appropriate. There is no hard and fast rule about when to begin studying a second language.

5. Appropriate. Research indicates that proportional thinking emerges in early adolescence. Within the framework of Piaget's theory, eleventh graders should be in the formal operations stage and so should be capable of proportional thought.

6. Not appropriate. From Piaget's perspective, students in the elementary grades are not yet capable of reasoning about ideas that are contrary to fact.

7. Appropriate. Students of all ages, even those in high school, often think they have learned things that they really haven't learned. By giving students questions they must answer from their reading assignment, Mr. Rodriguez is providing them with a way of testing themselves to find out what they actually do and do not understand.

8. Appropriate. According to Vygotsky, teachers should convey how culture interprets the world, and the terms *vertebrate* and *invertebrate* are examples of such cultural interpretation. Furthermore, from Piaget's perspective, eighth graders (who are typically at least thirteen years old) are capable of both multiple classification and abstract thought.

9. Not appropriate. Young children tend to overestimate how much they will be able to remember. One time through is probably insufficient even for an adult, let alone for a second grader, but Marnie is undoubtedly unaware of this fact.

10. Appropriate. From Piaget's perspective, high school students are capable of formal operational thought and so should be able to separate and control variables. They should be able to demonstrate the effect of more or less heat while keeping other variables (size and shape of container, amount of water, etc.) constant.

11. Appropriate. Many children in the early elementary grades don't realize they should ask questions when they don't understand. Ms. James is trying to teach them that asking questions is perfectly acceptable.

12. Not appropriate. The teacher is describing processes that students have never directly observed; thus, the ideas he is presenting are somewhat abstract. Fourth graders tend to have difficulty with strictly abstract ideas.

13. Not appropriate. Rehearsal is a commonly used learning strategy in the elementary grades. But older students are capable of elaboration, which is a more effective strategy (see Chapter 1).

Answers to Selected Margin Notes

- Page 39: *Recall our earlier discussion of the importance of separating and controlling variables in experimental research (Chapter 1).*

  In an experimental study, the experimenter manipulates (i.e., controls) one variable at a time in order to observe its effect on a second variable. Other possibly influential factors are separated out and held constant so that the manipulated variable must, by process of elimination, be the cause of any changes observed in that second variable.

- Page 53: *Might you see better performance in "low ability" students if you encourage them to work with a topic they know a lot about?*

  Yes, you should see better performance in these students when they have a rich knowledge base to which they can relate school subject matter.

Sample Test Questions

Items marked with a "1)" on the left-hand side are lower-level questions that assess your general knowledge and understanding of the material. Items marked with a "2)" on the left-hand side are higher-level questions that assess your ability to apply what you have learned to a new situation.

Multiple-Choice

2) 1. Irene knows how to count to 10. She counts the coins she has in her pocket (2 quarters, 5 dimes, and 3 nickels) and says, "I have 10 cents." From Piaget's perspective, Irene is:

    a. Accommodating the counting task to the fact that the different coins have different values
    b. Assimilating the counting task to the way she has counted things in the past
    c. Experiencing disequilibrium about how to count money
    d. Showing insufficient physiological maturation to perform the task correctly

2) 2. Roy gets confused when his chemistry teacher talks about a gas freezing at −100° Fahrenheit. "How can you have *minus* degrees, Ms. Lewis? Temperature can't be less than zero." Roy is showing _____, indicating that he may not yet have made the transition to Piaget's _____ stage.

    a. single classification; concrete operational
    b. multiple classification; formal operational
    c. dependence on concrete reality; concrete operational
    d. dependence on concrete reality; formal operational

2) 3. Which one of the following is the best example of *scaffolding*?

    a. Before her beginning saxophone students start to play "Jingle Bells," Ms. Arnold reminds them where each finger should be on their instruments.
    b. Mr. Baker gives a detailed lecture about the events leading up to the Gulf War.
    c. Mr. Christian has his students write a ten-page research paper on the African country of their own choosing.
    d. Ms. DiCicco equips her kindergarten classroom with a variety of art supplies that her students can use during free time.

2) 4. Imagine that you and your students have certain opinions about issues being addressed in an upcoming election and that you all agree to communicate your opinions by writing a group letter to the editor of the local newspaper. Together you brainstorm about different strategies for expressing your thoughts in a logical and persuasive manner, and then you translate the best strategy into an outline of the major points that you, as a class, want to make in the letter. In doing these things with your students, you demonstrate the value of both brainstorming and outlining as strategies for developing a persuasive essay. Your approach can best be described as:
  a. Teaching a task outside students' zone of proximal development
  b. The process of equilibration
  c. Helping students separate and control variables
  d. A cognitive apprenticeship

1) 5. The following statements describe the development of information processing abilities as children progress through the school years. Three of the statements are accurate. Which one is *not*?
  a. Older children are more likely to be aware of what they do and do not know as they study.
  b. Children develop more effective learning strategies as they move into the junior high school and high school years.
  c. Older children are more likely than younger children to overestimate how much they can remember from something they've read or studied.
  d. As they grow older, children are more likely to find interrelationships among the various things they learn.

2) 6. Which one of the following statements illustrates *undergeneralization* as psychologists define the term?
  a. "Christopher Columbus sailed to the New World, where he found the Pilgrims already living at Plymouth."
  b. "An igloo can't be a house because houses are always made of wood or bricks."
  c. "A sea horse must be a mammal, because all horses are mammals."
  d. "He runned all the way to school, then turned around and runned all the way home again."

Essay

2) 7. Using Piaget's perspective of cognitive development, describe a *strength* and a *weakness* of children's logical thinking in each of these three stages: the preoperational stage, the concrete operational stage, and the formal operational stage. To illustrate your discussion, give specific examples of how children in each stage are likely to think or behave.

1) 8. Explain what psychologists mean by the terms *receptive language* and *expressive language*. Provide two concrete examples of how students' receptive language skills continue to develop during the school years; also provide two concrete examples of how their expressive language skills continue to develop during the school years.

Answers to Sample Test Questions

1. b—Irene is showing assimilation: She is dealing with a new situation in a way that is consistent with something she already knows how to do (see textbook page 30).

2. d—Roy is unable to comprehend the concept of a negative number—an abstract concept that has little basis in concrete reality. Roy's inability to deal with abstract ideas indicates that he has not yet made the transition to formal operations (see the discussion of Piaget's formal operations stage beginning on textbook page 37).

3. a—Ms. Arnold is providing guidance to help her students perform a complex task successfully. (See the discussion of scaffolding on textbook pages 46-47.)

4. d—In a cognitive apprenticeship, a teacher and one or more students work together to accomplish a challenging task. In the process, the teacher models effective ways to think about the task. (Cognitive apprenticeships are discussed on textbook page 48.)

5. c—The reverse is true: Younger children tend to overestimate what they will be able to remember. They become increasingly more accurate as they grow older. (See the discussion of metacognition on textbook pages 53-55.)

6. b—The speaker has too narrow a definition of the concept *house*. (Undergeneralization is defined on textbook page 60.)

7. Strengths and weaknesses of each stage can be found in the following locations:
   Preoperational stage:
   • Strengths are described on textbook page 33.
   • Weaknesses are described on textbook pages 33-35, including the left-hand column of Table 2-1.
   Concrete operational stage:
   • Strengths are described on textbook page 35 and in the right-hand column of Table 2-1 (textbook page 34).
   • Weaknesses are described in the left-hand column of Table 2-2 (textbook page 36).
   Formal operational stage:
   • Strengths are described on textbook pages 37-39 and in the right-hand column of Table 2-2 (textbook page 36).
   • A weakness is described in the last paragraph on textbook page 39.
   Your response should include at least three concrete examples to illustrate your discussion, with at least one example for each of the three stages you have described. You can use some of the examples presented in the pages listed above, or you can develop examples of your own.

8. Receptive language is the ability to understand spoken and printed language; thus, it involves both listening and reading. Expressive language is the ability to communicate one's thoughts effectively; it includes both speaking and writing. Developmental changes in students' receptive and expressive language skills can be found on textbook pages 59-63.

Chapter 3

PERSONAL, SOCIAL, AND MORAL DEVELOPMENT

Chapter Overview

This chapter describes how personality, interpersonal skills and relationships, and moral reasoning and behavior develop over the course of childhood and adolescence. You will consider the concepts *self-concept* and *self-esteem*, seeing how these aspects of personality develop during the school years and learning what conditions influence their development. You will look at the process of *socialization*—the means through which society shapes growing children into responsible and productive adults—and see how parents, teachers, and peers all play a critical role in this process. You will also learn about moral development, discovering how students' moral reasoning, perspective taking, and prosocial behavior are likely to change during the elementary and secondary school years. Finally, you will discover some ways in which your students (including your students with special educational needs) are likely to be a diverse group with respect to their personal, social, and moral development.

Throughout the chapter, you will find numerous educational applications. For example, you will discover several strategies for enhancing students' self-concepts and self-esteem, including the most effective strategy of all—enabling students to experience success in academic, social, and physical activities. And you will see how, by promoting students' moral development, you can also enhance their ability to work productively and cooperatively in your classroom.

Common Student Beliefs and Misconceptions Related to Chapter Content

Below are several beliefs that college students often have before studying personal, social, and moral development—misconceptions that may interfere with an accurate understanding of what they read. As you read Chapter 3, be on the lookout for evidence that contradicts these common misconceptions:

1. Some students think that the terms *authoritative* and *authoritarian* are synonyms (see Table 3-1 on textbook page 78 for the difference between them).

2. Many students believe that to promote the development of positive self-concepts, we must never give negative feedback.

3. Some students think of *socialization* in terms of socializing with their friends. Developmentalists' meaning for this term is quite different.

4. Some students equate morality with religion or otherwise have a limited view of what morality encompasses. As a result, they may believe that morals and morality have no place in the schools.

CHAPTER OUTLINE	FOCUS QUESTIONS
HOW THE ENVIRONMENT INFLUENCES PERSONAL, SOCIAL, AND MORAL DEVELOPMENT	• What aspects of the environment are influential in students' personal, social, and moral development?
PERSONAL DEVELOPMENT How Parents Influence Their Children's Personal Development Self-Concept and Self-Esteem Developmental Differences in Personality	• What roles do parents play in children's development? In what ways are children raised with different parenting styles apt to be different? Which aspects of an authoritative parenting style are relevant for teachers? • What characteristics do a student's self-concept and self-esteem encompass? What effect do self-concept and self-esteem have on behavior? • What factors influence the development of self-concept and self-esteem? What implications do these factors have for classroom practice? • How do self-concept and self-esteem change during the school years? Why does a student's self-concept become increasingly stable over time? • How are students' personalities apt to be different during the preschool, elementary, and secondary school years? With these developmental changes in mind, identify some age-appropriate strategies for the grade level at which you will be teaching.
SOCIAL DEVELOPMENT Socialization Peer Relationships Fostering Social Skills Promoting Social Interaction Among Diverse Groups	• What do developmentalists mean by the term *socialization*? What kinds of behaviors develop through socialization? • What kinds of behaviors do teachers typically socialize in students? Why are such behaviors important for students over the long run? • What important roles do peers play in children's development? How do peer relationships change during the school years? • How can teachers help students develop more effective social skills? How can they promote interaction among diverse groups?

CHAPTER OUTLINE	FOCUS QUESTIONS

MORAL AND PROSOCIAL BEHAVIOR
 	
  How Emotions Reflect Moral Development
 	
  Development of Moral Reasoning: Kohlberg's Theory
 	
  Gender Differences in Moral Reasoning: Gilligan's Theory
 	
  Development of Perspective Taking: Selman's Theory
 	
  Development of Prosocial Behavior: Eisenberg's Theory
 	
  Integrating the Stages of Moral Reasoning, Perspective Taking, and Prosocial Behavior
 	
  Promoting Moral Development in the Classroom
	• What emotions reflect moral development?
	
	• What is a moral dilemma? Can you think of moral dilemmas that might arise in your own classroom?
	
	• How do individuals at each of Kohlberg's three levels and six stages reason about moral issues? According to Kohlberg, what factors affect a person's progression to the next higher stage? Which aspects of Kohlberg's theory have been confirmed by research?
	
	• In what way does Gilligan think males and females reason differently?
	
	• What changes occur in perspective taking and prosocial behavior during the school years? How can teachers promote these aspects of development?
	
	• What forms of moral reasoning, perspective taking, and prosocial behavior can you expect to see in students at the grade level you will be teaching?
	
	• What implications do the factors affecting moral and prosocial development have for classroom practice?

CONSIDERING DIVERSITY IN PERSONAL, SOCIAL, AND MORAL DEVELOPMENT Accommodating Students with Special Needs	• In what ways are students likely to be diverse with respect to their personal, social, and moral development? What characteristics are students with special educational needs likely to have?
THE BIG PICTURE: RECURRING THEMES IN PERSONAL, SOCIAL, AND MORAL DEVELOPMENT	• What three themes appear throughout the discussion of social, personal, and moral development?

Using the Compact Disk

"Assessing Moral Reasoning" on the *Simulations in Educational Psychology* CD is a hands-on activity similar to the "Heinz's Dilemma" Experiencing Firsthand exercise presented in the textbook.

Chapter Glossary

Attachment. A strong, affectionate bond formed between a child and another individual (e.g., a parent); usually formed early in the child's life.

Authoritarian parenting style. A parenting style characterized by rigid rules and expectations for behavior that children are expected to obey without question.

Authoritative parenting style. A parenting style characterized by emotional warmth, high expectations and standards for behavior, consistent enforcement of rules, explanations regarding the reasons behind these rules, and the inclusion of children in decision making.

Culture shock. A sense of confusion that occurs when students encounter a culture with very different expectations for behavior than the expectations with which the students have been raised.

Empathy. Experiencing the same feelings as someone in unfortunate circumstances.

Guilt. The feeling of discomfort that individuals experience when they know that they have caused someone else pain or distress.

Identity. A self-constructed definition of who a person thinks he or she is and what things are important in life.

Imaginary audience. The belief that one is the center of attention in any social situation.

Induction. Explaining why a certain behavior is unacceptable, often with a focus on the pain or distress that someone has caused another.

Moral dilemma. A situation in which there is no clear-cut answer regarding the morally correct thing to do.

Norms. Society's rules for acceptable and unacceptable behavior. (Note that we will use the term differently when we talk about assessment in Chapter 16.)

Parenting style. The general pattern of behaviors that a parent uses to raise his or her children.

Peer pressure. A phenomenon whereby a student's peers strongly encourage some behaviors and discourage others.

Peers. One's equals or age-mates.

Permissive parenting style. A parenting style characterized by emotional warmth but few expectations or standards for children's behavior.

Personal fable. The belief that one is completely unlike anyone else and so cannot be understood by other individuals.

Personality. Set of relatively enduring traits that characterize the way in which a person typically interacts with his or her physical and social environments.

Prosocial behavior. Behavior directed toward promoting the well-being of someone else.

Roles. Patterns of behavior acceptable for individuals having different functions within a society.

Self-concept. One's beliefs about oneself.

Self-esteem. The extent to which one believes oneself to be a capable and worthy individual.

Shame. A feeling of embarrassment or humiliation that children feel after failing to meet the standards for moral behavior that adults have set.

Socialization. The process of shaping a child's behavior to fit the norms and roles of the child's society.

Social skills. Behaviors that enable an individual to interact effectively with others.

Uninvolved parenting style. A parenting style characterized by a lack of emotional support and a lack of standards regarding appropriate behavior.

Application Exercise #5: Identifying Typical and Atypical Behaviors

Of the students described below, which ones are exhibiting behaviors typical for their age group, and which ones are not? Justify your decisions on the basis of theories and/or research findings described in Chapter 3.

1. When Larry gets a poor grade in his high school math class, he quickly jumps to the conclusion that he is not a good student—that he probably won't do well in any of his other classes (in science, Spanish, physical education, etc.) either.

2. Even though all the ninth graders at Harrison High School must take a required health class, many of them ignore the teacher's remarks about the dangers of unprotected sex. "I won't get pregnant," one girl says to a classmate, "and AIDS is something that only poor people get."

3. A seventh grader named Roger gets visibly angry when he sees several "skinheads" taunt an African-American classmate. "Racism is wrong," he says. "Everyone on this planet is equal. We are all entitled to human dignity and the respect of our fellow human beings."

4. Fifteen-year-old Linda is obviously quite upset about something. When her teacher tries to find out what's wrong, Linda replies, "I need to talk to my best friend Tara. No one else can possibly understand."

5. Several of the boys in Mr. Woodward's second-grade class are worried about the fact that they don't yet know what they want to be when they grow up.

6. Chip is well known for his obnoxious behavior in the school lunchroom at Monroe Junior High. He delights in knocking other students' lunch trays onto the floor, thereby making the lunches inedible. When Ms. McCartney confronts Chip about his behavior, he shows no understanding that his classmates will have to go hungry for the rest of the day.

7. Many of the students at Piedmont Junior High School try to dress and act like their most popular classmates.

8. A high school senior is depressed most of the time. "I'm no good at anything," she tells her teacher day after day.

9. A third grader thinks that it's okay to copy someone else's math homework as long as she doesn't get caught in the act.

10. A class of fourth graders is discussing the plight of homeless children. They readily acknowledge that these children might not have enough to eat and must often be very cold at night. However, they believe that the best course of action that these children can take is to get a job of some sort (for example, selling flowers on the street) rather than going to school.

Answers to Application Exercise #5

1. Not typical. Students usually make distinctions among various aspects of themselves. This is especially true at the high school level, when they are likely to realize that they may be more capable in some disciplines than in others.

2. Typical. Characteristic of the personal fable so common during adolescence is a belief that one is invulnerable to life's normal risks.

3. Not typical. From Kohlberg's perspective, Roger is showing postconventional moral reasoning—something that is rare before college.

4. Typical. High school students often have close, intimate friends with whom they share their innermost thoughts. They may also suffer from a "personal fable"—a belief that no one else (certainly not a teacher) has ever had the feelings or problems that they themselves have.

5. Not typical. Such behavior characterizes Erikson's stage of Identity vs. Role Confusion, which doesn't emerge until adolescence. Elementary students are more likely to be in Erikson's Industry vs. Inferiority stage.

6. Not typical. From Selman's perspective, Chip is showing egocentric perspective taking (Level 0). Such behavior is common in preschool and the early elementary years; however, most junior high school students are at Level 3 or 4.

7. Typical. Peer influences are the strongest during the junior high school years.

8. Not typical. Although self-esteem drops temporarily when students make the transition to junior high school, most older adolescents have positive self-concepts. If the student is seriously and chronically depressed, the teacher should consult with the school counselor or psychologist and be on the lookout for signs that the student may be contemplating suicide (see the section on "Emotional and Behavioral Disorders" in Chapter 5 of the textbook).

9. Typical. Most elementary students are in Kohlberg's preconventional level of moral reasoning: They define right and wrong behavior in terms of its consequences.

10. Typical. From Eisenberg's perspective, these students are showing a superficial "needs of others" orientation (Level 2). Such prosocial behavior is typical of many students in the elementary grades.

Application Exercise #6: Identifying Developmentally Appropriate Teaching Practices

Which of the following teacher behaviors are appropriate for the age level of the students, and which are not? Defend your decisions based on the principles, theories, and research findings described in Chapter 3.

1. Early in the school year, a kindergarten teacher explains that students should raise their hands and wait to be called on when they want to speak. He also insists that students follow these instructions; for example, he ignores students when they speak out of turn.

2. A junior high school student asserts that skipping school occasionally is okay because her older brother says that it is. Mr. Castaneda tells her that going to school is one of our society's rules and that society will function more smoothly when its citizens know how to read and write.

3. A kindergarten teacher tries to motivate Wayne to print his lowercase letters more neatly. She tells him, "Look at how your letters compare to Jeremy's. See how his are neat and yours are messy?"

4. As Ms. Ferguson teaches her high school English class how to write a good resumé, she reminds them, "Now that you're sophomores, most of you should have a good idea about what you'll be doing after you graduate."

5. Early in the school year, a second-grade teacher tells her students that they must never take things from another student's plastic storage box, or "cubby." She also tells them what the consequence will be if this rule is disobeyed.

6. Madison Elementary School is having its annual open house for parents tonight. In preparation for the event, Mr. Brock has his students put some of their best papers in a folder on their desks for their parents to see. He also has students' numerous art projects hanging on the walls.

7. A high school driver education teacher warns his students, "Be sure to stay within the speed limit. After all, there may be a traffic officer lurking in wait when you least expect one."

8. Before his first-grade class walks to the local park for a picnic lunch, Mr. Brillhart reminds his students that littering is not right because it makes the world an uglier place for others to live in.

Answers to Application Exercise #6

1. Appropriate. Teachers play an important role in the socialization of children; they teach them some of the behaviors they will need in adult society.

2. Appropriate. The student is reasoning at Kohlberg's Stage 3, looking to an authority figure (her older brother) for guidance about what's right and wrong. Mr. Castaneda is using Stage 4 reasoning (law and order)—something that she should be able to understand and that may therefore promote the development of more mature moral reasoning.

3. Not appropriate. For many children, the first year of school is an unsettling one that leads to a temporary drop in self-concept. Comparisons with other students, especially if those comparisons are unfavorable ones, are likely to be counterproductive.

4. Not appropriate. As high school sophomores, Ms. Ferguson's students are still in Erikson's Identity vs. Role Confusion stage, which continues throughout adolescence. Many of them probably do not yet have a clear idea of the role they want to play in adult society.

5. Appropriate. From Kohlberg's perspective, second graders are reasoning at a preconventional level: They are concerned primarily about what the consequences of their actions will be.

6. Appropriate. According to Erikson, elementary students are in the Industry vs. Inferiority stage—one in which they seek recognition for the things they produce.

7. Not appropriate. Most high school students reason at Kohlberg's conventional level—they define right and wrong in terms of meeting someone's approval (Stage 3) or obeying society's rules (Stage 4). By focusing on the potential consequences of speeding, the teacher is using preconventional reasoning with these students. Ideally, he should be presenting reasons for following the speed limit that reflect reasoning one stage above where students are (i.e., Stage 4 reasoning for some and Stage 5 reasoning for others).

8. Not appropriate. As first graders, Mr. Brillhart's students are probably reasoning at Kohlberg's preconventional level and so are concerned primarily about the consequences of their actions. They are also likely to be in Selman's Level 1 (subjective perspective taking), so they will view the needs of others in an overly simplistic fashion.

Answers to Selected Margin Notes

- Page 77: *Think about some television shows that depict family life (e.g., Roseanne, Full House, Married with Children). Which parenting styles best characterize each of these shows?*

  The parents in many shows have an authoritative parenting style; for example, they show genuine warmth and affection toward their children, have high expectations and standards for behavior, explain why household rules are important, and enforce those rules consistently. *Married with Children* is an exception; it illustrates elements of both permissive and uninvolved parenting.

- Page 82: *Have you ever seen one student say something that threatens a classmate's self-esteem? How might a teacher intervene in such a situation?*

  There is no single right or wrong answer to this question. However, if some students are continually behaving in ways that undermine another student's self-esteem, then teacher intervention is definitely in order. One strategy would be to use induction (see the discussion of this concept in the section "Promoting Moral Development in the Classroom") to help the culprits understand the effects of their thoughtless behavior. A second strategy would be to address any of the "victim's" characteristics or behaviors that lend themselves to ridicule (e.g., if the student is consistently being ridiculed for being dirty or smelly, then instruction in hygiene and/or needed hygienic supplies might be provided).

- Page 93: *Think back to our discussion of self-concept. What do Michelle's behaviors tell us about her self-perceptions of social competence?*

  Students tend to behave in ways that are consistent with their beliefs about themselves. Michelle apparently has a poor sense of social competence—a belief that is probably perpetuated by her lack of friends and the frequent insults she receives from others. Thus, she acts as if she isn't likely to make friends in any new social interaction, hurling insults before anyone else can say a word.

- Page 99: *Why is this level called preconventional?*

  People at this level are not yet considering society's conventions and norms for appropriate behavior.

- Page 104: *How is Selman's Level 0 similar to Piaget's preoperational stage of cognitive development?*

  Both are characterized by an inability to see a situation from any perspective except one's own; Piaget called this phenomenon *egocentrism*.

- Page 105: *What might you do to ease the transition of a new student into your classroom? How might you help other students see things from a new student's point of view?*

  One strategy for easing a new student's transition is to assign an especially prosocial child to act as a "buddy" for a few days, sitting with that student at lunch, making introductions in the schoolyard, and so on. To help other students see things from the new student's point of view, you might remind them of how they themselves feel when they are in a strange, possibly unreceptive situation. You may be able to identify additional strategies as well.

- Page 107: *In what ways is Eisenberg's Level 3 similar to Kohlberg's Stage 3?*

  Both Eisenberg's Level 3 and Kohlberg's Stage 3 involve doing the "right" thing in order to gain someone else's approval. Furthermore, both involve fairly conventional, stereotypical ideas of acceptable behavior.

Sample Test Questions

Items marked with a "1)" on the left-hand side are lower-level questions that assess your general knowledge and understanding of the material. Items marked with a "2)" on the left-hand side are higher-level questions that assess your ability to apply what you have learned to a new situation.

Multiple-Choice

1) 1. If you wanted to be an *authoritative* teacher, you would be most likely to:
      a. Focus attention on students' academic achievement, without regard for any personal or emotional problems that they might bring with them to the classroom.
      b. Establish strict rules for classroom behavior and refuse to tolerate any objections to these rules.
      c. Explain why the rules you've established will help students learn more effectively.
      d. Let students make most of their own choices about what they will do on any given school day.

2) 2. Three of the following teachers are likely to enhance their students' self-concepts and self-esteem. Which one is *least* likely to do so?
      a. Mr. Alvaro teaches students a technique that enables them to solve their geometry proofs more successfully.
      b. Ms. Berkowitz holds a class spelling bee to see which student is the best speller in the class.
      c. Ms. Caruso teaches her students how to do the butterfly stroke in swimming.
      d. Mr. Davidson uses a role-playing activity to help his students develop better interpersonal skills.

2) 3. Which one of the following is the best example of how an *imaginary audience* can be a factor in an adolescent's self-concept?
      a. Annette thinks that none of her friends can possibly understand how badly she feels about not having a date for the homecoming dance.
      b. Betsy doesn't like working in cooperative groups because she often has trouble understanding new concepts and doesn't want her classmates to think she's stupid.
      c. Christa doesn't think she could ever become a teacher because she doesn't like speaking in front of groups.
      d. Darlene is convinced that everyone in school has noticed that one of her ears sticks out more than the other.

1) 4. Socialization is best defined as the process through which children:
      a. Acquire such personality characteristics as friendliness or shyness
      b. Learn how to get along with others
      c. Learn what is acceptable behavior in their society
      d. Learn to appreciate being with other people

1) 5. Eisenberg's theory of prosocial behavior proposes that as children grow older, they:
      a. Become increasingly more concerned about helping others in need
      b. Acquire a more positive self-concept with regard to their social competence
      c. Develop more abstract notions about right and wrong
      d. Become increasingly more aware of the thoughts and feelings that motivate their own behaviors

2)   6.   Which one of the following statements is an example of *induction* as developmental theorists define the term?
  a.   "When you shout out the answers to my questions, you prevent anyone else from answering them."
  b.   "Under no circumstances will cheating be tolerated in this classroom."
  c.   "As soon as everyone has settled down, you can all go to lunch."
  d.   "Someone spilled blue paint all over the floor without telling me, and I think I know who that 'someone' is."

Essay

1)   7.   Imagine that you have just begun a new teaching job. You soon discover that most of the students in your class belong to one of two ethnic groups, that the two groups rarely interact with each another, and that most interactions that *do* occur between the groups are hostile rather than friendly. Keeping the textbook's discussion of social development in mind, use three short paragraphs to describe three different strategies that you and your teaching colleagues might use to promote more appropriate and productive interactions between the two groups.

2)   8.   Isaac says that stealing someone else's lunch money is okay as long as he doesn't get caught.
  a.   In which stage of moral reasoning does Isaac appear to be? Justify your choice.
  b.   How might a teacher promote Isaac's development to a more advanced stage of moral reasoning? Describe three different strategies that are consistent either with Kohlberg's theory or with research findings.

Answers to Sample Test Questions

1. c—The behaviors that authoritative parents exhibit are described in Table 3-1 (textbook page 78). An authoritative teacher would behave in a similar fashion.

2. b—Competition is usually *not* recommended as a way of promoting a positive self-concept (see textbook page 82).

3. d—An adolescent's imaginary audience is the belief that he or she is the center of everybody else's attention. (See the description on textbook page 87.)

4. c—Socialization is the process of shaping a child's behavior to fit society's norms and rules (see textbook page 89).

5. a—This trend is clearly seen in the right-hand column of Table 3-2 (textbook page 105).

6. a—Induction is giving students reasons why a behavior is unacceptable (see textbook page 110).

7. Strategies that you might use are described in the sections "Fostering Social Skills" and "Promoting Social Interaction Among Diverse Groups" on textbook pages 93-95.

8. a. Isaac is in Kohlberg's Stage 1: He will do anything he can get away with and has no recognition of anyone else's needs (see textbook page 100).
   b. Four possible strategies are these (you would need to identify only three):
   - Presenting reasoning one stage above a student's own reasoning (in Isaac's case, presenting reasoning at Stage 2)
   - Explaining why stealing is unacceptable (induction)
   - Modeling moral behavior (e.g., returning money that someone else has lost)
   - Asking students to wrestle with moral issues and dilemmas (e.g., a dilemma about a boy who cannot afford lunch money and sees a wealthy classmate leave her lunch money unattended)

   The first strategy is described in the discussion of *disequilibrium* on textbook page 102. The last three strategies are described in the section "Promoting Moral Development in the Classroom" beginning on textbook page 108.

Chapter 4

INDIVIDUAL AND GROUP DIFFERENCES

Chapter Overview

This chapter describes some important ways in which students at any particular grade level are likely to be different from one another. As you consider individual differences, you will explore the nature of intelligence and creativity, seeing how these characteristics play a role in students' classroom learning, behavior, and achievement. You will discover that both intelligence and creativity are clearly influenced by environmental factors, including the experiences and activities that students encounter at school. As you examine group differences later in the chapter, you will see how students may sometimes think and behave in very different ways, depending on their ethnicity, gender, and socioeconomic background. You will also learn more about students who are at risk for failing to achieve the skills they will ultimately need to be successful in the adult world.

Yet you must be careful not to jump too quickly to conclusions about how individual students are likely to perform in your classroom. As you will discover near the end of the chapter, unwarranted teacher expectations can have adverse effects on students' short-term achievement and long-term development. Our role as teachers is to maximize the academic and personal success of every student. Throughout the chapter, you will find many suggestions for adapting your instructional strategies and activities to the particular students you have in your classroom.

Common Student Beliefs and Misconceptions Related to Chapter Content

Below are several beliefs and misconceptions that college students often have before they study individual and group differences—beliefs and misconceptions that can interfere with an accurate understanding of the information they encounter in a textbook. As you read Chapter 4, be on the lookout for evidence that contradicts these commonly held ideas:

1. When average differences among groups are described, many people think of these differences as being much larger than they really are. For example, when they hear about gender differences in verbal ability or mathematics, they might think that most boys are better than most girls, or vice versa.
2. Some people think that intelligence is almost entirely inherited. Others believe that intelligence is exclusively the result of environmental factors.
3. Many people think of IQ scores as permanent characteristics, much as eye color and skin tone are.
4. Some people believe that IQ tests have no usefulness in school settings.
5. Many people see no advantage in acknowledging or accommodating cultural differences.
6. Some people believe that they were raised in a truly gender-equitable environment, even though research indicates that there are almost always differences in how parents treat their sons versus their daughters.

CHAPTER OUTLINE	FOCUS QUESTIONS
(introduction)	• What do psychologists mean by the terms *individual differences* and *group differences*?
KEEPING INDIVIDUAL AND GROUP DIFFERENCES IN PERSPECTIVE	• What general principles does the textbook present with regard to individual and group differences? What implications do these principles have for teachers?

INTELLIGENCE
 	
   Measuring Intelligence
   How Theorists Conceptualize Intelligence
   Heredity, Environment, and Group Differences
   Being Optimistic About Students' Potential
	• What characteristics are often associated with intelligent behavior?
	
	• What kinds of test items are often found on intelligence tests?
	
	• Which IQ scores appear frequently among students? Which scores appear infrequently? How are IQ scores related to school achievement? What limitations do intelligence tests have?
	
	• Why did Spearman believe that a general factor (*g*) underlies intelligence? What alternatives to the notion of *g* do Gardner and Sternberg offer?
	
	• What do theorists mean by the term *distributed intelligence*? What implications does this concept have for classroom practice?
	
	• What evidence exists to support the idea that both heredity and environmental factors contribute to intelligence?

CREATIVITY Fostering Creativity in the Classroom	• What is creativity? In what way does it often involve divergent thinking? • Is creativity a single entity? How consistently do students exhibit creativity across different content domains? • How can teachers foster creativity in students?

CHAPTER OUTLINE	FOCUS QUESTIONS

ETHNIC DIFFERENCES
 	
  The Problem of Cultural Mismatch
 	
  Examples of Ethnic Diversity
 	
  Creating a More Multicultural Classroom
    Environment
	• What is an *ethnic group*?
	
	• What conditions may contribute to a cultural mismatch between home and school?
	
	• What cultural differences exist among students of different ethnic groups? What can teachers do to maximize the classroom success of students from diverse ethnic backgrounds?
	
	• To what do the concepts *wait time* and *negative wait time* refer?
	
	• What strategies can teachers use to create a more multicultural classroom environment?

GENDER DIFFERENCES Origins of Gender Differences	• In what ways are boys and girls similar? In what ways are they different? • What environmental factors contribute to the development of gender differences? • How can teachers make education more equitable for both boys and girls?

SOCIOECONOMIC DIFFERENCES
 	
  Factors Interfering with School Success
 	
  Working with Homeless Students
 	
  Fostering Resilience
 	
  Building on Students' Strengths
	• What factors contribute to the generally lower school success of students from low-SES backgrounds? How can teachers counteract some of these effects?
	
	• What strategies are especially useful when working with homeless students?
	
	• What is *resilience*, and how can teachers foster it?

STUDENTS AT RISK
 	
  Characteristics of Students at Risk
 	
  Why Some Students Drop Out
 	
  Helping Students at Risk Stay in School
	• To which students does the term *at risk* refer? What characteristics do such students often exhibit?
	
	• Why do many students drop out prior to high school graduation?
	
	• What strategies can teachers use to help at-risk students be successful in school?

CHAPTER OUTLINE	FOCUS QUESTIONS
TEACHER EXPECTATIONS Effects of Teacher Expectations Guarding Against Unwarranted Expectations	• Teachers often have different expectations for different students. What effects do such expectations have on both teachers' and students' behaviors? • How can teachers guard against forming unnecessarily low expectations for students?
TAKING INDIVIDUAL AND GROUP DIFFERENCES INTO ACCOUNT Accommodating Students with Special Needs	• What general principles can guide teachers as they take individual and group differences into account? • What individual and group differences should teachers consider as they work with students who have special educational needs?

Chapter Glossary

African American dialect. A dialect of some African American communities that includes some pronunciations, grammatical constructions, and idioms different from those of Standard English.

Automaticity. The ability to respond quickly and efficiently while mentally processing or physically performing a task.

Convergent thinking. Pulling several pieces of information together to draw a conclusion or solve a problem.

Creativity. New and original behavior that yields an appropriate and productive result.

Cultural mismatch. A situation in which a child's home culture and the school culture hold conflicting expectations for the child's behavior.

Dialect. A form of English characteristic of a particular region or ethnic group.

Distributed intelligence. The idea that people are more likely to act "intelligently" when they have physical and/or social support systems to assist them.

Divergent thinking. Taking a single idea in many different directions.

Equity in instruction. Instruction without favoritism or bias toward particular individuals or groups of students.

Ethnic group. A group of people with a common set of values, beliefs, and behaviors. The group's roots either precede the creation of, or are external to, the country in which the group resides.

g. The theoretical notion that intelligence includes a general factor that influences people's ability to learn in a wide variety of content domains.

Group differences. Consistently observed differences, on average, among certain groups of individuals.

Higher-level question. A question that requires students to do something new with information they have learned—for example, to apply, analyze, synthesize, or evaluate it.

Individual differences. The ways in which people of the same age are different from one another.

Intelligence. The ability to modify and adjust one's behaviors in order to accomplish new tasks successfully. It involves many different mental processes, and its nature may vary, depending on the culture in which one lives.

Intelligence test. A general measure of current cognitive functioning, used primarily to predict academic achievement over the short run.

IQ score. A score on an intelligence test. It is determined by comparing one's performance on the test with the performance of others in the same age-group (see Appendix C of the textbook for more details).

Multicultural education. Education that includes the perspectives and experiences of numerous cultural groups on a regular basis.

Negative wait time. The tendency to interrupt someone who has not yet finished speaking.

Resilient students. Students who succeed in school despite exceptional hardships in their home lives.

Self-fulfilling prophecy. A situation in which one's expectations in and of themselves lead to the expected result.

Socioeconomic status (SES). One's general social and economic standing in society, encompassing such variables as family income, occupation, and level of education.

Sociolinguistic conventions. Specific language-related behaviors that appear in some cultures or ethnic groups but not in others.

Standard English. The form of English generally considered acceptable at school, as reflected in textbooks, grammar instruction, and so on.

Stereotype. A rigid, simplistic, and erroneous caricature of a particular group of people.

Students at risk. Students who have a high probability of failing to acquire the minimal academic skills necessary for success in the adult world.

Wait time. The length of time a teacher pauses, either after asking a question or hearing a student's comment, before saying something else.

Application Exercise #7: Identifying Typical Group Differences

Which of the situations below are consistent with what we know about gender, ethnic, and socioeconomic differences, and which are not? Defend your decisions.

1. When Mr. Russo asks his sophomore science students to raise their hands if they are planning to pursue a career in science, five students show an interest—Edith, Marilyn, Samantha, Rita, and Justin.

2. Carlos, a boy of Mexican American heritage, is beginning to work on his book report. "I'm going to see if I can do this better than anyone else in the class," he tells his teacher.

3. When teaching a unit on basketball in her physical education class, Ms. Martinez finds that boys who have trouble making a basket say that they need to try harder and practice more. In contrast, girls who have difficulty say that they were never very good at sports and so aren't likely to be so now.

4. Michael is an African American boy who lives in South Carolina. When his kindergarten teacher asks him, "What is this?" while pointing to a picture of a dog or a horse, Michael seems confused about how to respond. This puzzles his teacher, because she knows that he has seen numerous dogs and horses and is well aware of what they are called.

5. All of the girls in Ms. Tate's ninth-grade math class are proud of their friend Margaret, because she is clearly the smartest student in the class.

6. Mr. Friedman notices that the three Navajo students in his class never volunteer answers when he asks questions.

7. A high school counselor looks at the mathematics achievement records (class grades and test scores) of next year's senior class and selects the top 20 students for an advanced mathematics class. The class consists of 18 males and 2 females.

8. Harold is one of five children in a single-parent family living in a local public housing complex. He often seems stressed out; for example, he is easily frustrated and has a quick temper.

9. At the annual Great Plains Regional High School field day, a favorite event is the buffalo chip throwing contest. The winner and four runners up are all boys.

10. Ms. Jost gently scolds a Native American student named Felicia for coming to class late. Felicia looks Ms. Jost directly in the eye and appears to be listening closely.

11. A high school teacher notices that in the senior class, the girls tend to have closer, more intimate relationships with one another than the boys do.

12. When Mr. Jones asks an African American student named Joyce where her friend Wilma is, Joyce replies, "Oh, Wilma be comin' late today."

13. Mary and Bob are partners in chemistry lab. Mary usually takes charge of the pair's activities, and Bob sits back and watches.

14. An African American student won't answer when her teacher asks her what her father does for a living.

Answers to Application Exercise #7

1. Not consistent. We would expect most of the students interested in a science career to be boys. By high school, boys are more confident than girls about their ability to succeed in science. Furthermore, gender stereotypes influence the career choices that many students make, and science is traditionally thought to be a "masculine" discipline. (Keep in mind, however, that males and females probably have similar *ability* to succeed in science.)

2. Not consistent. Children raised in most Hispanic communities are more accustomed to working cooperatively than competitively.

3. Consistent. Males tend to blame their failures on a lack of effort, whereas females tend to blame their failures on a lack of ability. This gender difference is most often found in traditionally "male" activities.

4. Consistent. In some African American communities in the southeastern United States, parents are more likely to ask their children questions involving comparisons (e.g., "What's that like?"), rather than questions involving labels. Michael may be unaccustomed to answering "What is this?" questions about things that he already knows.

5. Not consistent. Students are more likely to ridicule or avoid students who engage in traditionally counterstereotypical behaviors.

6. Consistent. The question/answer sessions so typical in many classrooms are unlike the experiences Native American students usually have in their local communities. Furthermore, many of these students have learned to allow a certain amount of wait time before responding to an adult's question—wait time that may be nonexistent in Mr. Friedman's classroom.

7. Not consistent. Any gender differences in mathematics achievement are quite small during the K-12 years. We would expect a more equal representation of males and females in the class.

8. Consistent. High stress levels are common in children of lower-SES families.

9. Consistent. After puberty, males tend to be stronger than females (in large part because of their increased testosterone levels).

10. Not consistent. Native American students are more likely to look down when an adult speaks to them, usually as a way of showing respect.

11. Consistent. Girls tend to be more affiliative than boys.

12. Consistent. African American students raised in some parts of the country often speak a dialect other than Standard English. A statement such as Joyce's is grammatically correct within the context of that dialect.

13. Not consistent. When boys and girls are paired together, the boys usually take the more active role.

14. Consistent. Children in some African American communities are taught not to answer questions about their families and home life.

Answers to Selected Margin Notes

- Page 124: *Under what circumstances might it be appropriate for a teacher to use intelligence test results? What potential dangers are there in relying solely on IQ scores as a measure of students' abilities?*

  IQ scores are one source of information that teachers can use to help them select instructional materials and activities appropriate for every child. However, such scores should be used *only* within the context of other data about each student. Intelligence tests do not assess every aspect of intelligent behavior, and students may be quite capable in ways that a single test score does not reflect. IQ scores, especially when used in isolation from other information, may lead a teacher to form unwarranted expectations about a student's future classroom performance.

- Page 140: *Why do you think some teachers encourage competition among their students?*

  To my knowledge, no research has been conducted to answer this question. I suspect that many teachers believe that competition will motivate their students. As you will discover when you read Chapter 12, most students do *not* find competition motivating.

- Page 154: *What are possible reasons why some students don't participate in their school's extracurricular activities?*

  Here are several possibilities (you can probably think of others as well):
  - They feel intimidated by the "popular" students who dominate those activities, or else they lack confidence that they will be accepted by those students.
  - Their friends don't participate in the activities.
  - They lack the athletic abilities and skills necessary for team sports.
  - They find the activities irrelevant to their own interests.
  - They have no means of transportation for getting to school earlier than usual or getting home later than usual.
  - They have jobs or family commitments after school.

Sample Test Questions

Items marked with a " 1)" on the left-hand side are lower-level questions that assess your general knowledge and understanding of the material. Items marked with a " 2)" on the left-hand side are higher-level questions that assess your ability to apply what you have learned to a new situation.

Multiple-Choice

2) 1. Franklin is a fourth grader who has just obtained a score of 110 on an intelligence test. Which one of the following is a correct interpretation of his score?
   a. Franklin is showing below-average performance for a fourth grader.
   b. Franklin has done better on the test than most students his age.
   c. Franklin should probably be moved to the next higher grade level.
   d. Franklin is beginning to understand school material at an abstract level.

2) 2. Martha has trouble reading, and she is a bit clumsy when it comes to sports and athletics. However, she does well in her math classes, and she is quite popular among her classmates. Which view of intelligence is best reflected in Martha's pattern of strengths and weaknesses?
   a. Sternberg's triarchic theory
   b. Gardner's multiple intelligences
   c. Spearman's concept of *g*
   d. The notion of distributed intelligence

1) 3. Three of the following are accurate statements about the differences between boys and girls. Which one is *not* accurate?
   a. Boys are more motivated than girls to achieve in areas that are stereotypically "masculine."
   b. Boys are likely to think their academic failures are due to insufficient effort; girls are more likely to think the same failures are due to a lack of ability.
   c. Boys show greater inherited athletic ability than girls as early as preschool.
   d. Girls form closer friendships than boys do.

1) 4. Three of the following statements are consistent with the textbook's description of students from low-SES backgrounds. Which statement is *not*?
   a. Students from low-SES backgrounds have less exposure to television than students from middle-income families.
   b. Students from low-SES backgrounds are less likely to have been read to as young children.
   c. Students from low-SES backgrounds are likely to have a less healthful diet than is true for other students.
   d. Students from low-SES backgrounds are often "stressed out" about circumstances at home.

2) 5. Three of the students below show warning signs for being at risk. Which student is *least* likely to be at risk?
   a. Andrea is absent from school about two days out of every five.
   b. Bill is still in sixth grade, even though he is almost fourteen years old.
   c. Connie has been getting low grades since elementary school, and her reading comprehension skills are poor.
   d. Dwayne has spent so much time at practice for the football and basketball teams that his grades have dropped considerably.

Essay

1) 6. Drawing on research findings presented in the textbook, identify at least four ways that students from diverse cultural backgrounds may have difficulty adjusting to a traditional classroom in our country.

1) 7. Explain what psychologists mean when they refer to students as being *at risk*. Describe four characteristics commonly associated with at-risk students.

Answers to Sample Test Questions

1. b—With a score of 110, Franklin has done better than 74.8 percent of the students in his age group (see Figure 4-2 on textbook page 124).

2. b—Martha appears to have high logical-mathematical and interpersonal intelligence, but lower linguistic and bodily-kinesthetic intelligence (see Table 4-2 on textbook page 127).

3. c—Before puberty, boys and girls have similar physiological capabilities (see Table 4-3 on textbook page 146).

4. a—The other three alternatives are consistent with the discussion of socioeconomic differences (beginning on textbook page 151). Television viewing habits are not discussed in the textbook, and in fact there is no evidence to indicate that children from low-income families watch less television than other children do.

5. d—Students at risk engage in few if any extracurricular activities. By participating in school sports, Dwayne is showing psychological attachment to his school. (See the section "Characteristics of Students at Risk" on textbook page 154.)

6. Characteristics of certain cultural groups that may influence classroom performance are described in the section "Examples of Ethnic Diversity" beginning on textbook page 138. Your response should describe at least four of these.

7. Students at risk are those with a high probability of failing to acquire the minimal academic skills (reading, writing, spelling, math, etc.) necessary for success in the adult world. Characteristics of at-risk students are described on textbook page 154; your response should include at least four of them.

Chapter 5

STUDENTS WITH SPECIAL EDUCATIONAL NEEDS

Chapter Overview

This chapter describes students with special needs—those who are different enough from their classmates that they require specially adapted instructional materials and practices to help them maximize their school success. You will find that as a result of the *inclusion* movement and federal legislation, many students with special needs are now enrolled in general education classrooms for part or all of the school day.

After considering the advantages and disadvantages of categorizing and labeling special needs, you will read about five general categories of students with special needs: (1) students with specific cognitive or academic difficulties (learning disabilities, attention-deficit hyperactivity disorder, speech and communication disorders), (2) students with social or behavioral problems (emotional or behavioral disorders, autism), (3) students with general delays in cognitive and social functioning (mental retardation), (4) students with physical or sensory challenges (physical and health impairments, visual impairments, hearing loss, severe and multiple disabilities), and (5) students with advanced cognitive development (giftedness).

Throughout the chapter, you will find numerous suggestions for adapting academic materials, instruction, and activities for students with special needs. You will also find strategies for helping these students develop friendships with their classmates—social successes that are undoubtedly just as important as academic ones.

Common Student Beliefs and Misconceptions Related to Chapter Content

Below are four misconceptions that college students often have about students with special needs—misconceptions that may interfere with an accurate understanding of what they read in their textbooks. As you read Chapter 5, be on the lookout for evidence that contradicts these common misconceptions:

1. Some people believe that the labels assigned to various disabilities (e.g., *learning disability*) always reflect permanent, lifelong conditions.
2. Some people who are studying to become regular classroom teachers think that they will rarely, if ever, have students with special educational needs (e.g., those with mental retardation or those with emotional and behavioral disorders) in their classrooms.
3. Many people believe that autism is an emotional disorder. In fact, the characteristics associated with autism are probably due to cognitive factors (e.g., an undersensitivity or oversensitivity to sensory stimulation).
4. Some people believe that students who are gifted don't need special educational services.

CHAPTER OUTLINE	FOCUS QUESTIONS

INCLUSION: EDUCATING ALL STUDENTS IN GENERAL EDUCATION CLASSROOMS
 	
   An Historical Overview of the Inclusion Movement
 	
   Public Law 94-142: The Individuals with Disabilities Education Act (IDEA)
 	
   Is Inclusion in the Best Interest of Students?
 	
   The Current Conception of Inclusion
	• How has the education of students with special needs changed over the past century?
	
	• In the United States, what rights does the Individuals with Disabilities Education Act (IDEA) ensure for students with special needs? What implications do these rights have for teachers?
	
	• What is an IEP, and what are its components?
	
	• In what ways do students with special needs benefit from being educated in general education classrooms?

GENERAL CATEGORIES OF STUDENTS WITH SPECIAL NEEDS
 	
   Using People-First Language
 	
   An Overall Organizational Scheme
	• What are the problems associated with categorizing special needs? What are the advantages in categorizing them?
	
	• What is *people-first language*? Why is it recommended?

STUDENTS WITH SPECIFIC COGNITIVE OR ACADEMIC DIFFICULTIES
 	
   Learning Disabilities
 	
   Attention-Deficit Hyperactivity Disorder (ADHD)
 	
   Speech and Communication Disorders
 	
   General Recommendations for Students with Specific Cognitive or Academic Difficulties
	• What are *learning disabilities*, and how might they affect students' academic achievement?
	
	• What is *attention-deficit hyperactivity disorder*? What characteristics are associated with ADHD?
	
	• What are *speech and communication disorders*? How might they affect students' classroom performance?
	
	• How can teachers enhance the learning and achievement of students with various cognitive or academic difficulties? What strategies are useful with *all* of these students?

CHAPTER OUTLINE	FOCUS QUESTIONS
STUDENTS WITH SOCIAL OR BEHAVIORAL PROBLEMS Emotional and Behavioral Disorders Autism General Recommendations for Students with Social or Behavioral Problems	• What are *emotional and behavioral disorders*? How are *externalizing behaviors* different from *internalizing behaviors*? How are the characteristics associated with such disorders apt to affect academic achievement? • How is *autism* different from an emotional or behavioral disorder? What characteristics are often seen in students with this disability? • How can teachers adapt classroom practices to facilitate the classroom success of students with emotional and behavioral disorders and students with autism?
STUDENTS WITH GENERAL DELAYS IN COGNITIVE AND SOCIAL FUNCTIONING Mental Retardation	• What criteria are used to identify students with *mental retardation*? How can teachers accommodate the specific academic and social needs of these students?
STUDENTS WITH PHYSICAL AND SENSORY CHALLENGES Physical and Health Impairments Visual Impairments Hearing Loss Severe and Multiple Disabilities General Recommendations for Students with Physical and Sensory Challenges	• What conditions characterize students with *physical and health impairments*, *visual impairments*, *hearing loss*, and *severe and multiple disabilities*? What other characteristics might students in each of these categories have? • How can teachers enhance the learning and achievement of students with various physical and sensory challenges? What strategies are useful with *all* of these students?
STUDENTS WITH ADVANCED COGNITIVE DEVELOPMENT Giftedness	• In what areas might students show exceptional talent? Why is giftedness so difficult to pin down? • What strategies can teachers use to enhance the learning and achievement of students who are gifted?
CONSIDERING DIVERSITY WHEN IDENTIFYING AND ADDRESSING SPECIAL NEEDS	• What groups tend to be overrepresented among students identified as having special needs? What are some possible explanations for such disproportionate representation?
THE BIG PICTURE: HELPING ALL STUDENTS WITH SPECIAL NEEDS	• What general strategies can teachers use to adapt instruction more effectively to the needs of all students?

Chapter Glossary

Adaptive behavior. Behavior related to daily living skills and appropriate conduct in social situations; a deficit in adaptive behavior is used as a criterion for identifying students with mental retardation.

Attention-deficit hyperactivity disorder (ADHD). A category of special needs marked either by inattention or by both hyperactivity and impulsive behavior (or by all three of these); such characteristics probably have a biological origin.

Autism. A category of special needs characterized by impaired social interaction and communication, repetitive behaviors, restricted interests, and a strong need for a predictable environment; underlying the condition may be either an undersensitivity or an oversensitivity to sensory stimulation.

Cooperative teaching. A general education teacher and special education teacher collaborating to teach all students in a class, including students both with and without special educational needs, throughout the school day.

Emotional and behavioral disorders. A category of special needs characterized by behaviors or emotional states that have a substantial negative effect on students' classroom performance.

Externalizing behavior. A symptom of an emotional or behavioral disorder that has direct or indirect effects on other people (e.g., aggression, disobedience, stealing).

Giftedness. A category of special needs characterized by unusually high ability in one or more areas, to the point where students require special educational services to help them meet their full potential.

Hearing loss. A category of special needs characterized by malfunctions of the ear or associated nerves that interfere with the perception of sounds within the frequency range of normal human speech.

Inclusion. The practice of educating all students, even those with severe and multiple disabilities, in neighborhood schools and general education classrooms.

Individualized education program (IEP). A written description of an appropriate instructional program for a student with special needs; mandated by the Individuals with Disabilities Education Act (IDEA) for all students with disabilities.

Individuals with Disabilities Education Act (IDEA). U.S. legislation granting educational rights to people with cognitive, emotional, or physical disabilities from birth until age 21; it guarantees a free and appropriate education, fair and nondiscriminatory evaluation, education in the least restrictive environment, an individualized education program, and due process.

Internalizing behavior. A symptom of an emotional or behavioral disorder that primarily affects the student with the disorder, with little or no effect on others (e.g., anxiety, depression).

Learning disabilities. A category of special needs characterized by average or above-average intelligence, lower academic achievement than would be predicted from students' IQ scores, and a deficiency in one or more specific cognitive processes.

Least restrictive environment. The most typical and standard educational environment that can reasonably meet a student's needs.

Mainstreaming. The practice of having students with special needs join general education classrooms primarily when their abilities enabled them to participate in normally scheduled activities as successfully as other students.

Mental retardation. A category of special needs characterized by significantly below-average general intelligence and deficits in adaptive behavior.

Mnemonic. A special memory aid or trick designed to help students learn and remember information.

People-first language. Language in which a student's disability is identified *after* the student (e.g., "student with a learning disability" rather than "learning disabled student").

Physical and health impairments. A category of special needs characterized by general physical or medical conditions (usually long-term) that interfere with students' school performance to such an extent that special instruction, curricular materials, equipment, or facilities are necessary.

Savant syndrome. A syndrome characterized by an extraordinary ability to perform a specific task despite difficulty in other aspects of mental functioning; occasionally observed in students with autism.

Self-contained class. A class in which students with special needs are educated as a group apart from other students.

Severe and multiple disabilities. A category of special needs in which students have two or more disabilities, the combination of which requires significant adaptations and highly specialized services in their educational programs.

Speech and communication disorders. A category of special needs characterized by abnormalities in spoken language or language comprehension that significantly interfere with students' classroom performance.

Students with special needs. Students who are different enough from their peers that they require specially adapted instructional materials and practices.

Visual impairments. A category of special needs characterized by malfunctions of the eyes or optic nerves that prevent students from seeing normally even with corrective lenses.

Application Exercise #8: Identifying Special Needs

Identify the special need that each of the following students is most likely to have.

1. Meghan must be supervised closely during recess. She picks fights with other students, especially those younger than herself, and she has no real friends. Meghan's father has a history of alcoholism and becomes violent when he gets drunk.

2. Even with his thick glasses, Ronald has trouble reading what his teacher writes on the board. He squints while looking at his textbooks and often misreads words that he should be able to recognize.

3. Although Rachel is a fifth grader, her knowledge and skills are more typical of a first grader, and she seems happiest playing with children who are several years younger than she is. One of her fifth-grade classmates says that she "acts silly, like my little brother."

4. As a junior high school student, Matthew plays the trombone in the school orchestra and is a standout on the cross-country team. He does quite well in math but is having difficulty in his history, geography, and English classes, all of which require a fair amount of reading. His mother reports that he spends at least three hours doing homework every night but often finds his assignments difficult and frustrating.

5. Calvin's performance on school tasks is inconsistent. Curiously, he usually does better on challenging tasks than on easy ones. He has many friends at school, although they describe him as being a bit pompous, because he sometimes uses words that they don't understand— words like "venerable," "capricious," and "anachronism."

6. Nadine tires easily and must rest often. She visits the school nurse twice a day for her medication, and she often stays in the nurse's office to take a short nap. Participating in the regular physical education program is out of the question, because Nadine doesn't have the endurance to keep up with her classmates.

7. Harlan's written work—homework assignments, compositions, and exams—reveals a young man with a great deal of academic potential. However, Harlan is extremely quiet in class; when his teacher calls on him, he has trouble putting his thoughts into words.

8. As a middle school student, Sandra has trouble paying attention in class for more than five minutes at a time. She is exceptionally hyperactive for her age; for example, she gets out of her seat frequently and talks incessantly to those around her. Her parents say she has always been this way; they have taken her to several specialists over the years, but none has been able to pinpoint a physical or emotional source for her behavior.

9. Valerie does exceptionally well on exams; in fact, she often has the highest score in the class. Yet during class sessions, she never says a word unless she is specifically called on; however, she converses readily with her friends in other situations. On several occasions in class, her teacher has asked Valerie questions that he knows she can answer correctly, but she says nothing and acts as if she's forgotten everything she has learned.

10. Lucy rarely talks in her first-grade class and prefers to spend most of her time alone. She is often preoccupied with the pencils in her pencil box.

11. Luis seems extremely depressed much of the time. He frequently describes himself as a "complete zero." He spends his study hall time writing poems that usually depict despair, destruction, and death.

Answers to Application Exercise #8

1. Meghan's difficulty interacting appropriately with others and establishing any long-term interpersonal relationships suggests a possible <u>emotional or behavior disorder</u>.

2. Ronald has a <u>visual impairment</u>.

3. Although we don't know anything about what Rachel's performance on an intelligence test might be, low achievement in all areas of the school curriculum and social behaviors inappropriate for her age group are both indicative of <u>mental retardation</u>.

4. Matthew's uneven record in academic achievement and his particular difficulty with reading indicate a possible <u>learning disability</u>.

5. Calvin's behavior indicates possible <u>giftedness</u>. His poor performance on easy tasks is probably due to boredom rather than to a lack of ability.

6. Nadine has a <u>physical or health impairment</u> that may require special educational services (e.g., in physical education) to meet her needs.

7. Harlan's difficulty with spoken language indicates a possible <u>speech or communication disorder</u>.

8. Sandra's behaviors are consistent with <u>attention-deficit hyperactivity disorder</u>.

9. Valerie is showing signs of <u>giftedness</u> but may be trying to hide her ability from her peers.

10. Lucy's lack of social interaction and communication, combined with her unusual interest in certain objects, indicates possible <u>autism</u>.

11. Long-term depression indicates an <u>emotional or behavioral disorder</u>. The teacher should worry that Luis might be contemplating suicide and immediately contact the school psychologist or counselor.

Answers to Selected Margin Notes

- Page 169: *What additional concerns might people have had about self-contained classes?*
  They may have had any number of concerns, including these:
  - Students were not getting the "normal" school experiences that would maximize academic and social development.
  - Students in self-contained classrooms had few if any opportunities to interact and form friendships with nondisabled peers.
  - Expectations for students may have been lower in self-contained classrooms and the curriculum watered down accordingly.
  - Special class placement might adversely affect students' self-esteem.

- Page 170: *Why is it important for parents to be included in the multidisciplinary team?*
  For one thing, parents often have useful information and observations about their child that can provide a more complete and accurate understanding of his/her strengths and weaknesses. Second, it is often advantageous to coordinate strategies being implemented at school with things parents are doing at home. And third, an instructional program is most likely to be effective when the child's parents are fully supportive of a teacher's efforts.

- Page 174: *Why do you think students placed in regular classrooms often have more appropriate classroom behavior? Why do you think they may have better self-concepts and more positive attitudes about school?*
  By being in a general education classroom, they are probably getting the message that they are, to some extent, like everyone else rather than being "different" in some way. Furthermore, they are more likely to see models of appropriate classroom behavior than they would if they were in, say, a self-contained class for students with emotional and behavioral problems. And perhaps most important, their teachers are more likely to hold high expectations for both their academic achievement and their classroom behavior.

- Page 176: *Why do you think it is so difficult to define some categories of special needs?*
  Although students may be similar in some ways, they are likely to be very different in others.

- Page 189 *Why are [students with emotional and behavioral problems] so often disliked by their classmates?*
  They often interact with their peers in inappropriate and perhaps counterproductive ways.

- Page 209: *Why else might some individuals oppose special services for gifted students?*
  We can only speculate as to why some people might be opposed to gifted education. One possible concern is that special services for gifted programs might divert funds and personnel that might otherwise be devoted to other students. Another possibility is that when some students are given special services for the gifted and others are not, the latter are essentially being told that they have lower ability than some of their classmates.

Sample Test Questions

Items marked with a "1)" on the left-hand side are lower-level questions that assess your general knowledge and understanding of the material. Items marked with a "2)" on the left-hand side are higher-level questions that assess your ability to apply what you have learned to a new situation.

Multiple-Choice

1)   1. In the United States, three of the following are mandated by Public Law 94-142 (IDEA). Which one is *not* mandated by this legislation?
    a. Special educational services must be provided for gifted students as well as for students with cognitive, emotional, and physical disabilities.
    b. Students with special needs must be educated in the most "typical" school environment that can meet their specific needs.
    c. Decisions about the best program for a student with special needs should be made only after a fair evaluation of all available information.
    d. The instructional program developed for a student with special needs must be described in terms of the specific objectives to be accomplished and the methods by which those objectives will be achieved.

2) 2. Which one of the following students is most likely to be identified as having a *learning disability*?
   a. Alan gets tired very easily and must often stop to rest in the middle of an assignment.
   b. Barbara has trouble reading despite a recently obtained IQ score of 110.
   c. Carl prefers to play with younger children and demonstrates low achievement in all areas of the school curriculum.
   d. Dolly often stutters when she's called on in class.

1) 3. Some students with emotional or behavioral disorders may exhibit one of the following behaviors. Which one is an *internalizing behavior*?
   a. Stealing other people's possessions
   b. Setting fires
   c. Refusing to interact with peers
   d. Hitting and biting other people

2) 4. Students with mental retardation have deficits in *adaptive behavior*. Which one of the following students shows such a deficit?
   a. Angela spends much of the school day rocking back and forth.
   b. At least once a week, Beth threatens to commit suicide.
   c. Craig can't seem to sit still for more than two minutes at a time.
   d. David has trouble remembering and following normal classroom routines.

1) 5. Experts recommend three of the following strategies for teaching students who are gifted. Which strategy do they *not* necessarily recommend?
   a. Identifying mentors who can teach students specialized skills
   b. Forming study groups of students with similar abilities
   c. Focusing instruction on the areas in which students are weakest
   d. Providing opportunities for independent study

Essay

1) 6. Why are students with special educational needs often included in general education classrooms for most or all of the school day? Describe three distinct benefits that inclusion may have.

1) 7. The textbook identifies a number of strategies that are applicable to most or all students with special educational needs. Describe three of these strategies, and illustrate each one with a concrete example of what a teacher might do.

Answers to Sample Test Questions

1. a—PL 94-142 does not address the special educational needs of gifted students. The categories addressed by IDEA are listed on textbook page 176.

2. b—Students with learning disabilities have difficulty with one or more cognitive processes even though they often have average or above-average intelligence (see the section on "Learning Disabilities" beginning on textbook page 179).

3. c—An internalizing behavior primarily affects the student with the disorder (see textbook page 188). The other three alternatives are externalizing behaviors, which affect other people as well.

4. d—Students with mental retardation may have difficulty with self-direction (following a schedule, completing required tasks, etc.) See Figure 5-4 on textbook page 195.

5. c—Much of the instruction for gifted students is aimed at challenging them and helping them develop their special talents further (see the section on "Adapting Instruction" beginning on textbook page 209).

6. Inclusion has benefits for students both with and without disabilities. Several advantages are listed in the section "Is Inclusion in the Best Interest of Students?" beginning on textbook page 172.

7. Your response should describe three of the strategies presented in "The Big Picture" on textbook pages 212-215. It should also include a specific example of how a teacher might carry out each strategy.

Chapter 6

LEARNING AND COGNITIVE PROCESSES

Chapter Overview

This chapter introduces you to the psychological study of how human beings learn. It then explores basic principles of learning and memory from the perspective of cognitive psychology, a perspective that focuses on how people think about and mentally "process" the information they receive. You will find that human memory may have several components, including a sensory register, working memory, and long-term memory. You will read about the various cognitive processes through which students put (store) information in memory and discover that some processes are more effective than others. You will also examine the nature of "remembering" (retrieval) and examine several possible explanations for why your students may sometimes forget the things that you have taught them. Near the end of the chapter, you will consider examples of diversity in cognitive processing, with a particular focus on students who have special educational needs.

Throughout the chapter, you will find applications of cognitive psychology for classroom practice. For example, you will learn numerous strategies for helping students process information in ways that will help them remember it and be able to use it. You will also discover the many advantages of *wait time*—of simply giving students the time that they need to think things through.

Common Student Beliefs and Misconceptions Related to Chapter Content

Below are several beliefs that college students often have before studying cognitive psychology—beliefs that may interfere with an accurate understanding of what they read. As you read Chapter 6, be on the lookout for evidence that contradicts these common beliefs:

1. Some students believe that we don't necessarily have to *think about* the information we receive—that mere exposure to the information is enough.

2. Some students believe that rote memorization—repeating something over and over without really thinking about it—is an effective way to learn.

3. Some students think of *rehearsal* only in terms of practicing lines in a play or oral presentation. Cognitive psychologists' meaning of this term is quite different.

CHAPTER OUTLINE	FOCUS QUESTIONS
LOOKING AT LEARNING FROM DIFFERENT PERSPECTIVES Learning as a Change in Behavior Learning as a Change in Mental Associations Keeping an Open Mind About Theories of Learning	• In what two ways is learning commonly defined? With which learning theories is each definition associated? • Why did behaviorists propose that the study of learning should focus exclusively on stimuli and responses? How have cognitive psychologists responded to behaviorists' concern about the study of nonobservable, mental phenomena (i.e., thinking)?
BASIC ASSUMPTIONS OF COGNITIVE PSYCHOLOGY	• What basic assumptions underlie cognitive psychology? What implications does each assumption have for teaching practice? • Why do many cognitive psychologists believe that learning often involves a process of construction?
BASIC TERMINOLOGY IN COGNITIVE PSYCHOLOGY Memory Storage Encoding Retrieval	• What do cognitive psychologists mean by the terms *memory, storage, encoding,* and *retrieval*? Can you think of a new example of each one of these?
A MODEL OF HUMAN MEMORY The Nature of the Sensory Register Moving Information to Working Memory: The Role of Attention The Nature of Working (Short-Term) Memory Moving Information to Long-Term Memory: Connecting New Information with Prior Knowledge The Nature of Long-Term Memory Critiquing the Three-Component Model	• What roles do the sensory register, working memory, and long-term memory play in learning? How much capacity does each component have? How long does information stored in each component last? • What role does attention play in the memory system? How can teachers encourage students to pay attention? • Which aspects of the memory system have a limited capacity? What implications does this limited capacity have for classroom instruction? • At what point in the memory system do students connect new information with existing knowledge? • What alternative view of memory have some theorists offered?

CHAPTER OUTLINE	FOCUS QUESTIONS
LONG-TERM MEMORY STORAGE The Various Forms of Knowledge How Declarative Knowledge Is Learned How Procedural Knowledge Is Learned Prior Knowledge and Working Memory in Long-Term Memory Storage Using Mnemonics in the Absence of Relevant Prior Knowledge	• What different forms does knowledge take? Why are multiple encodings of a single piece of information beneficial? • What five long-term memory storage processes may be involved in acquiring declarative knowledge? Describe these processes in your own words, and think of a new example of each one. • Which of the five storage processes are clearly effective? Which one is relatively ineffective, and why? • What three conditions are necessary for meaningful learning to occur? What implications do these conditions have for classroom instruction? • What processes may be involved in acquiring procedural knowledge? How can teachers help students learn new skills? • Why does students' prior knowledge affect their ability to store new information effectively? • When are mnemonics most useful? Can you describe *verbal mediation*, the *keyword method*, and a *superimposed meaningful structure* and apply each technique to a new learning task?
LONG-TERM MEMORY RETRIEVAL The Nature of Long-Term Memory Retrieval Factors Affecting Retrieval Why People Sometimes "Forget"	• How do cognitive psychologists think that retrieval of information from long-term memory occurs? What conditions facilitate retrieval, and why? • What teaching strategies can facilitate retrieval of previously learned information and skills? • What are five different reasons why students may "forget" what their teachers have taught them? With these reasons in mind, can you identify several teaching strategies that can minimize the chances that students will forget important material?
GIVING STUDENTS TIME TO PROCESS: EFFECTS OF INCREASING WAIT TIME	• What do theorists mean by the term *wait time*? After what two events are teachers "waiting"? • How much wait time do teachers typically allow? How much time appears to be beneficial? • When wait time increases, what changes are seen in students' behavior? in teachers' behavior?

CHAPTER OUTLINE	FOCUS QUESTIONS
ACCOMMODATING DIVERSITY IN COGNITIVE PROCESSES Facilitating Cognitive Processing in Students with Special Needs	• How might students' cognitive processes differ as a function of ethnic differences: How might they differ as a function of special needs?

<u>Chapter Glossary</u>

Activation. The degree to which a particular piece of information in memory is currently being attended to and mentally processed.

Attention. The focusing of mental processes on particular environmental stimuli.

Automaticity. The ability to respond quickly and efficiently while mentally processing or physically performing a task.

Behaviorism. A theoretical perspective in which learning and behavior are described and explained in terms of stimulus-response relationships. Adherents to this perspective are called *behaviorists*.

Cognitive psychology. A theoretical perspective that focuses on the mental processes underlying human learning and behavior.

Construction. The process of taking many separate pieces of information and using them to build an overall understanding or interpretation of an event.

Constructivism. A theoretical perspective that proposes that learners construct a body of knowledge from their experiences—knowledge that may or may not be an accurate representation of external reality. Adherents to this perspective are called *constructivists*.

Decay. A hypothesized weakening over time of information stored in long-term memory, especially if the information is used infrequently or not at all.

Declarative knowledge. Knowledge related to "what is"—how things are, were, or will be.

Elaboration. A cognitive process in which learners expand on new information based on what they already know.

Encoding. Changing the format of new information as it is being stored in memory.

Failure to store. One's failure to mentally process information in ways that promote its storage in long-term memory.

Inability to retrieve. Failing to locate information that currently exists in long-term memory.

Information processing theory. A theoretical perspective that focuses on the specific ways in which individuals mentally think about and "process" the information they receive.

Interference. A phenomenon whereby something stored in long-term memory inhibits one's ability to remember something else correctly.

Keyword method. A mnemonic technique in which an association is made between two ideas by forming a visual image of one or more concrete objects (*keywords*) that either sound similar to, or symbolically represent, those ideas.

Knowledge base. One's knowledge about specific topics and the world in general.

Learning. A relatively permanent change, due to experience, in either behavior or mental associations.

Long-term memory. The component of memory that holds knowledge and skills for a relatively long period of time.

Meaningful learning. A cognitive process in which learners relate new information to the things they already know.

Meaningful learning set. An attitude that one can make sense of the information one is studying.

Memory. A learner's ability to save something (mentally) that he or she has previously learned, *or* the mental "location" where such information is saved.

Mnemonic. A special memory aid or trick designed to help students learn and remember information.

Organization. A cognitive process in which learners find connections (e.g., forming categories, identifying hierarchical relationships) among the various pieces of information they need to learn.

Procedural knowledge. Knowledge concerning how to do something.

Recall task. A memory task in which one must retrieve information in its entirety from long-term memory.

Recognition task. A memory task in which one must recognize correct information among irrelevant information or incorrect statements.

Reconstruction error. Constructing a logical but incorrect "memory" by using information retrieved from long-term memory plus one's general knowledge of the world.

Rehearsal. A cognitive process in which information is repeated over and over as a possible way of learning and remembering it. When it is used to maintain information in working memory, it is called **maintenance rehearsal**.

Response (R). A specific behavior that an individual exhibits.

Retrieval. The process of "finding" information previously stored in memory.

Retrieval cue. A hint about where to "look" for a piece of information in long-term memory.

Rote learning. Learning information primarily through verbatim repetition, without understanding it in a meaningful fashion.

Sensory register. A component of memory that holds incoming information in an unanalyzed form for a very brief period of time (probably less than a second for visual input and two or three seconds for auditory input).

Social cognitive theory. A theoretical perspective in which learning by observing others is the focus of study.

Stimulus (S) (pl. stimuli). A specific object or event that influences an individual's learning or behavior.

Storage. The process of "putting" new information into memory.

Superimposed meaningful structure. A mnemonic technique in which a familiar shape, word, sentence, poem, or story is imposed on information and thereby used to remember it.

Verbal mediator. A mnemonic technique in which a word or phrase is used to form a logical connection or "bridge" between two pieces of information.

Visual imagery. The process of forming mental "pictures" of objects or ideas.

Wait time. The length of time a teacher pauses, either after asking a question or hearing a student's comment, before saying something else.

Working memory. A component of memory that holds and processes a limited amount of new information; also known as *short-term memory*. The duration of information stored in working memory is believed to be approximately five to twenty seconds.

Application Exercise #9: Analyzing Cognitive Processes

Identify the cognitive processes and/or components of memory involved in each of the following.

1. When Michelle reads about the assassination of Martin Luther King, Jr., she associates it with the racist attitudes that many people have toward African Americans.

2. Alex remembers that Juneau is the capital of Alaska by thinking, "<u>D'you know</u> the capital of <u>Alaska</u>?"

3. Walt studies his spelling words by writing each one three times in a row.

4. Candace is studying her multiplication tables, including $6 \times 9 = 54$ and $7 \times 8 = 56$. When she is multiplying 7 and 8 on a homework assignment, she erroneously writes "54."

5. Dominic's physical education teacher is demonstrating how to dribble a basketball past an opponent. Dominic thinks to himself, "Aha! To keep the ball away from my opponent, I need to move the ball as unpredictably as I can."

6. As her teacher reads the first chapter of *Stuart Little,* Juanita tries to imagine the little mouse washing himself in a human-size bathroom sink.

7. Just before a mathematics quiz, Frank looks at the formula for computing the area of a circle ($A = \pi r^2$) one last time. He repeats the formula to himself until he receives his exam sheet, at which point he quickly writes it down in the margin so he won't forget it.

8. When Kevin's teacher asks him, "In the biological classification system, in which class do we find spiders?" Kevin's mind goes blank. Later, he and his friend Joey are talking about old movies, and Joey mentions *Arachnophobia* as one of his all-time favorites. Suddenly Kevin remembers the answer to his teacher's question—arachnids.

9. James remembers that *le chien* is French for "the dog" by picturing a dog with a big *chain* around its neck.

10. As his teacher explains how *The Scarlet Letter* reflects the values of Puritan New England, Joel is thinking about the fight that he had with his best friend at lunch.

11. When the music teacher asks, "Which operas did Mozart write?" her students cannot remember a single one. She gives them a hint: "One of his operas involves a wedding." At this point, Tom immediately shouts out, "*The Marriage of Figaro*!"

12. Gail is reading about the American Revolution. To help herself remember what she is reading, Gail lists the various events that occurred before and during the war on a piece of paper; she then draws arrows to indicate possible cause-effect relationships among them.

13. Once a week, Suzanne reviews the vocabulary words she has learned in Spanish I this year.

14. Ben is reading a college-level textbook that he is having trouble understanding. "Surely I can make sense of this if I work at it a while," he thinks to himself.

15. Rhonda remembers the biological classification system—kingdom, phylum, class, order, family, genus, species—by remembering "King Philip comes over for good spaghetti."

Answers to Application Exercise #9

1. Michelle is engaging in <u>meaningful learning</u>. She is understanding King's assassination in terms of something she already knows—racism.

2. Alex is using a mnemonic—<u>verbal mediation</u>—to connect Juneau ("d'you know") to Alaska.

3. Walt is using <u>rehearsal</u> in an attempt to store how the words are spelled.

4. Candace may be suffering from <u>interference</u>—she is confusing the answer to 6×9 with the answer to 7×8.

5. Dominic is engaging in <u>elaboration</u>. The teacher did not specifically say that one should dribble the ball unpredictably, but Dominic is inferring so from the teacher's behavior.

6. Juanita is storing part of the story in terms of a <u>visual image</u>.

7. Frank is engaging in <u>maintenance rehearsal</u>, a process that will keep the formula in his working memory until he has a chance to write it down.

8. In class, Kevin is suffering from an <u>inability to retrieve</u> the word *arachnid*. The movie title later provides him the <u>retrieval cue</u> he needs.

9. James is using the <u>keyword</u> mnemonic to make the connection between *le chien* and "the dog."

10. The teacher's explanation is not getting beyond Joel's <u>sensory register</u> because he isn't <u>paying attention</u>.

11. The teacher provides a <u>retrieval cue</u> that enables Tom to retrieve one of Mozart's operas.

12. By identifying the connections among events, Gail is <u>organizing</u> the material.

13. Suzanne apparently knows that occasional review will enhance her ability to <u>retrieve</u> those words when she needs them.

14. Ben has a <u>meaningful learning set</u>—an intention to learn something at a meaningful level.

15. Rhonda is using a <u>superimposed meaningful structure</u> to help her remember the list.

Application Exercise #10: Identifying Effective Classroom Practices

Decide whether each of the following teaching practices is consistent with cognitive psychology's principles of learning, and why.

1. Mr. Hendricks asks his students to multiply 623×59 in their heads.

2. As Ms. Ziolkowski describes how Japanese culture is different from our own, she occasionally stops to ask students a question for them to think about and answer.

3. Even though Mr. Stolte's students are now studying multiplication and division, he occasionally has them do problems requiring addition and subtraction.

4. Ms. Tipton warns Sam, an avid reader, that he may be reading too much. She tells him, "I'm afraid that your mind will get so cluttered with the things you read that you won't have room for the things you're supposed to learn in school."

5. Before beginning a lesson on mammals, Ms. Thomas asks, "How many of you have pets at home? How many have dogs? cats? fish? birds? lizards? Can you think of ways in which all of these animals are alike?"

6. Ms. Durocher teaches in a Boston suburb, close to where many early events of the American Revolution took place. When she begins to talk about the revolution in a history lesson, she describes each local event as it comes to mind.

7. Mr. Urquhart reminds his students, "All eyes should be on me as I explain tonight's homework assignment."

8. Mr. Palermo's class has just read Nathaniel Hawthorne's *The Scarlet Letter*. "I don't think Hester Prynne did anything wrong," says Karen. Mr. Palermo waits several seconds to see if other students agree or disagree before sharing his own opinion about Hester's behavior.

9. As Mr. Gotthardt describes World War II's D-Day, he passes around pictures from an old issue of *Life* magazine that show Allied troops landing at Omaha Beach.

10. Mr. Davis says, "Now that we know the properties of acids, what things might acids help us do?"

11. Ms. Gibbs is preparing her students for a standardized achievement test they will be taking next Monday. "Listen closely and put this in your short-term memories," she advises them. "Be sure to get a good night's sleep and eat a good breakfast before you come to school that day."

12. Mr. Li's class is studying South America. He has them study a different aspect of the continent each month—the topography in September, the culture in October, major cities in November, economics in December, and so on—so that they won't get all these things confused.

13. Mr. Nakamura wants his students to be as relaxed as possible while he describes a difficult concept, so he gives them paper and crayons to draw pictures as he talks.

14. Ms. Ellis is showing members of the high school majorette squad how to do a butterfly spin. "You hold the baton in the middle and keep your arm out straight," she says. "You move the large end and then the small end of the baton *over* your arm. With the next spin, you move both the large end and small end *under* your arm. Then over, over, and under, under. As the baton goes up, your arm goes down, and vice versa. See?" Ms. Ellis has the students practice the spin in slow motion and encourages them to say "Over, over, under, under" as they do so.

15. Ms. Montgomery says, "OK, students, we've studied a number of basic elements, including aluminum, boron, calcium, carbon, copper, iodine, iron, potassium, silicon, tin, and zinc. Let's classify them into two groups—metals and nonmetals."

16. To keep her students' attention, Ms. Peterson engages in a rapid-fire presentation of facts they need to know.

17. When scoring her students' physics tests, Ms. Tobias gives credit only when students describe things exactly as presented in the book. This way, she can score their answers consistently and fairly.

18. Mr. Joslin isn't pleased with the geography textbook he must use with his students; he thinks that it presents far too many details about each region that the class will be studying. So before he assigns each chapter, he tells his students what parts they should focus on as they read.

19. Ms. Freitag has her second graders practice reading commonly used English words over and over again. Such practice sometimes involves responding to flash cards, but more often, it involves reading many short stories that include the words.

20. Mr. Sheehan says, "Now that we have studied three simple machines—levers, wedges, and pulleys—who can tell me what kind of machine an axe is?" When the students don't raise their hands immediately, he tells them, "An axe is a wedge."

21. Ms. Sanderson tells students in her French class that they can remember that *marcher* means "to walk" by thinking about "marching."

22. Mr. Wolfe is reviewing yesterday's discussion of poetry. "What do we call the word for a poem's rhythmic pattern?" When no one responds after several seconds, he says, "See if you can remember. It begins with the letter *M*." At that point several students shout out, "Meter!"

23. Ms. Flanagan is trying to give her students an idea of how long humans have populated the earth. She tells them, "Think of the earth's history as being a 24-hour day. Human beings have only been in existence between 11:59 p.m. and midnight."

Answers to Application Exercise #10

1. Not consistent. Such a problem would probably exceed the limits of students' working memory capacity.

2. Consistent. Her questions may serve one or more of several purposes—to keep students' attention, check for possible misinterpretations, and promote elaboration.

3. Consistent. Occasional review of things already learned will promote better retrieval over the long run.

4. Not consistent. Long-term memory has a capacity that is, for all intents and purposes, unlimited in capacity. Furthermore, a rich knowledge base facilitates meaningful learning and elaboration.

5. Consistent. Ms. Thomas activates students' prior knowledge about mammals before beginning the lesson, thereby promoting connections between the information she will present and the things that students already know.

6. Not consistent. If Ms. Durocher wants her students to understand how various events of the revolution were interrelated, she should make their relationships clear. A stream-of-consciousness presentation will not help students organize the information she presents.

7. Consistent. Although eye contact alone does not guarantee that students will pay attention, it does increase the likelihood that they will.

8. Consistent. Mr. Palermo is allowing wait time after a student's response—something that should promote greater student participation.

9. Consistent. The pictures should help students form visual images that can supplement what they read and hear about the invasion.

10. Consistent. By asking students to apply what they have learned, he is promoting elaboration.

11. Not consistent. Short-term (working) memory lasts a few seconds, not a few days.

12. Not consistent. Students can probably better understand South America if they see how its various characteristics are related. They will have difficulty interrelating (organizing) all they learn if they study different characteristics at different times.

13. Not consistent. Students may be paying more attention to their artwork than to Mr. Nakamura's explanation.

14. Consistent. By encouraging students to practice the spin and repeat the steps to themselves, she is helping them convert declarative knowledge into procedural knowledge.

15. Consistent. She is helping students organize what they have learned.

16. Not consistent. She is probably exceeding students' working memory capacity, in which case they won't be able to process or remember everything they hear.

17. Not consistent. She is encouraging rote learning rather than meaningful learning.

18. Consistent. People can process only so much information in a certain amount of time, so they must often be selective about what they learn. Mr. Joslin is helping them select important information.

19. Consistent. By having the students read the words over and over again, she is helping them learn to recognize common English words to a level of automaticity. Given the limited capacity of working memory, students are more likely to comprehend the things they read if word recognition is automatic.

20. Not consistent. Mr. Sheehan is probably allowing insufficient wait time to retrieve and/or construct an answer.

21. Consistent. She is helping students make the connection between *marcher* and "walk" by providing a verbal mediator.

22. Consistent. He allows students several seconds to retrieve the answer, but they are unable to do so. The letter *M* provides a retrieval cue that focuses their search of long-term memory.

23. Consistent. She is using an analogy to help students relate the incomprehensible length of the earth's history to something they already know.

Answers to Selected Margin Notes

- Page 221: *From a teacher's perspective, what are the potential advantages of defining learning as a change in behavior? as a change in mental associations?*
  By defining learning as a change in behavior, teachers can specify ahead of time exactly what they want students to be able to do. Furthermore, they can easily observe the extent to which learning is taking place. By defining learning as a change in mental associations, teachers are more likely to identify important connections that students should make; they are also more likely to consider the role that students' prior knowledge must play in new classroom learning tasks. (You may have identified additional advantages of either definition.)

- Page 222: *Can you think of examples of how scientists in other disciplines have drawn inferences about unobservable phenomena?*
  Inference drawing is hardly unique to psychology. For example, chemists developed the concepts *molecule* and *atom* to explain chemical reactions long before such tiny entities were ever observed. Similarly, astronomers have developed the notion of *black hole* solely from the patterns of light and dark that reach their high-powered telescopes.

- Page 232: *Do you see why this process is called maintenance rehearsal?*
  Maintenance rehearsal *maintains* information in working memory indefinitely.

- Page 241: *What implications does this second condition—relevant prior knowledge—have for teaching students from diverse cultural backgrounds?*

  Students from different cultural backgrounds are likely to have the same *amount* of background knowledge (because they have had as many years of experience as their age-mates have), but they may be less familiar with aspects of mainstream culture and so have less background related to a traditional school curriculum. Thus, it is important to determine what knowledge these students do and do not have and to build upon the things that they already know.

- Page 247: *Do you now see why Kanesha had such difficulty remembering the coccyx, ulna, sacrum, clavicle, and patella?*

  She had no knowledge that would help her understand why these bones have the names that they do.

Sample Test Questions

Items marked with a "1)" on the left-hand side are lower-level questions that assess your general knowledge and understanding of the material. Items marked with a "2)" on the left-hand side are higher-level questions that assess your ability to apply what you have learned to a new situation.

Multiple-Choice

2)   1. In which one of the following situations would a *behaviorist* be most likely to say that learning has taken place?
   a. Ruth starts writing her short stories in cursive letters after she studies cursive writing in school.
   b. Matt finally figures out the logic behind a particular geometry proof.
   c. Lucius feels both anger and sadness when he reads about the Holocaust.
   d. JaNeane suddenly realizes that the expression "Look before you leap" isn't necessarily meant to be taken literally.

2)   2. Thursday night, Jennifer studies for a test on Friday morning. She remembers the material quite accurately on Friday and gets an A on the test. However, when she takes a review test two weeks later, she can no longer remember that same material. How far in Jennifer's memory did the material get?
   a. It reached her sensory register.
   b. It reached her working memory.
   c. It reached her long-term memory.
   d. It never got into her memory at all.

2)   3. After her French teacher says, "Merci beaucoup," Henrietta repeats the phrase and then immediately turns to talk to her friend. How far in Henrietta's memory did the material get?
       a. It reached her sensory register.
       b. It reached her working memory.
       c. It reached her long-term memory.
       d. It never got into her memory at all.

2)   4. Justin is trying to learn information in his textbook. His eyes are focused on the words in front of him, but he is thinking about the fishing trip he has planned for this weekend. How far in Justin's memory did the material get?
       a. It reached his sensory register.
       b. It reached his working memory.
       c. It reached his long-term memory.
       d. It never got into his memory at all.

2)   5. In which situation is a student *elaborating* on new information?
       a. Gloria thinks, "Hmm, World War I ended on November 11. That's my friend Cecily's birthday."
       b. Martin thinks, "I see that many California cities have Spanish names. So early settlers in California were probably Spanish."
       c. Francine says to herself, "The capital of South Dakota is Pierre. Pierre, South Dakota. Pierre, South Dakota. Pierre, South Dakota."
       d. Neil says, "The first ten elements in the periodic table are hydrogen, helium, lithium, beryllium, boron, carbon, nitrogen, oxygen, fluorine, and neon. Let's see if I can remember all ten in the correct order."

2)   6. Mr. Wang wants his physical education students to learn how to dribble a basketball so well that they can perform the skill almost without thinking. In other words, he wants them to learn the task to a level of *automaticity*. Which one of the following strategies will best help his students achieve that goal?
       a. Tell students how important it is for them to learn to dribble.
       b. Explain the logic behind dribbling it one way rather than another.
       c. Demonstrate dribbling while students observe.
       d. Give students a lot of practice dribbling.

Essay

1)   7. According to the textbook, three conditions are necessary for meaningful learning to occur. Describe these three conditions, and identify a teaching strategy that you might use to make sure each condition is present while students are learning.

2)   8. The nine planets of the solar system, in order of their distance from the sun, are Mercury, Venus, Earth, Mars, Jupiter, Saturn, Uranus, Neptune, and Pluto. Develop a mnemonic for remembering this list using a *superimposed meaningful structure*.

Answers to Sample Test Questions

1. a—Only Ruth is demonstrating a change in behavior (see the discussion of "Learning as a Change in Behavior" on textbook pages 221-222). The other three situations involve nonobservable, mental phenomena.

2. c—Because Jennifer remembered the material from one day to the next, it was in her long-term memory. The duration of working memory is less than a minute; the duration of the sensory register is only a second or two (See "The Nature of the Sensory Register" on textbook pages 229-230.)

3. b—Henrietta had to pay attention in order to repeat the phrase, so she stored it in her working memory. But because she immediately turned to talk to her friend, she probably didn't process it sufficiently to store it in long-term memory. (See the section "Moving Information to Long-Term Memory" beginning on textbook page 233.)

4. a—Everything sensed is stored in the sensory register. But because Justin is not giving his *mental* attention to the page, he is not storing the words in his working memory. (See the section "Moving Information to Working Memory" beginning on textbook page 230.)

5. b—Martin is the only one going beyond the information itself—in this case, by drawing an inference. (Gloria is relating the information to something she already knows—the process of meaningful learning—but is not extending the new information in any way.) See the discussion of elaboration beginning on textbook page 243.

6. d—Automaticity develops primarily through repetition and practice (see the section entitled "Learning Things to Mastery and Beyond" on textbook page 252).

7. The three conditions—a meaningful learning set, relevant prior knowledge, and awareness of the relevance of that knowledge—are described on textbook pages 240-241. Examples of strategies that you might use to promote each one are these:
   • <u>A meaningful set</u>: Insist that students explain things in their own words rather than verbatim from a textbook.
   • <u>Relevant prior knowledge</u>: Begin instruction with what students already know and proceed from there.
   • <u>Awareness of the relevance of prior knowledge</u>: Draw an analogy between a new idea or concept and a personal experience students have previously had.

8. A superimposed meaningful structure (described on textbook page 249) is a word, phrase, sentence, or the like, that represents a list of items. In this case, we might use a sentence such as this one: "<u>M</u>y <u>v</u>ery <u>e</u>ager <u>m</u>other <u>j</u>ust <u>s</u>ent <u>u</u>s <u>n</u>ew <u>p</u>etunias." The first letters of each word correspond to the planets in terms of their relative distance from the sun.

Chapter 7

KNOWLEDGE CONSTRUCTION

Chapter Overview

In this chapter, we continue our exploration of cognitive psychology, this time focusing on how people pull together what they learn into more general understandings of the world. You will discover that storage and retrieval processes are often *constructive* in nature—that students may add their own ideas to classroom material and, as a result, may "learn" or "remember" something very different from what you anticipated. You will examine several ways in which students organize their experiences, including *concepts, schemas, scripts,* and *personal theories*.

Later in the chapter, you will find that the process of meaningful learning, though usually beneficial, can be counterproductive if students relate new material to incorrect beliefs (misconceptions) about the world. You will learn instructional strategies both for helping students construct meaningful understandings of complex phenomena and for encouraging students to revise existing misconceptions (i.e., to undergo *conceptual change*). Finally, you will consider how constructive processes may be influenced by students' cultural backgrounds and how some students with special needs may construct meaning differently from their classmates.

Common Student Beliefs and Misconceptions Related to Chapter Content

Listed below are three commonly held beliefs that may interfere with an accurate understanding of processes related to knowledge construction. As you read Chapter 7, be on the lookout for evidence that contradicts these ideas:

1. Many people erroneously think that knowledge is absorbed exactly as it is received, so that what is stored in memory is an accurate representation of the world.
2. Some people may believe that an especially vivid memory of an event must certainly be an accurate recollection of the event.
3. Many people think that an individual's misconception about the world will quickly disappear once a correct explanation is presented; they don't realize that misconceptions are often quite resistant to change.

CHAPTER OUTLINE	FOCUS QUESTIONS

CONSTRUCTIVE PROCESSES IN LEARNING AND MEMORY
 	
   Construction in Storage
 	
   Construction in Retrieval
 	
   Knowledge Construction: An Individual Activity and a Social Process
	• How is the process of construction involved in storage? How is it involved in retrieval?
	
	• What is individual constructivism? What is social constructivism? Speculate about possible implications that each perspective might have for classroom practice.

ORGANIZING KNOWLEDGE
 	
   Concepts
 	
   Schemas and Scripts
 	
   Personal Theories
	• What is a *concept*? Why do undergeneralization and overgeneralization reflect incomplete concept learning?
	
	• Explain how students' knowledge of concepts might take the form of *feature lists*, *prototypes*, and *exemplars*. With these ideas in mind, identify several strategies for teaching concepts.
	
	• What are *schemas* and *scripts*? How do they influence learners' construction of meaning?
	
	• How do students' *personal theories* influence learning?

WHEN KNOWLEDGE CONSTRUCTION GOES AWRY: ORIGINS AND EFFECTS OF MISCONCEPTIONS	• What kinds of misconceptions about the world are students likely to have? How do misconceptions affect learning?

PROMOTING EFFECTIVE KNOWLEDGE CONSTRUCTION
 	
   Providing Opportunities for Experimentation
 	
   Presenting the Ideas of Others
 	
   Emphasizing Conceptual Understanding
 	
   Promoting Dialogue
 	
   Using Authentic Activities
	• What strategies do cognitive psychologists recommend for helping students construct accurate understandings? Why is each of these strategies likely to be effective?
	
	• What is an *authentic activity*? Think of examples of authentic activities that you might use related to the subject matter you will be teaching.

CHAPTER OUTLINE	FOCUS QUESTIONS

PROMOTING CONCEPTUAL CHANGE
 	
    Identifying Existing Misconceptions Before Instruction Begins
 	
    Convincing Students That Existing Beliefs Are Inadequate
 	
    Motivating Students to Learn Correct Explanations
 	
    Monitoring for Persistent Misconceptions
	• What is *conceptual change*? Under what conditions is it most likely to occur? What implications do these conditions have for promoting conceptual change in the classroom?

CONSIDERING DIVERSITY IN CONSTRUCTIVE PROCESSES Accommodating Students with Special Needs	• Why might students from different backgrounds sometimes form different interpretations of the same situation? • What characteristics are teachers likely to see related to knowledge construction in students with special needs? How can teachers facilitate effective knowledge construction for these students?

Using the Compact Disk

Two activities on the *Simulations in Educational Psychology* CD are relevant to this chapter:

- "Bartlett's Ghosts" is similar to the "War of the Ghosts" Experiencing Firsthand exercise presented in the textbook.
- "Intuitive Physics" illustrates principles related to misconceptions and presents recommendations for promoting conceptual change.

Chapter Glossary

Authentic activities. Classroom activities similar to those that students are likely to encounter in the outside world.

Concept. A mental grouping of objects or events that have something in common.

Conceptual change. Revising one's knowledge and understanding of a topic in response to new information about that topic.

Conceptual understanding. Knowledge acquired in an integrated and meaningful fashion.

Correlational feature. A characteristic present in many positive instances of a concept but not essential for concept membership.

Defining feature. A characteristic that must be present in all positive instances of a concept.

Exemplar. A specific example that is an important part a learner's general knowledge and understanding of a concept. Several exemplars taken together give the learner a sense of the variability that exists within any category of objects or events.

Individual constructivism. A theoretical perspective that focuses on how people, as individuals, construct meaning from the events around them.

Misconception. Previously learned but incorrect information.

Negative instance. A nonexample of a concept.

Overgeneralization. Having too broad a meaning for a word, applying the word in situations where it's not appropriate; identifying objects or events as examples of a concept when in fact they are not.

Personal theory. A self-constructed explanation for one's observations about a particular aspect of the world; it may or may not be consistent with generally accepted explanations of scientific phenomena.

Positive instance. A specific example of a concept.

Prototype. A mental representation of a "typical" positive instance of a concept.

Reconstruction error. Constructing a logical but incorrect "memory" by using information retrieved from long-term memory plus one's general knowledge of the world.

Salience. In concept learning, the degree to which a particular feature or characteristic is obvious and easily noticeable.

Schema. An organized body of knowledge about a specific topic.

Script. A schema that involves a predictable sequence of events related to a common activity.

Social constructivism. A theoretical perspective that focuses on people's collective efforts to impose meaning on the world.

Undergeneralization. An overly restricted meaning for a word, excluding some situations to which the word does, in fact, apply; an overly narrow view of what objects or events a concept includes.

Application Exercise #11: Analyzing Constructive Processes

Explain each of the following situations using concepts or principles related to knowledge construction:

1. James is trying to remember how to spell the word *permanent*. He can remember the first four letters (p-e-r-m) and the last four letters (n-e-n-t), but he's not sure what the middle vowel is. He correctly decides that the middle vowel must be an *a* based on how the word is pronounced.

2. As a third-grade teacher begins to read *Black Beauty* to her class, eight-year-old Casey pictures the main character—a horse—with a shiny coat, flowing mane, and long black tail.

3. Ms. Forbes explains that objects are buoyant in water when they are, on average, less dense than the water they displace. Yvonne misinterprets the teacher's statement as confirming something she already "knows": Light things float and heavy things sink.

4. Several students get together to read and interpret William Shakespeare's *Julius Caesar*. One student describes the benefits of the group discussion this way: "I like hearing my friends' ideas about what the characters are really trying to say. Shakespeare isn't always an easy guy to understand, you know."

5. As students in Nadia's band class are warming up to play their instruments, an announcement comes over the school intercom. Nadia catches bits and pieces of the announcement—she hears "Student Council" and "Thursday"—and guesses that the Student Council must be meeting Thursday after school.

6. Mr. Holder shows his sixth graders a large map of Africa and explains how the Nile River flows north to the Mediterranean Sea. Although his students hear what he says, his comment doesn't really "register" with many of them. In a class discussion a few days later, Paul describes the river as running south, *away* from the Mediterranean. "No, Paul," Linda volunteers, "I used to think that that was true. But rivers must run *toward* the sea, not away from it. So the Nile must run north."

7. Maureen remembers this "fact" from a previous lesson about the French Revolution: "Marie Antoinette had her head chopped off because she couldn't bear Henry VIII any children."

8. Sandy reads a story about a family going to a fast-food restaurant for lunch. The story never mentions that the family members order and pay for their meals at the counter before they sit down. Nevertheless, Sandy assumes that they do these things.

<u>Answers to Application Exercise #11</u>

1. James is demonstrating <u>construction in retrieval</u>. He combines the letters that he can actually remember with other information that he has (i.e., how the word is pronounced) to construct a reasonable (and, in this case, accurate) guess as to how the word must be spelled.

2. Casey is constructing a visual image of Black Beauty based on his knowledge of what horses typically look like.

3. Yvonne is imposing a <u>misconception</u> on what the teacher is saying and so learns something that is not completely accurate. Even a very heavy object (e.g., a metal battleship) will float if its average density is less than that of the water it displaces.

4. Learners can sometimes construct meaning more effectively when they work together to make sense of a situation—a process consistent with the <u>social constructivist</u> view of knowledge construction.

5. Nadia is demonstrating <u>construction during storage</u>: She must construct meaning from incomplete information.

6. Paul's <u>misconception</u> that rivers always run south prevails over Mr. Holder's statement that the Nile flows north. In contrast, Linda has undergone <u>conceptual change</u> and now realizes that rivers must flow downhill toward the sea.

7. Maureen combines things she recalls from French history (Marie Antoinette and her encounter with the guillotine) with a piece of English history (Henry VIII and his treatment of his wives), thus showing <u>reconstruction error</u> in what she remembers.

8. Sandy uses her knowledge of typical procedures at a fast-food restaurant—a <u>script</u>—to fill in details that the story leaves out.

Application Exercise #12: Identifying Effective Classroom Practices

Decide whether each of the following teaching practices is consistent with principles of learning related to knowledge construction, and *why*.

1. Ms. Forbes discovers that, despite instruction to the contrary, Yvonne still believes that heavy objects cannot possibly float. "What will happen when I put a heavy casserole dish in a sink full of water?" Ms. Forbes asks her. "It will sink, of course," Yvonne replies. Ms. Forbes places such a casserole dish in water to show her that it floats.

2. Mr. Goldberg's class has already learned that insects have three body parts, six legs, wings, and antennae. Then he says, "Let's take a look at a picture of a wasp. See? It has all the parts that insects have, so it must be an insect."

3. In a unit on clouds, Ms. Lavoie shows a picture of a cloud and says, "One type of cloud is a cumulonimbus cloud. Here is what a typical cumulonimbus cloud looks like." She then moves on to a discussion of cumulus clouds.

4. In her French class, Ms. Malnati makes sure that her students have frequent opportunities to converse with one another in French.

5. Mr. Huang is teaching a unit on buoyancy and asks his students why it's easier to swim in salt water. Marla replies, "It's easier because the salt holds you up." Mr. Huang realizes that her understanding of buoyancy isn't quite right, but he lets it go because he figures that a more correct understanding will evolve over time.

6. Mr. Sawyer has his middle school students read a short story about a Bar Mitzvah. Knowing that many of his students are not Jewish, he first describes what a typical Bar Mitzvah is like.

7. Mr. Rochelle knows that he needs to move quickly if he's going to cover all the material that he has planned for his pre-calculus students. So he introduces two or three new topics or procedures each day, giving his students homework problems every night that allow them to review and practice the things they are studying in class.

8. After a hard practice session after school, Coach DiStephano calls the members of the girls' soccer team together and asks them to discuss and debate various strategies for defeating the Westview Warriors—a team whose defense has a reputation for being almost impenetrable—in next Saturday's game.

9. Mr. Robichaud decides that his geology students will learn general principles of geology most effectively if they discover everything for themselves, so he dispenses with a textbook for his class and devotes class time almost entirely to hands-on experiences with rocks.

10. As Ms. Shump describes an upcoming quiz in her language arts class, she tells her students, "Yesterday I gave you a list of definitions for the week's new vocabulary words. As long as you learn those definitions, you should be in good shape for the quiz."

Answers to Application Exercise #12

1. Consistent. When she sees that Yvonne is holding fast to her misconception that heavy objects cannot float, Ms. Forbes presents a phenomenon that contradicts Yvonne's belief—a recommended strategy for promoting <u>conceptual change</u>.

2. Consistent. Mr. Goldberg is asking students to use something they already know to interpret new information.

3. Not consistent. Ms. Lavoie provides a <u>prototype</u> of a cumulonimbus cloud, but she does nothing else to help students learn the concept. Ms. Lavoie should also identify defining features and present several positive instances of cumulonimbus clouds. Furthermore, she should show students some negative instances, so that they learn what a cumulonimbus cloud is *not*.

4. Consistent. Conducting a conversation in French is an example of an <u>authentic activity</u>—one in which students use what they have learned in a real-world task.

5. Not consistent. Students are unlikely to correct their <u>misconceptions</u> if they get no feedback that their beliefs are incorrect.

6. Consistent. Mr. Sawyer is providing a <u>script</u> that should help his students make sense of the story.

7. Not consistent. Mr. Rochelle is probably moving too quickly through the material for students to develop a <u>conceptual understanding</u> of the mathematical concepts and procedures that they are studying.

8. Consistent. <u>Dialogue</u> among students is often an effective way of promoting knowledge construction. In this situation, dialogue may be especially useful as a means of helping the girls clarify their own thinking about how to play soccer strategically; it should also expose the girls to perspectives that may be more useful than their own.

9. Not consistent. Although experimentation is one effective way of promoting knowledge construction, the students can probably learn only so much from "experimenting" with rocks. Another effective way of promoting knowledge construction is to expose students to how others have tried to make sense of the world—an idea that has emerged from <u>social constructivism</u>. A textbook provides one means through which students can encounter the ideas (e.g., concepts, principles) that others have developed to help them understand the nature of rocks.

10. Not consistent. The vocabulary words are, in essence, <u>concepts</u> that she wants her students to learn. She is encouraging the students only to learn definitions, perhaps at a rote level; there is no guarantee that students will relate these words to anything else they know. Ms. Shump should use other strategies that facilitate concept learning. For instance, she might ask students to use each word in a sentence (thereby having them generate their own examples), or she might have them explain how each word relates to other words (concepts) in their vocabularies.

Answers to Selected Margin Notes

- Page 268: *Adult readers often skip over letters, and even over entire words, as they read, yet may still understand what they are reading quite accurately. Can you explain this phenomenon using the idea of knowledge construction?*

  Using the letters and words that they've read, as well as context cues (what the topic of the reading passage is about, what they expect the author will say, etc.) and their prior knowledge, they can construct a reasonable interpretation of what the text is probably trying to communicate.

- Page 269: *What implications does the notion of reconstruction error have for the credibility of eyewitness testimony?*

  Eyewitness testimony is sometimes an inaccurate representation of what actually happened (Buckhout, 1974; Lindsay, 1993; Loftus, 1991, 1992). People's descriptions of the crime may vary considerably, depending on prior knowledge about the individuals involved, expectations about what typically happens in such a situation, and additional information presented at a later time.

- Page 273: *Are definitions likely to be effective when students learn them at a rote level? Why or why not?*

  Learning definitions at a rote level is unlikely to be effective. When students learn a definition in a word-for-word fashion, they may not relate the concept and its meaning to anything else in their knowledge base. As a result, they may not realize that objects or events with which they are familiar are positive instances of that concept.

- Page 276: *What is a typical script for a trip to the grocery store? to the movies? to a fast-food restaurant?*

  Going to the grocery store often includes parking in the parking lot, getting a grocery cart, going up and down the aisles putting desired items in the cart, waiting in line at the check-out counter, paying for the groceries, and using the cart to take the purchased items to your car. Going to the movies often includes waiting in line, purchasing a ticket, buying popcorn or a soft drink, sitting down in the theater, watching previews and commercials, and watching the movie. Going to a fast-food restaurant usually involves waiting in line at the counter while looking at the menu items, telling the cashier what you want, paying for what you've ordered, waiting at the counter until the food is handed to you on a tray, carrying the tray to a table, sitting down and eating, and disposing of trash and leftovers in a trash bin.

- Page 282: *Unfortunately, the researchers didn't eliminate several other possible explanations for their results. Besides the fact that one group used teacher-prescribed procedures and the other used self-chosen procedures, what other differences between the two groups might account for the results obtained in this study?*

  Additional differences between the two groups included:
  - Raising rabbits versus raising goldfish
  - Raising pets at school versus raising them at home
  - Sharing responsibility for pet care at school versus doing it alone at home

Sample Test Questions

Items marked with a "**1**)" on the left-hand side are lower-level questions that assess your general knowledge and understanding of the material. Items marked with a "**2**)" on the left-hand side are higher-level questions that assess your ability to apply what you have learned to a new situation.

Multiple-Choice

2) 1. John learns that the capital of South Dakota is Pierre. A few days later, as he is trying to recall this information, he thinks for a while and then finally says, "Oh, I remember now. It's Perry." Which one of the following statements best explains John's error?
    a. John uses his script for state capitals to develop a logical conclusion as to what South Dakota's capital must be.
    b. John is exhibiting construction during retrieval; he remembers parts of the capital city's name and then fills in the rest.
    c. John has developed an incorrect schema for Pierre.
    d. John has undergone conceptual change between the time when he first learned the information and the time when he has to remember it.

2) 2. Ms. Eisenstadt wants her students to understand what a *dribble* is in basketball. Given what we know about effective concept learning, her best strategy would be to:
    a. Show them the correct way to dribble a ball
    b. Show them how *not* to dribble a ball
    c. Show them both what dribbling is and what it isn't
    d. Keep it simple by bouncing the ball just twice in a row

2) 3. For which one of the following concepts would a definition be *most* helpful to students?
    a. *invertebrate*
    b. *green*
    c. *duck*
    d. *pencil*

2) 4. Margaret says that the earth is flat. When her teacher tells her that the earth is round, Margaret pictures a world shaped like a pancake—both round *and* flat. From the perspective of cognitive psychology, how can we best explain Margaret's error?
    a. People's working memories are insufficient to hold two complex pieces of information simultaneously.
    b. People rarely learn effectively when they must encode verbal input in a visual form.
    c. People's prior beliefs affect their interpretations of new information.
    d. People must pay attention in order to learn.

2) 5. Which one of the following is the best example of an *authentic activity*?
    a. Spelling words aloud before a spelling test
    b. Reading the "chapter objectives" at the beginning of a textbook chapter
    c. Doing mathematics word problems
    d. Drawing a map of the school building

1) 6. If we apply the idea of knowledge construction to an understanding of students from diverse cultural backgrounds, we are most likely to say that:

   a. Different students interpret their experiences differently because they have different knowledge bases and schemas from which to draw.

   b. Students from some cultures are likely to interpret classroom material at face value, whereas students from other cultures are likely to derive abstract, underlying ideas from that same material.

   c. Some cultures value cooperation more than others, and students from "cooperative" cultures are the only students who are likely to engage in the social construction of knowledge.

   d. Students from some cultures are more likely to have had exposure to authentic activities than students from other cultures.

Essay

2) 7. Explain the difference between a concept's *defining features* and *correlational features*. Illustrate your discussion by identifying two defining features and two correlational features of the concept *beach*.

1) 8. Using principles of cognitive psychology, explain why students' misconceptions are often so resistant to change.

1) 9. Imagine that you are a new teacher. You discover that your students have several misconceptions about the subject matter your class will be studying over the next few weeks. Describe three different strategies you might use to help your students correct those misconceptions. Base your response on the textbook's discussion of promoting conceptual change.

Answers to Sample Test Questions

1. b—John remembers part of what he is trying to retrieve—the beginning *P* and the *err* in the middle—and uses those letters to construct a logical, although incorrect, city name. See the section "Construction in Retrieval" beginning on textbook page 268.

2. c—Concepts are learned more effectively when students see both positive and negative instances. (See the section "Concepts as Feature Lists" beginning on textbook page 271.)

3. a—Definitions are most helpful when a concept's defining features are not obvious. In the case of *invertebrate,* the defining feature "lack of a backbone" isn't readily apparent. (See the section "Concepts as Feature Lists" beginning on textbook page 271.)

4. c—Margaret interprets her teacher's statement that the world is round in light of her own misconception that the world is flat (see the section "When Knowledge Construction Goes Awry" on textbook pages 279-281). Note that you need to draw on information from both Chapter 6 and Chapter 7 to answer this question.

5. d—Drawing a map is the alternative most similar to something one might eventually do in an out-of-school context. Authentic activities are described on textbook pages 285-286.

6. a—The textbook's description of cultural differences in knowledge construction is most consistent with this alternative (see "Considering Diversity in Constructive Processes" on textbook page 292). No evidence exists to support the other three alternatives.

7. Defining features must be present in all positive instances of the concept. Correlational features are present in many positive instances but are not essential for concept membership. (See the explanations of both terms on textbook page 271.) Two defining features of *beach* are sand and proximity to a large body of water. Correlational features of *beach* include waves, seaweed, shells, swimmers, sunbathers, lifeguards, and beach umbrellas; you may have identified other correlational features as well.

8. The essence of your answer should be that students often interpret new information within the context of what they already know. You should include at least one of these concepts in your response: *rote learning, meaningful learning, elaboration,* or *construction.* (See "When Meaningful Learning Goes Awry" beginning on textbook page 279.)

9. You can find several strategies in the section "Promoting Conceptual Change" on textbook pages 286-292. Your response should include at least three of these strategies.

Chapter 8

HIGHER-LEVEL THINKING SKILLS

Chapter Overview

This chapter focuses on some of the more complex ways that human beings think and learn; these are often referred to as *higher-level thinking skills*. Early in the chapter, you will look at the process of *transfer*—the ability to apply what one has learned to new situations—and identify the conditions under which students are most likely to transfer the knowledge and skills they acquire in the classroom. As you examine one particular form of transfer—problem solving—you will identify several cognitive processes that influence students' problem-solving success. Later in the chapter, you will read about *critical thinking*, discovering that it often takes different forms in different content domains. You will then explore the topic of *metacognition*—students' knowledge and regulation of their own thinking and learning processes—and identify the kinds of study strategies that can help students learn classroom material most effectively. Finally, you will consider some ways in which your students, including those who had special educational needs, are likely to exhibit diversity in higher-level thinking skills.

Suggestions for facilitating higher-level thinking skills appear throughout Chapter 8. For example, you will find that the *less is more* principle is relevant to both transfer and critical thinking skills. You will learn that students are more likely to solve problems successfully when they know the subject matter well and have acquired basic knowledge and skills to a level of automaticity. You will also discover that students are most likely to develop effective study strategies when they learn those strategies within the context of specific academic disciplines.

Common Student Beliefs and Misconceptions Related to Chapter Content

Below are three misconceptions that college students often have before reading about higher-level thinking processes—misconceptions that may interfere with an accurate understanding of what they read. As you read Chapter 8, be on the lookout for evidence that contradicts these common misconceptions:

1. Many people believe that general mental "exercise" improves the mind.
2. Many people believe that children and adolescents naturally know how to learn classroom material—that effective learning and study strategies don't need to be taught.
3. Some people believe that note taking interferes with learning.

CHAPTER OUTLINE	FOCUS QUESTIONS
THE NATURE OF HIGHER-LEVEL THINKING	• How are higher-level questions different from lower-level ones?

TRANSFER
 	
    Basic Concepts in Transfer
    Factors Affecting Transfer
    Theories of Transfer
	• What is transfer? How are positive and negative transfer different? How are specific and general transfer different? Think of new examples of each of these concepts.
	
	• What factors promote transfer? What implications do these factors have for teachers?
	
	• What is the *formal discipline* view of transfer? What common teaching practices are based on this notion? What is the current status of this perspective?
	
	• What cognitive process is essential for transfer to occur? With this process in mind, what implications for teaching practice can you identify?
	
	• What do theorists mean by *situated cognition*? What implications does this concept have for classroom practice?

PROBLEM SOLVING
 	
    Basic Concepts in Problem Solving
    Cognitive Factors Affecting Problem Solving
	• How are well-defined and ill-defined problems different? Think of examples of each kind of problem in your own life.
	
	• What are *algorithms* and *heuristics*? Think of examples of each of these concepts.
	
	• What cognitive factors affect problem solving? What implications does each factor have for facilitating students' problem solving?
	
	• What is a *mental set*? Why does it sometimes interfere with effective problem solving?

CRITICAL THINKING	• What is *critical thinking*? What forms might it take? • How can teachers promote critical thinking in the classroom?

CHAPTER OUTLINE	FOCUS QUESTIONS

METACOGNITION AND STUDY STRATEGIES
  Effective Study Strategies
  Factors That Affect Strategy Use
	• What is *metacognition*? What knowledge and abilities does it include? Why is it especially important at the upper grade levels?
	
	• What study strategies does research indicate to be effective? Are there special circumstances under which each strategy is more or less effective?
	
	• Why do students often have trouble identifying important information? How can teachers help them identify it more accurately?
	
	• What functions does note taking serve? What kinds of notes are most effective?
	
	• How does a *concept map* facilitate learning?
	
	• Describe how a teacher might use *elaborative interrogation* to promote elaboration.
	
	• What is *comprehension monitoring*? How does self-questioning promote this process? What happens when students don't monitor comprehension as they read and study?
	
	• What factors influence the extent to which students use effective study strategies?
	
	• What components does study skills training often include? How can teachers help students develop more effective learning strategies?

CONSIDERING DIVERSITY IN HIGHER-LEVEL THINKING SKILLS Accommodating Students with Special Needs	• How do students' backgrounds affect their use of higher-level thinking skills? • To what extent do students with various kinds of special needs exhibit higher-level thinking skills? How can *metacognitive scaffolding* facilitate their use of effective learning strategies?
THE BIG PICTURE: PROMOTING HIGHER-LEVEL THINKING IN THE CLASSROOM	• In what way are complex cognitive processes related to intelligence?

Using the Compact Disk

"Intuitive Physics" on the *Simulations in Educational Psychology* CD is relevant to the textbook's discussion of transfer.

Chapter Glossary

Algorithm. A prescribed sequence of steps guaranteeing a correct problem solution.

Comprehension monitoring. The process of checking oneself to make sure one understands the things being read or heard.

Concept map. A diagram of concepts within an instructional unit and the interrelationships among them.

Critical thinking. Evaluating information or arguments in terms of their accuracy and worth.

Elaborative interrogation. A study strategy in which students develop and answer elaborative questions about the material they are trying to learn.

Epistemological beliefs. One's beliefs regarding the nature of knowledge and knowledge acquisition.

Formal discipline. A view of transfer that postulates that the study of rigorous subjects enhances one's ability to learn other, unrelated things.

General transfer. An instance of transfer in which the original learning task and the transfer task do not overlap in content.

Heuristic. A general problem-solving strategy that may or may not yield a problem solution.

Higher-level question. A question that requires students to do something new with information they have learned—for example, to apply, analyze, synthesize, or evaluate it.

Higher-level thinking. Thought that involves going beyond information specifically learned (e.g., application, analysis, synthesis, evaluation).

Ill-defined problem. A problem in which the desired goal is unclear, information needed to solve the problem is missing, and/or several possible solutions to the problem exist.

Illusion of knowing. Thinking one knows something that one actually does not know.

Lower-level question. A question that requires students to express what they have learned in essentially the same way they learned it—for example, by reciting a textbook's definition of a concept or describing an application that their teacher presented in class.

Mental set. Encoding a problem in a way that excludes potential problem solutions.

Metacognition. One's knowledge and beliefs regarding one's own cognitive processes, and one's resulting attempts to regulate those cognitive processes to maximize learning and memory.

Metacognitive scaffolding. A supportive technique that guides students in their use of metacognitive strategies.

Negative transfer. A phenomenon whereby something learned at one time interferes with learning or performance at a later time.

Positive transfer. A phenomenon whereby something learned at one time facilitates learning or performance at a later time.

Self-questioning. The process of asking oneself questions as a way of checking one's understanding of a topic.

Situated cognition. Knowledge and thinking skills that are acquired and used primarily within certain contexts, with limited if any transfer to other contexts.

Specific transfer. An instance of transfer in which the original learning task and the transfer task overlap in content.

Transfer. A phenomenon whereby something that an individual has learned at one time affects how the individual learns or performs in a later situation.

Well-defined problem. A problem in which the goal is clearly stated, all information needed to solve the problem is present, and only one correct answer exists.

Table 8-2—Which Study Strategies Do You Use, and When?

Here is a copy of the table presented on page 331 of your textbook. You may wish to fill it out here, rather than in your textbook.

Study Strategy	In which classes or subjects do you use this strategy frequently?	In which classes or subjects might you benefit from using this strategy more often?	What factors affect your ability to use this strategy successfully?
Identifying important information			
Taking notes			
Retrieving relevant prior knowledge			
Organizing			
Elaborating			
Summarizing			
Monitoring comprehension			

Application Exercise #13: Predicting Transfer and Problem Solving

For each of the following situations, decide whether successful transfer or problem solving is likely to occur. Justify your decisions on the basis of the principles and theories of transfer and problem solving described in Chapter 8.

1. When Clarence learns about the law of inertia in his science class, it suddenly makes sense to him why his father's motor boat continues to move forward after the engine is turned off.

2. Mr. Montey teaches students in his middle school math class how to calculate the area of a triangle (area = 1/2 base × height). He presents an example of how to use the formula with a triangle that has a base of 4 centimeters and a height of 7 centimeters and makes sure that all his students arrive at the correct answer of 14 square centimeters. He then proceeds to a discussion of how to calculate a triangle's perimeter.

3. Mr. Swetzig dictates this algebra problem and asks students to solve for x in their heads:
$$x^4 + x^3 + 4x^2 + 2x = 84$$

4. Ryan has been studying Spanish for three years now. He is hoping that his knowledge of Spanish will help him learn Italian when he goes on a student exchange program to Rome this summer.

5. A one-semester high school psychology course is designed to give students an introduction to the field of psychology—to physiological psychology, perception, child development, human learning, social psychology, individual differences, industrial psychology, and so on.

6. Janice is learning how to sew cuffs on the sleeves of the shirt she is making in her "life skills" class. She realizes that the process is very similar to sewing on a collar—something she already knows how to do.

7. Teresa studies the state capitals until she knows them all at a level of automaticity.

8. When Peter's mother asks him what he is learning in history, he says, "A bunch of stuff. It's all just history."

9. In a unit on softball, Ms. Warren teaches her students to keep their eye on the ball as it comes toward the bat and to swing the bat out to meet the ball. She is hoping that her students will use the same strategy when they begin the tennis unit in two weeks.

10. In her woodworking class, Lucy learns how to use a miter box to cut 45° angles for the corners of a picture frame she is working on. Next week, she will need to use the miter box again when Mr. Nesbitt shows the class how to frame a doorway.

11. Vanessa studies computer programming, hoping that it will help her think more logically in her other classes.

12. Heath memorizes the formula $E = mc^2$ and recites it perfectly. He knows that E stands for energy and m stands for mass, although he's not sure what c refers to.

Answers to Application Exercise #13

1. Likely. Clarence is learning the law of inertia in a meaningful fashion, because he is relating it to something he already knows.

2. Not likely. Students are more likely to transfer information they have learned when they have *numerous* examples and opportunities to practice using the information.

3. Not likely. Students will probably have insufficient working memory capacity to remember the entire problem as they simultaneously try to solve it.

4. Likely. Spanish and Italian are languages with common roots and similar vocabulary. Transfer is more likely to occur when the previously learned information (in this case, Spanish) and the knowledge to be learned in the transfer situation (in this case, Italian) are obviously similar.

5. Not likely. The course provides superficial coverage of many topics. Transfer is more likely to occur when students learn a specific topic in depth.

6. Likely. Janice is retrieving relevant knowledge at the time she needs it.

7. Not likely. Although thorough learning facilitates transfer, students are more likely to transfer general principles than specific facts. The state capitals are specific facts that have little applicability to anything else.

8. Not likely. Peter is thinking of the subject matter as something that is context-bound—as being a part of history but nothing else. He isn't relating the subject matter to anything else he knows.

9. Likely. The behaviors involved in both situations (keeping one's eye on an approaching ball and swinging to meet it) are similar.

10. Likely. Both tasks require cutting 45-degree angles to form corners and so are clearly similar. Furthermore, the second task will occur soon after the first task.

11. Not likely. The logic that one uses in computer programming is not necessarily the same logic that one uses in other disciplines. Vanessa is basing her assumption on the notion of formal discipline—the idea that studying rigorous subjects strengthens the mind. Most psychologists have rejected this view of transfer.

12. Not likely. Students are unlikely to apply things they learn in a meaningless fashion.

Application Exercise #14: Facilitating Effective Study Strategy Use

Which of the following techniques are likely to promote more effective study strategies, and which are not? Defend your choices.

1. Ms. Randolph reminds her seventh graders that they should be taking notes in class today. Then, throughout the class session, she identifies specific concepts and ideas that they should include in their notes.

2. Mr. Rangel begins a unit on how mountains are formed by telling his class, "Before we look at how mountains are formed, I want you to try to erase from your memories anything you think you already know about mountains. Let's all begin as blank slates on this subject and start totally from scratch."

3. Ms. Valentine gives students questions they should ask themselves tonight as they read the chapter on cell division.

4. During the last five minutes of class each day, Mr. Benedetti has students take out a sheet of paper and write a brief summary of the day's lesson.

5. Mr. Murphy recommends that a struggling student take a study skills course during the summer when she is not distracted by her regular school schedule. In this two-week course, a variety of strategies will be described, and a specific example of how each strategy might be used will be presented.

6. At the beginning of a lecture on World War II, Mr. Quesenberry says, "There are two things you should learn from today's class: why the United States entered the war and what influence its involvement had on the war's final outcome."

Answers to Application Exercise #14

1. Will promote better strategies. Generally speaking, note taking promotes learning. Students' class notes are most likely to be helpful when they include the main ideas presented in class. Seventh graders have probably not had much prior experience taking notes and may be at a loss as to what things they should be writing down. By telling them what things are important to include, Ms. Randolph is providing scaffolding that should enable them to develop a good set of notes.

2. Will not promote better strategies. Students are more effective learners when they relate new information to what they already know. Mr. Rangel is urging them *not* to make such meaningful connections.

3. Will promote better strategies. Questions can help focus students' attention on the things that are important for them to learn. Questions also provide a means through which students can monitor their comprehension. After reading the chapter, the students should be able to answer Ms. Valentine's questions. If they cannot do so, they will know that they haven't yet learned the things they need to learn from the chapter.

4. Will promote better strategies. Summarizing is an effective study strategy. It helps students identify important ideas and the interrelationships among them.

5. Will not promote better strategies. Students learn study skills more effectively when they encounter them within the context of specific academic subject areas and when they have numerous opportunities to practice using those skills.

6. Will promote better strategies. Providing objectives for a lesson helps students identify the important ideas to be gleaned from that lesson.

Answers to Selected Margin Notes

- Page 307: *Is this an instance of specific transfer or general transfer?*
  Learning how to learn is an example of general transfer, because there is often little overlap in content from one situation to the next.

- Page 315: *How could you use algebra to solve this problem?*
  Let x be the number of pigs and $21 - x$ be the number of chickens. Because the pigs have four legs each and the chickens have two legs each, the total number of pig legs is $4x$ and the total number of chicken legs is $2(21 - x)$. The total number of legs is 60, so:
  $$4x + 2(21 - x) = 60$$
  Solving for x, we find that $2x + 42 = 60$, so $2x = 18$ and $x = 9$ (the number of pigs). The number of chickens is $21 - 9$, or 12.

- Page 324: *Look through this textbook. Can you find paragraphs in which the main idea is located in the middle or near the end of the paragraph rather than at the beginning?*
  An example of where the main idea appears near the middle is the first paragraph on page 310, which defines the term *heuristic*. An example of where the main idea appears near the end is the first paragraph after the "Rain Forests" exercise on page 299.

- Page 324: *Do such prompts remind you of the concept of scaffolding?*
  They should. *Scaffolding* is a support structure that enables students to perform a difficult task successfully. Scaffolding sometimes involves providing hints about how the task should be done (see Chapter 2).

- Page 326: *Does this approach also remind you of scaffolding?*
  Modeling is another form that scaffolding may take (see Chapter 2).

- Page 330: *As you read a textbook, when is the information in working memory? in long-term memory? With your answers in mind, explain why students should monitor their comprehension not only as they read but also at a later time.*
  Information is in working memory as soon as you pay attention to it and remains there as long as you continue to think about it actively. If you process it in some way beyond just paying attention to it, it will be stored in long-term memory within a few seconds. If you monitor your comprehension of the information as you are learning it, you are considering it while it is still in working memory—where it probably won't last very long—and you are likely to be overly optimistic about how well you know it (Nelson & Dunlosky, 1991; Weaver & Kelemen, 1997). If you monitor your comprehension at a later point in time, you are assessing your ability to retrieve it effectively from long-term memory, which is what you will need to be able to do over the long run.

- Page 333: *Do you study a little bit each day or procrastinate until the last minute? Why is the former approach more likely to be effective?*
  Regular studying allows you to monitor your comprehension from one day to the next. It also provides periodic review of information, which facilitates retrieval (see Chapter 6). Furthermore, if you leave everything to the last minute, you may be too tired or anxious to process information effectively (see Chapter 12's discussion of anxiety).

Sample Test Questions

Items marked with a "**1)**" on the left-hand side are lower-level questions that assess your general knowledge and understanding of the material. Items marked with a "**2)**" on the left-hand side are higher-level questions that assess your ability to apply what you have learned to a new situation.

Multiple-Choice

2) 1. In which of the following situations is *negative transfer* occurring?
   a. A student who has used a typewriter for many years discovers that the letters are in the same places on a computer keyboard.
   b. A student who is studying Portuguese finds many similarities in vocabulary and grammar with the Spanish she already knows.
   c. A middle school student has tests in science and language arts this week.
   d. After learning to add two fractions by simply adding their numerators, a student begins to multiply fractions in a similar fashion, getting an incorrect result.

2) 2. Three of the following teachers are using strategies that should facilitate students' ability to transfer the things that they are learning. Which teacher is *not* using a strategy that should promote transfer?
   a. Ms. Arons has members of her soccer team practice shooting at the goal during the warm-up period before a game.
   b. Mr. Bartoli makes sure his students have mastered addition before he moves on to subtraction.
   c. Mr. Chen shows students many different examples of volcanic mountains (Mount St. Helens, Mount Rainier, Mount Vesuvius, etc.).
   d. Ms. Drew tells students in her sociology class that many principles of sociology are very different from those of psychology.

1) 3. Three of the following strategies should promote effective problem solving. Which one will *not*?
   a. Help students understand the logic behind mathematical procedures.
   b. Make sure that students master each topic before moving to the next one.
   c. Have students practice mathematical principles on just one or two particularly vivid examples.
   d. Teach students general principles more than specific facts.

1) 4. Only one of the following is *always* found in critical thinking. Which one?
   a. Separating and controlling variables
   b. Evaluating information or arguments
   c. Visual-spatial thinking
   d. Algorithmic problem solving

2) 5. Which one of the following statements reflects an *epistemological belief*?
   a. "If I can't make sense of something right away, I'll never make sense of it at all."
   b. "I'll do my homework first and then treat myself by watching a video."
   c. "It takes the sun's rays seven minutes to reach the earth. That's amazing!"
   d. "Why is it that people at the South Pole don't fall into outer space?"

1) 6. Three of the following statements are consistent with what research tells us about study skills training. Which one is *not*?
   a. Students should focus on learning just one specific study strategy very, very well.
   b. Students should have lots of practice applying the study strategies they learn.
   c. Students must have high self-efficacy that they can succeed in the classroom before they will use the strategies they are taught.
   d. Students should be given reasons why a study strategy is helpful.

Essay

2) 7. Steven wants to become a surgeon. His teacher urges him to take computer programming to develop his logical thinking skills for medical school. Is the teacher's reasoning accurate? Why or why not?

1) 8. Define *comprehension monitoring,* and explain why students who engage in comprehension monitoring learn more successfully than those who do not.

<u>Answers to Sample Test Questions</u>

1. d—Negative transfer occurs when knowledge or skills learned in one situation are applied inappropriately in another situation (see textbook page 300).

2. d—Ms. Drew is stressing the differences between sociology and psychology. Students are more likely to show transfer from one situation to another when they are aware of the similarities between the two (see textbook pages 303-304).

3. c—Problem solving is one form of transfer, and students are more likely to transfer what they learn when they have numerous examples and opportunities to practice (see textbook page 303 in the section on transfer and textbook page 316 in the section on problem solving).

4. b—By definition, critical thinking involves evaluating information or arguments in terms of their accuracy and worth (see textbook page 319).

5. a—Epistemological beliefs are beliefs about the nature of knowledge and knowledge acquisition (see textbook page 332). The first statement reflects the speaker's belief that learning occurs either quickly or not at all.

6. a—Study strategies training is more effective when students learn a variety of strategies rather than just one (see Table 8-3 on textbook page 334).

7. The teacher is incorrect. Learning in one situation is unlikely to facilitate learning and performance in another situation if the information and cognitive processes required in the two situations are very different. In Steven's case, the logical thinking skills necessary for computer programming and those necessary for medical school are not necessarily the same. The teacher's reasoning is an example of the formal discipline perspective of transfer—a perspective that has largely been discredited (see textbook page 306).

8. Comprehension monitoring is a process of periodically checking one's own understanding during a learning activity (e.g., reading, studying). Students who engage in comprehension monitoring know when they haven't fully learned something and so can take steps to remediate their incomplete knowledge. (See the discussion on textbook pages 330-331.)

Chapter 9

LEARNING IN THE CONTENT AREAS

Chapter Overview

In this chapter, you will apply concepts and principles of cognitive psychology to an understanding of reading, writing, mathematics, science, and social studies. You will discover that each of these content areas involves fairly specialized skills and cognitive processes. Yet you will discover, too, that several principles are common to all of them. First, learning involves constructive processes and is influenced by students' prior knowledge; for instance, reading involves constructing meaning from the words on the page, and skilled writing involves putting previously learned ideas together in a way that communicates meaning effectively to someone else. Second, metacognitive knowledge and strategies influence students' academic achievement; for instance, students' epistemological beliefs about math influence their problem-solving success, and their beliefs about the nature of science affect how they study. Third, students think about and understand the subject matter in qualitatively different ways at different points in their development; for instance, children in the primary grades interpret maps in a very literal fashion (e.g., thinking that roads depicted in red are paved in red concrete), whereas high school students understand the symbolic nature of maps.

Throughout the chapter you will find numerous strategies for enhancing students' learning and achievement in the various academic disciplines. You will also find ways of adapting instruction for students with special educational needs.

Common Student Beliefs and Misconceptions Related to Chapter Content

Below are several beliefs that clash with principles and recommendations presented in Chapter 9. As you read the chapter, look for evidence that contradicts these beliefs:

1. Some future teachers have previously heard that a whole-language approach to reading instruction is definitely the most effective. Others have heard that a focus on letter-sound correspondences (e.g., "phonics") and other basic reading skills is more effective. In general, research does *not* indicate that one approach is superior to the other. In fact, many theorists urge us to strike a balance between whole-language and basic-skills approaches.

2. Some college students have previously learned (perhaps in a high school writing course) that writing should proceed through three steps—planning, writing a first draft, and revising—in a somewhat lockstep fashion. But skilled writing actually involves moving back and forth among these processes in a flexible manner.

3. Some college students have epistemological beliefs about mathematics, science, history, and geography that interfere with a true understanding of these disciplines; for instance, they may believe that mathematical problem-solving procedures are to be memorized rather than understood, or that history and geography are nothing more than a collection of facts and figures.

CHAPTER OUTLINE	FOCUS QUESTIONS
APPLYING GENERAL PRINCIPLES TO TEACHING CLASSROOM SUBJECT MATTER	• What four general principles apply to learning in all of the content areas?

READING
 	
   Emergent Literacy
 	
   The Nature of Skilled Reading
 	
   Developmental Changes in Reading
 	
   General Strategies for Teaching Reading
	• What is *emergent literacy*? How does it develop, and why is it important for later reading achievement?
	
	• What knowledge and skills are involved in skilled reading? How can teachers foster them?
	
	• How does the quality of students' reading change with development? What implications do developmental changes have for instruction at different grade levels?
	
	• What general instructional strategies can foster students' reading skills?

WRITING
 	
   The Nature of Skilled Writing
 	
   Writing as a Facilitator of Learning
 	
   Developmental Changes in Writing
 	
   General Strategies for Teaching Writing
	• What processes does skilled writing involve? How can teachers help students develop each of these processes?
	
	• How are *knowledge telling* and *knowledge transforming* different? Why is the latter preferred?
	
	• Why does writing facilitate learning?
	
	• How does the quality of students' writing change over time?
	
	• What general strategies for teaching writing do experts recommend?

MATHEMATICS
 	
   The Nature of Mathematical Reasoning
 	
   Developmental Changes in Mathematical Understanding
 	
   General Strategies for Teaching Mathematics
	• What processes does mathematical reasoning involve? How can teachers foster each one?
	
	• Why is it important for students to understand the logic behind mathematical procedures?
	
	• What common epistemological beliefs can interfere with success in mathematics?
	
	• How do students' mathematical abilities change with development? What implications do such changes have for instruction?
	
	• What general instructional strategies can enhance students' achievement in mathematics?

CHAPTER OUTLINE	FOCUS QUESTIONS
SCIENCE The Nature of Scientific Reasoning Developmental Changes in Science General Strategies for Teaching Science	• How do students' *personal theories* influence learning in science? • What processes does scientific reasoning involve? How can teachers foster them in the classroom? • How do students' scientific reasoning abilities change over time? What implications do developmental trends in science have for instruction? • What general strategies for teaching science do experts recommend?
SOCIAL STUDIES The Nature of Historical Knowledge and Thinking The Nature of Geographic Knowledge and Thinking Developmental Changes in Thinking About History and Geography General Strategies for Teaching Social Studies	• What processes are involved in knowledge and thinking about history? about geography? How can teachers foster these processes? • How does students' understanding of history and geography change with development? What implications do developmental differences have for instruction? • What general instructional strategies are useful in teaching social studies?
TAKING STUDENT DIVERSITY INTO ACCOUNT Accommodating Students with Special Needs	• What ethnic and gender differences should teachers keep in mind in their efforts to maximize the achievement of all students? • How can teachers adapt instruction in the various content areas to accommodate the strengths and weaknesses of students with special needs?
THE BIG PICTURE: REVISITING THE FOUR GENERAL PRINCIPLES	• How does each of the four general principles manifest itself in reading, writing, mathematics, science, and social studies?

Using the Compact Disk

Two activities on the *Simulations in Educational Psychology* CD are relevant to this chapter:
- "The Pendulum Experiment" is similar to Chapter 2's "Pendulum Problem" Experiencing Firsthand exercise, which is discussed again in the section "Investigating Scientific Phenomena."
- "Intuitive Physics" illustrates principles related to the section "Revising Theories and Models."

Chapter Glossary

Benchmark lesson or experiment. Lesson or experiment that begins a new unit by illustrating the issues that the unit will address.

Confirmation bias. A tendency to look for evidence that confirms a hypothesis and to ignore evidence that contradicts the hypothesis.

Emergent literacy. Knowledge and skills that lay a foundation for reading and writing; typically develops in the preschool years as a result of early experiences with oral and written language.

Model. In science, knowledge of the components of a particular scientific entity and the interrelationships among those components. (Note that we will use the term differently in Chapter 11.)

Personal theory. A self-constructed explanation for one's observations about a particular aspect of the world; it may or may not be consistent with generally accepted explanations of scientific phenomena.

Phonological awareness. The ability to hear the distinct sounds (phonemes) within a word.

Theory. An organized body of concepts and principles developed to explain certain phenomena; a description of possible underlying mechanisms to explain why certain principles are true.

Translating. In writing, the process of converting one's ideas into written language.

Whole language instruction. An approach to teaching reading and writing in which basic skills are taught solely within the context of authentic reading and writing tasks.

Word decoding. In reading, identifying the sounds associated with a word's letters and then determining what the word probably is.

Application Exercise #15: Identifying Effective Classroom Practices

Of the following teaching strategies, which are consistent with guidelines presented in Chapter 9 and which are not? Defend your decisions.

1. Mr. Zeskind uses a plastic model of a heart to show his sixth graders how a heart pumps blood.

2. Mr. Holliday asks his high school biology students to write a two-page paper describing the processes involved in human digestion. "The best approach is just to write down the things you've learned about digestion as various thoughts come to mind," he tells them.

3. When Ms. Yount introduces the concept *negative number* in her junior high school math class, she first defines the concept as "a number less than zero" and presents this basic principle: "When you add a negative number to a positive number, it's the same as subtracting a positive number from a positive number." She then gives students several practice problems, such as 7 + (-4) and 12 + (-10).

4. Mr. Honig discourages his first graders from using their fingers when they solve simple addition problems. He instead wants them to rely on their memories of addition facts.

5. Ms. Powell has her middle school geography class look at a map of Canada. On the chalkboard, she lists all the cities with populations of more than 100,000. "Why are there high concentrations of people in these cities?" she asks. "Can you think of some reasons why a lot of people want to live in these locations?"

6. Mr. Stranko asks his kindergartners to think of words that rhyme with *goat*.

7. Ms. Stoff has her high school history students read excerpts from the journals of several members of the Lewis and Clark expedition through what is now the northwestern United States. Included in the excerpts are journal entries in which different members of the expedition describe the same event somewhat differently.

8. Mr. Moser wants his fourth graders to apply what they are learning in math to real-world situations, so he gives them many word problems to solve.

9. Mr. Weinstock is asking his ninth graders to write their first research paper. He gives them a specific format to follow: (1) an introduction that provides an overview of the paper; (2) a presentation of research findings, including at least three sections on three different aspects of the topic (with each section having its own subheading); and (3) a conclusion that summarizes and identifies implications of the research described in the paper.

10. Ms. Umanoff asks her fifth graders to conduct experiments to see whether salt water makes things float more than regular water and whether water's temperature affects how well objects float. She has the students conduct experiments using eggs as the floating objects, and she provides containers of cold water and very warm water. As the students work in pairs to conduct their experiments, she circulates through the classroom, occasionally asking a question such as, "How do you know that the amount of salt in the water is making the difference, rather than the temperature of the water?"

11. A boy in Ms. Finch's third-grade class is reading aloud to his reading group. He pauses when he gets to the word *enough* and obviously doesn't know what the word is. "Just ignore the rest of the words on the page," Ms. Finch advises him. "Focus on the word you're having trouble with and try to sound it out."

12. Mr. Peluso has his junior high school science students study two contrasting theories of how human beings see color.

13. Ms. Rothman encourages her second graders to use a number line to help them as they work out challenging subtraction problems.

14. Ms. Olenick gives her eighth-grade history students twenty minutes to write an essay describing the events leading up to the American Revolutionary War. She tells them that she expects correct spelling and punctuation throughout the essay.

15. As he teaches his third graders map interpretation skills, Mr. Campanella introduces the concept of *scale*.

16. Mr. DeSeife allows his seventh-grade language arts students to choose their next book from among several classic works of literature (e.g., *The Yearling, To Kill a Mockingbird, The Red Pony*). Over the next two weeks, students who are reading the same book get together in small groups to discuss the book.

17. In the unit on the solar system, Ms. Smeriglio has her eighth-grade science students focus on learning the characteristics of the nine planets and each one's distance from the sun..

18. Ms. McElroy tells students in her high school mathematics class, "You can use the mnemonic FOIL to remember how to simplify an expression such as $(x + 3)(x - 2)$. FOIL stands for *first, outer, inner, last*. Multiply together the first terms within the parentheses, then multiply the two outer terms, then the inner terms, and finally the last terms. Don't worry about why FOIL works; just remember that it will always give you the correct answer."

19. To help his second graders understand important events in North American history, Mr. Kandetzki draws a time line on the chalkboard and shows them where such events as Columbus's voyage, the Pilgrims' landing, and the French and Indian War fall on the line. He puts his students' birth years on the time line as well to "personalize" it somewhat for them.

20. When Ms. Liu asks her seventh graders to read a chapter in their social studies textbook, she also asks them to write a brief summary of the chapter.

Answers to Application Exercise #15

1. Consistent. Physical models help students form mental models of scientific phenomenon.

2. Not consistent. Mr. Holliday is asking students to engage in knowledge telling, a process that is unlikely to help them organize their thoughts into a cohesive whole.

3. Not consistent. Ms. Yount has provided only an abstract explanation of negative numbers. Even at the high school level, mathematical concepts and principles are more meaningful to students when they are related to concrete objects and situations.

4. Not consistent. Many theorists recommend letting children use mathematical strategies they've developed on their own (including using their fingers). Over time, children will discard these strategies as they master more efficient ones—for instance, as they become capable of retrieving basic number facts quickly and automatically.

5. Consistent. Studying geography involves learning not only where things are but also *why* they are located where they are. For instance, geography includes principles regarding why people are more likely to settle in some areas than others.

6. Consistent. Rhyming exercises are one means of enhancing students' phonological awareness, which contributes to reading success.

7. Consistent. Particularly at the high school level, students should learn that history is often as much a matter of perspective as it is a matter of fact.

8. Not consistent. Many theorists believe that word problems alone are insufficient to promote transfer to real-world situations. In addition, Mr. Moser should engage students in real-world tasks that involve mathematics (grocery shopping, collecting and analyzing data, etc.).

9. Consistent. Giving students a structure to follow provides the scaffolding that many students need to guide their writing efforts. Such a structure becomes less necessary over time, as students gain experience with various forms of writing.

10. Consistent. Students in upper elementary grades are more likely to separate and control variables when they work with familiar situations and have only two or three variables to control. Only two variables need to be controlled in this situation: temperature of the water and the presence or absence of salt. Furthermore, Ms. Umanoff is asking questions that encourage students to reflect on their observations.

11. Not consistent. Students in the elementary grades should be encouraged to use context clues (e.g., surrounding words) to help them identify an unfamiliar word. Context clues may be especially useful when a word's letters do not enable a student to zero in on a single pronunciation; for instance, *enough* could conceivably be pronounced in ways that rhyme with *through, though,* or *bough.*

12. Consistent. Students should learn that science is as much theory as it is fact and that it continues to evolve over time as new data emerge.

13. Consistent. A number line can help young children develop an understanding of how numbers relate to one another.

14. Not consistent. The students probably have time for only one draft of the essay. Students may have insufficient working memory capacity to worry about writing mechanics at the same time that they worry about getting their thoughts on the page in a coherent fashion.

15. Not consistent. Understanding scale involves proportional reasoning, which doesn't emerge until early adolescence.

16. Consistent. Students who can choose their reading material use more sophisticated metacognitive strategies when they read, and they remember more content. Furthermore, group discussions help students construct meaning from what they read.

17. Not consistent. Especially at the secondary level, learning science should be more than learning a collection of discrete facts; it should also involve learning interrelationships among concepts and principles, perhaps in the form of theories or models.

18. Not consistent. Students are more likely to use mathematical procedures correctly when they understand the mathematical logic behind the procedures.

19. Not consistent. Second graders have little understanding of historical time.

20. Consistent. Writing about classroom subject matter enhances students' learning.

Answers to Selected Margin Notes

- Page 345: *What other misconceptions do you see in the children's responses?*
  Bill believes that the English named a state "America" and that the state existed before their arrival. Lisa thinks the country was formed after the American Civil War (she spells it "saver wore"); she also thinks that England gave the country the Statue of Liberty and that the statue is, in and of itself, liberty. Meg thinks (so it appears) that the dinosaurs lived as recently as six thousand years ago. Ben says that George Washington gave us the country only 2000 days ago.

- Page 358: *Why is it so difficult for people to detect ambiguities in their own writing*
  People read their own written work with their ideas already clearly in mind; what they *expect* to read will influence the meanings they construct as they read. Other readers, who don't necessarily have the writer's knowledge and beliefs, may not be able to construct a precise meaning based solely on what appears on the page.

- Page 363: *How might you set up (encode) the "carpet" problem using algebra?*
  Let x be the carpet's width and $x = 4$ be its length. The carpet's area (width times length) is $x(x + 4)$, so we can encode the problem this way:

  $$x(x + 4) = 45$$

  We can then solve for x as follows:

  $$x^2 + 4x = 45$$
  $$x^2 + 4x - 45 = 0$$
  $$(x + 9)(x - 5) = 0 \quad \text{(here we're factoring the equation)}$$
  $$x = -9 \text{ or } +5 \quad \text{(one expression within the parentheses must equal zero)}$$

  The carpet's width must be a positive number, so we eliminate –9. The carpet is therefore 5 feet wide and 9 feet $(x + 4)$ feet long.

Sample Test Questions

Items marked with a "**1**)" on the left-hand side are lower-level questions that assess your general knowledge and understanding of the material. Items marked with a "**2**)" on the left-hand side are higher-level questions that assess your ability to apply what you have learned to a new situation.

Multiple-Choice

2) 1. Which one of the following is an example of *emergent literacy*?
   a. Jessie, a first grader, reads *The Cat in the Hat* aloud to her classmates.
   b. Layne, a seventh grader, is just beginning to read adult fiction.
   c. Michael, a three-year-old, recognizes the symbol for Nike footwear.
   d. Paulette, a third grader, can write a short story but misspells many of the words.

2) 2. A fifth-grade teacher looks at the new history textbook that her school district has purchased for her class. She is disappointed to discover that the book describes events in American history only from the perspective of the European settlers; it gives no account of how early Native Americans must have felt about the settlers' encroachment on the land. "Oh, well," she rationalizes, "my students will certainly realize that the book is offering a biased account of history." From a developmental perspective, the teacher is making an erroneous assumption. She is forgetting that students in the upper elementary grades:
   a. Take what they read at face value
   b. Devote more effort to word recognition than to comprehension
   c. Can, from Piaget's perspective, classify objects and events as belonging to only one category at a time
   d. Cannot learn history in a meaningful fashion

1) 3. Three of the following are recommended strategies for fostering students' writing skills. Which one is *not* recommended?
    a. Teach students letter-sound correspondences and common spelling patterns.
    b. Tell students not to worry about spelling and punctuation in their first draft.
    c. Have students envision a particular person or group of people for whom they are writing, and encourage them keep the knowledge and beliefs of the audience in mind as they write.
    d. Have students write a first draft as ideas come to mind and then organize those ideas better as they write the second draft.

1) 4. From the perspective of cognitive psychology, should students learn basic number facts to a level of automaticity?
    a. No, because doing so prevents students from learning the facts in a meaningful fashion.
    b. No, because doing so will inhibit the development of appropriate epistemological beliefs about mathematics.
    c. Yes, because automatic retrieval of basic number facts lessens the burden on working memory.
    d. Yes, because research indicates that automaticity facilitates problem encoding.

2) 5. To test their belief that heavy objects fall faster than light ones, Gerard and Damon drop a golf ball and a marble from a third-story window. Their classmate Martha is at ground level to see which object lands first. "Wow!" Martha exclaims. "They landed at almost the same time. But I think maybe the golf ball landed just a little bit sooner. So I guess heavy objects *do* fall faster than light ones." Which one of the following concepts does Martha's statement illustrate?
    a. A benchmark
    b. Confirmation bias
    c. Problem encoding
    d. An epistemological belief

1) 6. When students learn why historical figures behaved as they did during important historical events, they are apt to:
    a. Empathize with those individuals and so understand historical events better.
    b. Acquire a better understanding of historical time.
    c. Develop an appreciation for general, abstract principles of history.
    d. Express a desire to read about diverse perspectives of the same event.

Essay

1) 7. The textbook recommends that teachers teach writing not just in language arts but in *all* areas of the curriculum. Identify a subject area you might teach and a grade level at which you might teach it. Then describe three strategies you might use to help your students write more effectively within that subject area.

2) 8. Describe at least one advantage of conducting whole-class or small-group discussions to promote students' learning and achievement in each of the following areas: reading, writing, mathematics, and science.

Answers to Sample Test Questions

1. c—Emergent literacy includes the knowledge and skills that lay a foundation for reading and writing; it typically develops in the preschool years. (See the section "Emergent Literacy" on textbook page 346.)

2. a—Students in the upper elementary grades typically take the things they read at face value (see the section "Developmental Changes in Reading" on textbook page 350).

3. d—This approach encourages knowledge telling rather than knowledge transforming. It is usually more effective to have students organize what they are going to write about before they begin to write. (See the section "Writing a First Draft" beginning on textbook page 355.)

4. c—Automaticity for basic number facts allows students to devote most of their working memory capacity to the more complex aspects of solving a problem (see the section "Mastering Problem-Solving Procedures" on textbook pages 366-367).

5. b—Confirmation bias is the tendency to look for evidence that confirms a hypothesis. See the section entitled "Investigating Scientific Phenomena" beginning on textbook page 372.

6. a—Students develop greater empathy for historical figures when they learn about the goals, motives, and personality characteristics that these people had (see the section "Thinking of Historical Figures as Real People" on textbook pages 381-382).

7. Numerous strategies are presented in the section "Writing" on textbook pages 352-361; your response should include at least three of them. The strategies you identify should be appropriate for the grade level at which you will be teaching, so you should take developmental changes in writing into account (see textbook page 359).

8. The textbook provides several justifications for conducting group discussions. In reading, group discussions enhance metacognitive skills and meaning construction (textbook pages 350-351). In writing, they facilitate retrieval of relevant knowledge and editing (textbook pages 354 and 358). In mathematics, they enhance students' understanding of concepts and problem-solving procedures (textbook page 371). In science, they promote conceptual change (textbook page 378). Your response should include at least one justification for *each* of the four subject areas.

Chapter 10

BEHAVIORIST VIEWS OF LEARNING

Chapter Overview

In this chapter, you will look more closely at *behaviorism,* a theoretical perspective that focuses primarily on relationships between the behaviors that people make and the environmental stimuli that promote and sustain those behaviors. As you examine *classical conditioning,* you will discover that some of the responses that people learn (many emotional responses, for example) become involuntary reactions to particular stimuli. And as you examine *operant conditioning,* you will find that the consequences (in particular, the *reinforcers*) of people's behaviors influence how those individuals behave on future occasions.

Throughout the chapter, you will encounter recommendations for classroom practice. For instance, you will find suggestions for helping students become less anxious about tasks and activities that they have associated with frustration and failure in the past. You will also learn numerous strategies for encouraging productive behaviors and reducing nonproductive and counterproductive ones. Ultimately, the classroom environment you create will have a strong influence on the behaviors your students exhibit.

Common Student Beliefs and Misconceptions Related to Chapter Content

Below are several misconceptions that college students often have before studying behaviorist views of learning—misconceptions that may interfere with an accurate understanding of what they read. As you read Chapter 10, be on the lookout for evidence that contradicts these common beliefs:

1. Some students, especially if they have previously encountered only early behaviorist perspectives (e.g., Pavlov's work with dogs, Skinner's work with pigeons), may believe that behaviorists focus primarily on animal learning and that behaviorist research has little relevance to how children learn in the classroom.

2. Some students erroneously think that a *reinforcer* is always a concrete object.

3. Many students think that *negative reinforcement* is a synonym for *punishment.*

4. Future teachers often use the term *reinforce* to mean giving learners additional information or providing additional experiences related to a topic (e.g., "We can reinforce children's knowledge of math facts by giving them lots of practice"). They then confuse this meaning of the term with the behaviorist meaning.

5. Many future teachers say that punishment is something that a teacher should never use, yet they recommend other strategies for reducing inappropriate behavior (e.g., "imposing consequences") that, for all intents and purposes, mean the same thing as punishment.

CHAPTER OUTLINE	**FOCUS QUESTIONS**
BASIC ASSUMPTIONS OF BEHAVIORISM	• What basic assumptions underlie behaviorist views of learning? • What do behaviorists mean by the term *contiguity*?

CLASSICAL CONDITIONING
   Classical Conditioning of Emotional Responses
   Generalization
   Extinction
	• How did Pavlov's dog demonstrate *learning* as behaviorists define the term? Analyze Pavlov's experiment using classical conditioning terminology.
	
	• Can you explain classical conditioning in your own words? Can you think of examples of responses *you* may have learned through classical conditioning?
	
	• Explain how a person might learn an emotional response to a particular situation through classical conditioning.
	
	• What is generalization in classical conditioning? What is extinction? Think of new examples of these phenomena.
	
	• From the perspective of classical conditioning, how can teachers help reduce students' anxiety about school activities and subject matter?

OPERANT CONDITIONING
   Contrasting Classical and Operant Conditioning
   Three Essential Conditions for Operant Conditioning
	• Can you state the basic principle of operant conditioning in your own words?
	
	• How is operant conditioning different from classical conditioning?
	
	• What conditions are essential for operant conditioning to occur?

CHAPTER OUTLINE	FOCUS QUESTIONS

REINFORCEMENT IN THE CLASSROOM
    Primary Versus Secondary Reinforcers
    Positive Versus Negative Reinforcement
    Using Reinforcement Effectively
	• Why do behaviorists use the term *reinforcer* instead of *reward*? How are *primary reinforcers* and *secondary reinforcers* different?
	
	• What is *positive reinforcement*? What various forms does it take? Describe the difference between extrinsic reinforcers and intrinsic reinforcers.
	
	• What is *negative reinforcement*? What effect does it have on the behavior it follows? How is it different from punishment?
	
	• What guidelines does the textbook offer for using reinforcement effectively in the classroom?
	
	• What is a *terminal behavior*? What specific educational practice has been derived from this concept?
	
	• What is a *contingency contract*? What are its essential components?

SHAPING NEW BEHAVIORS	• Describe *shaping* in your own words. Can you think of a new example of this process?

EFFECTS OF ANTECEDENT STIMULI AND RESPONSES
    Generalization
    Discrimination
    Cueing
    Setting Events
    Behavioral Momentum
	• How does generalization occur within the context of operant conditioning? How does discrimination occur?
	
	• What is *cueing*? What is a *setting event*? What is *behavioral momentum*? How can teachers apply each of these concepts to encourage desired classroom behaviors?

REDUCING AND ELIMINATING UNDESIRABLE BEHAVIORS
    Extinction
    Cueing Inappropriate Behaviors
    Reinforcing Incompatible Behaviors
    Punishment
	• Compare extinction in operant conditioning to extinction in classical conditioning.
	
	• How can teachers use extinction, cueing, reinforcement of incompatible behavior, and punishment to discourage inappropriate behavior?
	
	• What forms does punishment take? What kinds of punishment are recommended in classroom settings, and what kinds are not? What guidelines should teachers follow if they believe that they have no alternative but to punish students for misbehavior?

CHAPTER OUTLINE	FOCUS QUESTIONS

MAINTAINING DESIRABLE BEHAVIORS OVER THE LONG RUN
 	
    Promoting Intrinsic Reinforcement
 	
    Using Intermittent Reinforcement
	• How can teachers encourage students to continue making desired responses over the long run?
	
	• What is intermittent reinforcement? How does it affect learning? How does it affect extinction?

ADDRESSING ESPECIALLY DIFFICULT CLASSROOM BEHAVIORS
 	
    Applied Behavior Analysis
 	
    Positive Behavioral Support
	• What strategies does *applied behavior analysis* include? What strategies does *positive behavioral support* include? What does research tell us about the effectiveness of these approaches?

POTENTIAL LIMITATIONS OF BEHAVIORIST TECHNIQUES	• What are potential disadvantages of using extrinsic reinforcement in the classroom?
CONSIDERING DIVERSITY IN STUDENT BEHAVIORS Accommodating Students with Special Needs	• Using a behaviorist point of view, explain why different students respond in different ways to the same situations. • What behaviorist principles can teachers use to help students with special needs achieve academic and social success?

Chapter Glossary

Activity reinforcer. An opportunity to engage in a favorite activity.

Antecedent response. A response that increases the likelihood that another, particular response will follow.

Antecedent stimulus. A stimulus that increases the likelihood that a particular response will follow.

Applied behavior analysis. The systematic application of behaviorist principles in educational and therapeutic settings; sometimes known as *behavior modification*.

Baseline. The frequency of a response before operant conditioning.

Behavioral momentum. An increased tendency for an individual to make a desired response immediately after making similar responses.

Behaviorism. A theoretical perspective in which learning and behavior are described and explained in terms of stimulus-response relationships. Adherents to this perspective are called *behaviorists*.

Classical conditioning. A form of learning whereby a new, involuntary response is acquired as a result of two stimuli being presented at the same time.

Concrete reinforcer. A reinforcer that can be touched.

Conditioned response (CR). A response that, through classical conditioning, begins to be elicited by a particular stimulus.

Conditioned stimulus (CS). A stimulus that, through classical conditioning, begins to elicit a particular response.

Conditioning. Another word for learning; commonly used by behaviorists.

Contiguity. The occurrence of two or more events at the same time. *Contiguous* is the adjective used to refer to events having contiguity.

Contingency. A situation in which one event happens only after another event has already occurred. One event is *contingent* on another's prior occurrence.

Contingency contract. A formal agreement between a teacher and a student regarding behaviors the student will exhibit and reinforcers that will follow those behaviors.

Continuous reinforcement. Reinforcing a response every time it occurs.

Cueing. A teacher's signal that a particular behavior is desired or that a particular behavior should stop.

Discrimination. Phenomenon in operant conditioning whereby an individual learns that a response is reinforced in the presence of one stimulus but not in the presence of another, similar stimulus.

Extinction. In classical conditioning, the eventual disappearance of a conditioned response as a result of the conditioned stimulus being repeatedly presented alone (i.e., in the absence of the unconditioned stimulus); in operant conditioning, the eventual disappearance of a response that is no longer being reinforced.

Extrinsic reinforcer. A reinforcer that comes from the outside environment, rather than from within the individual.

Generalization. A phenomenon in both classical conditioning and operant conditioning whereby an individual learns a response to a particular stimulus and then makes the same response in the presence of similar stimuli.

Group contingency. A situation in which an entire group must make a particular response before reinforcement occurs.

Incompatible behaviors. Two or more behaviors that cannot be performed simultaneously.

In-school suspension. A form of punishment in which a student is placed in a quiet, boring room within the school building. It often lasts one or more school days and involves close adult supervision.

Intermittent reinforcement. Reinforcing a response only occasionally, with some occurrences of the response going unreinforced.

Intrinsic reinforcer. A reinforcer supplied by oneself or inherent in the task being performed.

Logical consequence. A consequence that follows logically from a student's misbehavior; in other words, the punishment fits the crime.

Negative reinforcement. A consequence that brings about the increase of a behavior through the removal (rather than the presentation) of a stimulus.

Neutral stimulus. A stimulus that does not elicit any particular response.

Operant conditioning. A form of learning whereby a response increases in frequency as a result of its being followed by reinforcement.

Positive behavioral support. A modification of traditional applied behavior analysis that includes identifying the purpose that an undesirable behavior serves for a student and providing an alternative way for the student to achieve the same purpose.

Positive feedback. A message that an answer is correct or a task has been well done.

Positive reinforcement. A consequence that brings about the increase of a behavior through the presentation (rather than removal) of a stimulus.

Premack principle. A phenomenon whereby individuals do less-preferred activities in order to engage in more-preferred activities.

Presentation punishment. A form of punishment involving the presentation of a new stimulus, presumably one that an individual finds unpleasant.

Primary reinforcer. A stimulus that satisfies a basic physiological need.

Psychological punishment. Any consequence that seriously threatens a student's self-concept and self-esteem.

Punishment. A consequence that decreases the frequency of the response it follows.

Reinforcement. The act of following a particular response with a reinforcer and thereby increasing the frequency of that response.

Reinforcer. A consequence (stimulus) of a response that leads to an increased frequency of that response.

Removal punishment. A form of punishment involving the removal of an existing stimulus, presumably one that an individual views as desirable and doesn't want to lose.

Response cost. The loss either of a previously earned reinforcer or of an opportunity to obtain reinforcement.

Secondary reinforcer. A stimulus that becomes reinforcing over time through its association with another reinforcer.

Setting event. In behaviorism, a complex environmental condition in which a particular behavior is most likely to occur.

Shaping. A process of reinforcing successively closer and closer approximations to a desired terminal behavior.

Social reinforcer. A gesture or sign that one person gives another to communicate positive regard.

Terminal behavior. The form and frequency of a response at the end of operant conditioning.

Time-out. A procedure whereby a misbehaving student is placed in a dull, boring situation with no opportunity to interact with classmates and no opportunity to obtain reinforcement.

Token economy. A technique whereby desired behaviors are reinforced by tokens, reinforcers that students can use to "purchase" a variety of other reinforcers.

Unconditioned response (UCR). A response that, without prior learning, is elicited by a particular stimulus.

Unconditioned stimulus (UCS). A stimulus that, without prior learning, elicits a particular response.

Application Exercise #16: Recognizing Examples of Classical and Operant Conditioning

In each of the following situations, a response is being learned through either classical or operant conditioning. Decide which form of conditioning is occurring in each case. If classical conditioning is taking place, identify the UCS, UCR, CS, and CR. If operant conditioning is taking place, identify the response, the reinforcer, and, if applicable, the discriminative stimulus.

1. Lindsey's mother has told Lindsey that she must do her homework every day before she can get together with her friends. Lindsey finds that by doing her homework quickly (although not necessarily carefully or accurately), she can spend more time at the mall with Mayesha and Heather.

2. When it's time for his fourth graders to go to lunch, Mr. Linnebur lets each row of students line up only when the entire row is quiet. Mr. Linnebur finds that he rarely has discipline problems at lunch time if he uses this procedure.

3. When Rhonda plugs in the oscilloscope in physics lab, an electrical short in the instrument gives her a nasty shock and she quickly pulls her hand away. Rhonda refuses to touch the oscilloscope in the lab after that. In fact, she is reluctant to handle any of the lab's electrical equipment.

4. Ms. Fiscus praises John when he reads the word *cat* correctly. Sometimes, however, he reads the word *car* as "cat"; he receives no praise from Ms. Fiscus when he does so. Eventually he learns to tell the difference between *cat* and *car*.

5. In history class, Ms. Swanson gets angry about Tom's poor test performance and humiliates him in front of his classmates. This humiliation creates bad feelings in Tom—feelings about Ms. Swanson as well as about her behavior.

6. Will usually turns in lengthy assignments several days early so he doesn't have to worry about them anymore.

7. Shannon's friend lends her a novel by Stephen King. Although Shannon doesn't usually spend much time reading, she finds this novel exciting and fun to read. When she finishes it, she begins to borrow other Stephen King novels from the library and reads them from cover to cover.

8. In his attempts to get Ms. Steinberg's attention, Josh tries talking loudly at inappropriate times. This strategy works for a while, because Ms. Steinberg admonishes him sternly for his outbursts. However, Ms. Steinberg eventually decides that it would be better to ignore Josh's disruptive behavior rather than to reprimand him. At this point, Josh discovers that he can continue to get a rise out of his teacher only when he throws an occasional "four-letter word" into his outspoken remarks.

Answers to Application Exercise #16

1. Operant conditioning. Doing her homework quickly (the response) is reinforced by being able to spend time with her friends (the reinforcer). The <u>Premack principle</u> is operating here.

2. Operant conditioning. Sitting quietly (the response) is followed by being allowed to get in line for lunch (the reinforcer). A <u>group contingency</u> is in effect here, because everyone in the row must be quiet before the reinforcer is presented.

3. Classical conditioning. The shock (UCS) leads to an immediate withdrawal of the hand (UCR). By being associated with the shock, the oscilloscope (CS) begins to elicit an avoidance response (CR) as well. Rhonda is also <u>generalizing</u> this conditioned response to other equipment in the lab.

4. Operant conditioning. Saying "cat" (the response) is followed by praise (the reinforcer). John begins to <u>discriminate</u> between the stimuli *cat* and *car*.

5. Classical conditioning. The humiliation (UCS) elicits bad feelings (UCR). Because Ms. Swanson is associated with the humiliation, she becomes a CS that elicits similar bad feelings (CR).

6. Operant conditioning. Completing assignments early (the response) leads to a reduction in worry (a <u>negative reinforcer</u>).

7. Operant conditioning. Reading (the response) is reinforced by excitement and enjoyment (an <u>intrinsic reinforcer</u>). The reading response <u>generalizes</u> to other novels by Stephen King.

8. Operant conditioning. Talking out of turn (the response) is followed by Ms. Steinberg's attention (the reinforcer). Ms. Steinberg is attempting to <u>extinguish</u> Josh's behavior by ignoring him. By continuing to reinforce those statements that contain undesirable words, however, she is actually <u>shaping</u> Josh's inappropriate remarks.

Application Exercise #17: Identifying Effective Classroom Practices

From a behaviorist perspective, which of the following teaching strategies are likely to be effective and which are not? Using behaviorist terminology, develop a rationale for each of your decisions.

1. A reading teacher has several students who are at risk for dropping out of high school. She finds reading materials that relate to each student's particular interests (football, fashion, auto mechanics, and so on).

2. Mr. Turiel tells his students, "As soon as you complete your multiplication tables, you can go to one of the learning centers you all enjoy so much."

3. Hoping to boost Yvette's self-confidence, Mr. Evans praises her when she finally passes one of his tests, even though he knows that she cheated on the test.

4. In a unit on genetics, Mr. Lima has students separate fruit flies by gender. He explains that the females have more stripes on their abdomen than the males do and that the males have bristle-like "combs" on their front legs. He walks around the room as students work and gives them positive feedback when they are separating the flies correctly.

5. Ronny clearly wants to be "Mr. Cool" in Ms. LaBranche's middle school science class. It seems as if he provokes Ms. LaBranche just to gain the admiration of his friends. In an attempt to encourage more productive behavior, Ms. LaBranche begins praising Ronny every time she sees him on task.

6. Later in the school year, Ms. LaBranche finds that Ronny is quite a comedian and enjoys making his classmates laugh. Furthermore, she discovers that Ronny can often create very clever jokes out of classroom subject matter. She takes Ronny aside one day and says, "I'll make a deal with you, Ronny. If you can stay on task throughout class each day, I'll give you the last few minutes of the period to tell two or three jokes. Two conditions, however: The jokes have to relate to whatever topic we've been studying that day, and they can't hurt anyone's feelings."

7. Kathy is a student with a history of counterproductive social behavior; she insults, teases, and ridicules other students almost daily. Over a period of several weeks, Mr. Puzio meets with Kathy twice a week after school to teach her more appropriate ways of interacting with her classmates. Every time Kathy displays her newly learned interactive skills with another child, Mr. Puzio catches her eye and smiles at her.

8. In his instrumental music class, Mr. Salazar praises his students no matter how well they play their instruments, even if they don't show any signs of improvement over a period of several weeks.

9. As Mr. Pacheco takes his third graders on a nature walk through a local park, he asks them to pick up any litter that they find along the trail. The children develop quite an enthusiasm for the task and proudly show him some of the trash they are finding. When the class returns to school, Mr. Pacheco looks at his watch and says, "Hmm, we got back earlier than I thought we would. Before we go inside, let's pick up some of the litter we see on the playground."

10. At lunch time on the first day of school, Ms. Denton has her first graders line up to get ready to go to the cafeteria. "Remember what I told you earlier, children," she says. "We need to walk *quietly* down the hall so we don't disturb children in other classrooms."

11. In a unit on golf in her physical education classes, Ms. McDaniels is teaching her students how to swing a golf club. She begins by praising them for using good form even when they miss the ball altogether. Eventually she praises them only when they use good form *and* hit the ball, and then only when, by swinging the club appropriately, they hit the ball a reasonable distance and in the proper direction.

12. After recess, Ms. Yancey's fifth graders are having trouble settling down. She tells them, "Okay, you can have another ten minutes to talk among yourselves, but then you need to get back to work on your book reports."

13. Laura rarely turns in the homework that Ms. Jonassen assigns. One day Laura *does* turn in her homework, but Ms. Jonassen is not aware of the fact until that evening when she is grading her students' papers. The following day, Ms. Jonassen makes sure to give Laura positive feedback by telling her, "Nice work yesterday."

14. At the beginning of the school year, Mr. Kelsey gives free time at the end of each day to students who finish their in-class assignments on time. Once his students are regularly completing their assignments in a timely manner, he continues to reinforce this behavior on occasion but more frequently makes free time contingent on other desired responses.

15. Susan often blurts out answers in class, to the point where she usually dominates class discussions. To help Susan control her outspokenness, Mr. Krick develops a contingency contract for her. He meets with her after school to describe its contents; he then asks her to sign it.

Answers to Application Exercise #17

1. Effective. The students will be learning new things about topics of interest to them as they read, so reading behavior will be <u>intrinsically reinforced</u>.

2. Effective. Mr. Turiel is reinforcing completion of the multiplication tables with a desired activity. In other words, he is using the <u>Premack principle</u>.

3. Not effective. Mr. Evans is reinforcing an undesirable behavior—cheating.

4. Effective. Mr. Lima is reinforcing desired behavior by giving positive feedback. Furthermore, he is teaching students to <u>discriminate</u> between two different stimuli by reinforcing different responses to each one.

5. Not effective. Not all students find praise reinforcing. Because Ronny is trying to maintain his "cool" image, he is unlikely to appreciate Ms. LaBranche's well-intended words.

6. Effective. Ms. LaBranche has identified a new behavior that serves the same purpose as Ronny's disruptive behavior: to gain the admiration of classmates. This strategy is often used in <u>positive behavioral support</u>.

7. Effective. Mr. Puzio is using <u>continuous reinforcement</u> to increase appropriate behavior.

8. Not effective. Ideally, Mr. Salazar should be reinforcing closer and closer approximations to the desired behavior—playing a musical instrument competently. In other words, he should be <u>shaping</u> students' behavior. By continuing to reinforce the same behavior week after week, he is giving students no reason to improve.

9. Effective. Mr. Pacheco is taking advantage of <u>behavioral momentum</u>: The students are more likely to make desired responses after they have already been making similar responses.

10. Effective. Ms. Denton is <u>cueing</u> appropriate behavior.

11. Effective. Ms. McDaniels starts by reinforcing something her students can do and then <u>shapes</u> more skillful behavior over time.

12. Not effective. Ms. Yancey is presenting a potential reinforcer (allowing students to talk with one another) *before* the desired response.

13. Not effective. Ideally, reinforcement should be immediate. Delayed reinforcement is likely to be effective only when students know immediately that it is coming eventually. In this situation, Laura has no reason to expect reinforcement for turning in her homework. Furthermore, when Ms. Jonassen finally *does* reinforce Laura, she does not indicate what response is specifically being reinforced.

14. Effective. Mr. Kelsey switches from <u>continuous reinforcement</u> to <u>intermittent reinforcement</u> of a desired response (finishing assignments on time) as a way of maintaining this response over the long run.

15. Not effective. Effective contingency contracts are those that a teacher and student develop *together,* agreeing on both the desired behaviors and the reinforcers that will be contingent on those behaviors.

Answers to Selected Margin Notes

- Page 401: *Do you remember the earlier example of learning to respond negatively to an instructor's scowl? Can you explain your learning from the perspective of classical conditioning?*

  The question is referring to the first example on textbook page 398. Because the D– grade already gives you a bad feeling in your stomach, we can say that the semi-failure is an unconditioned stimulus (UCS) that elicits the unconditioned response (UCR) of feeling uncomfortable. The teacher's scowl occurs in conjunction with the UCS. When the scowl itself elicits the uncomfortable feeling, it has become a conditioned stimulus (CS) and the feeling in response to it alone (i.e., in the absence of the D–) has become a conditioned response (CR).

- Page 405: *How is the concept of <u>contingency</u> different from <u>contiguity</u>?*

  Contiguity exists when two or more events occur at the same time. Contingency exists when one event happens *only* after another event occurs.

- Page 406: *Can you think of other examples of primary and secondary reinforcers?*

  Other examples of primary reinforcers are a cool swim on an exceptionally hot day, an opportunity to release pent-up energy, and sex. Other examples of secondary reinforcers are trophies, certificates, high school diplomas, paychecks, and nods of approval.

- Page 409: *How might you determine which reinforcers are most effective for your students?*

  You can ask students or their parents. You can also observe students to see what kinds of consequences students consistently seek out.

- Page 410: *What stimulus is being removed in each of these situations? What response is being reinforced as a result?*

  1. Electric shock is being removed. Pressing the bar is being reinforced.
  2. Worry is being removed. Finishing the assignment is being reinforced.
  3. Confusion is being removed. Procrastinating on the assignment is being reinforced.
  4. The noise and rowdiness are being removed. Yelling is being reinforced.

- Page 413: *How might you use shaping to teach an eight-year-old to write in cursive? a twelve-year-old to swing a baseball bat? an aggressive high school student to behave prosocially?*

  - <u>Writing in cursive</u>: Teachers frequently use shaping to teach cursive writing. They may begin by having students trace cursive letters that have been lightly written between two horizontal lines. They may then present only part of a letter, having students trace that part and then complete the letter. Over a period of time, students copy rather than trace the letters, write the letters from memory, write the letters from memory between smaller and smaller lines, and eventually write the letters on unlined paper.
  - <u>Swinging a baseball bat</u>: One possibility is to begin with "T-ball," where the child swings and hits a stationary ball placed at the appropriate height on a plastic stand. After the child masters hitting the ball off the batting tee, the ball can be thrown from a short distance, then from a longer one, etc. An alternative approach is to begin with a very large ball and then gradually decrease the size of the ball that the child needs to hit.
  - <u>Teaching prosocial behavior</u>: You should begin by identifying and reinforcing a behavior that the student already exhibits frequently—one that, although perhaps not prosocial, is at least nonaggressive. Once this behavior is occurring frequently, you can selectively reinforce only a more "prosocial" form of the behavior, and then a more desirable form of *that* behavior, and so on, until eventually truly prosocial behavior is occurring regularly.

- Page 417: *How is extinction similar in classical and operant conditioning? How is it different?*
  In both cases, extinction involves a gradual reduction in the frequency of a response when the circumstances that originally led to conditioning are no longer present. In classical conditioning, extinction occurs when the conditioned stimulus (something that appears *before* the response) is repeatedly experienced in the absence of the unconditioned stimulus. In operant conditioning, extinction occurs when reinforcement no longer is presented *after* the response.

- Page 425: *One statement in this paragraph is based on the concept of* shaping. *Another statement reflects the concept of* scaffolding, *described in Chapter 2. Can you identify each of these statements?*
  Providing extrinsic reinforcement for little improvements is shaping. Breaking down a complex task into smaller pieces is an example of scaffolding.

- Page 426: *Which form of reinforcement—continuous or intermittent—would you use to teach your students to persist at difficult tasks?*
  Intermittent reinforcement is preferable, because it makes a response more resistant to extinction. With an intermittent schedule, students are essentially learning that not every response is going to pay off, but that some responses eventually *will* pay off.

- Page 427: *Can you think of other possible reasons for the success of behaviorist techniques?*
  Because the desired terminal behavior is identified at the very beginning, students' efforts can be directed toward a particular goal. Furthermore, the frequent success (i.e., reinforcement) that students experience is likely to increase their self-confidence (or *self-efficacy,* as we will call it in social cognitive theory) that they can do something successfully. There are undoubtedly other possible explanations as well.

- Page 428: *Why do you think extrinsic reinforcers might have such effects? Can you form some hypotheses before you read Chapter 12?*
  - Regarding the undermining of intrinsic motivation: Providing extrinsic reinforcers for a behavior may give students the message that the behavior is not worth doing in its own right. A second explanation comes from social cognitive theory: When extrinsic reinforcers stop unexpectedly, students sometimes feel that they have been punished.
  - Regarding the decrease of other desirable behaviors: Students are likely to direct their efforts toward obtaining the extrinsic reinforcers, especially if those reinforcers are highly desirably ones. Furthermore, extrinsic reinforcers will encourage students to focus on their accomplishments rather than on learning per se; in other words, they will focus on *performance goals* rather than *learning goals* (see Chapter 12).

- Page 429: *In a number of places throughout the chapter I have sneaked unobservable phenomena (e.g., thoughts, feelings) into my description of behaviorist principles. Can you find some places where I have done so?*
  Here are a few places where I have done so (there are many others as well):
  - On page 398, I refer to Alan's *anxiety* whenever he is up at bat.
  - On page 400, I say that Brenda *feels happy* when she hears a song.
  - On page 406, I say that not everyone *appreciates* secondary reinforcers.
  - On page 407, I define an activity reinforcer as an opportunity to engage in a *favorite* activity.
  - On page 409, I talk about *intrinsic* reinforcers.
  - On page 410, I say that Rhonda no longer has to *worry* about her assignment.

- On page 419, I describe removal punishment as involving a stimulus that a person finds *desirable* and doesn't *want* to lose.
- On pages 425-426, I say that it may take Maria longer to *realize* that she is no longer being reinforced.

Sample Test Questions

Items marked with a "**1**)" on the left-hand side are lower-level questions that assess your general knowledge and understanding of the material. Items marked with a "**2**)" on the left-hand side are higher-level questions that assess your ability to apply what you have learned to a new situation.

Multiple-Choice

1)   1.   Three of the assumptions below characterize behaviorist views of learning. Which one is *not* an assumption that behaviorists make?
   a. People are most likely to make connections between a stimulus and a response when the two occur close together in time.
   b. Rats and people often learn in similar ways.
   c. Thinking processes cannot be observed and so cannot be studied scientifically.
   d. People rarely learn anything when the stimuli around them are unpleasant.

2)   2.   Three of the following are examples of operant conditioning. Which one is *not*?
   a. When Alice's teacher praises her in class for her fine oral report, Alice is embarrassed and vows never to act so smart in front of her friends again.
   b. When Bart changes the way he throws the javelin, he finds that it goes farther than it ever has before, and so he continues to use the new technique.
   c. When Cordell tells a funny joke, his classmates all laugh. Cordell soon becomes the class clown, telling jokes at every opportunity.
   d. When Donna discovers that she can leave physical education class early by complaining about a stomachache, she begins to get these "stomachaches" about once a week.

2)   3.   Which one of the following is an example of *negative reinforcement*?
   a. Eric's friends think he's cool because he has the audacity to swear in class.
   b. Ophelia completes her English paper two days early so she won't have it hanging over her head anymore.
   c. Timothy's teacher scolds him when she finds a copy of *Playboy* hidden behind the textbook he's supposed to be reading.
   d. Myra gets the attention of all the boys when she wears tight, skimpy outfits to school.

2)   4. Raymond discovers that he gets better grades on his history tests when he studies a little bit every night than when he tries to cram at the last minute. Raymond starts applying the same strategy to his biology and geography classes as well. From the perspective of operant conditioning, Raymond is demonstrating:

    a. Generalization
    b. Baseline behavior
    c. Shaping
    d. Discrimination

2)   5. Sally has trouble sitting still in class. Mr. Torrentino begins praising Sally every time she sits quietly for a reasonable period of time. He notices improvement in Sally's classroom behavior and so continues reinforcing Sally in this fashion in the weeks that follow. By Thanksgiving, Sally is behaving as well as her classmates, so Mr. Torrentino concludes that he no longer has to reinforce her for sitting still. Soon after this, Sally's behavior begins to deteriorate, and by January she is back to her old, restless self. From an operant conditioning perspective, what should Mr. Torrentino *definitely* have done differently in this situation?

    a. He should have taught Sally to discriminate between situations in which sitting still was and was not appropriate.
    b. He should have punished her for getting out of her seat and for other similarly "restless" behaviors.
    c. He should have continued to reinforce her for sitting quietly on an intermittent basis.
    d. He should have used a reinforcer other than praise.

1)   6. Three of the following practices are consistent with the textbook's guidelines for using punishment to reduce inappropriate behavior. Which one is *not* consistent with these guidelines?

    a. Teach students more appropriate behavior and punish *in*appropriate behavior.
    b. Give reasons why the punished behavior cannot be tolerated.
    c. Let students know in advance what behaviors will be punished, and how.
    d. Assign extra classwork when students have been especially disruptive.

Essay

2)   7. Miriam was badly beaten by an aggressive classmate in the school corridor yesterday, and now she does not want to go to school. Explain this situation in terms of *classical conditioning*. Identify the UCS, UCR, CS, and CR.

2)   8. You want to teach Leon to catch a baseball. Describe how you might use *shaping* to teach this skill. Specify:

    a. An appropriate terminal behavior
    b. A reinforcer you might reasonably use
    c. The specific steps you would take during the shaping process

Answers to Sample Test Questions

1. d—People often learn from unpleasant stimuli. For examples, see the section "Classical Conditioning of Emotional Responses" beginning on textbook page 400.

2. a—Operant conditioning always leads to an increase in the reinforced behavior (see the basic principle of operant conditioning presented on textbook page 403). Alice probably won't increase her "acting smart" behavior. The teacher's praise is not reinforcing to Alice; instead, it is punishing.

3. b—By completing her paper, Ophelia gets rid of something unpleasant: She no longer has the assignment hanging over her head. See the discussion of negative reinforcement on textbook page 410.

4. a—Raymond learns to make a response in the presence of one stimulus (history classes) and begins to demonstrate the same response in the presence of similar stimuli (other classes). Textbook page 414 describes generalization within the context of operant conditioning.

5. c—When reinforcement stops, extinction often occurs. An intermittent schedule of reinforcement makes a learned response more resistant to extinction once reinforcement finally *does* stop (e.g., at the end of the school year). See the discussion of extinction on textbook page 417.

6. d—Extra classwork is usually *not* recommended as classroom punishment because it communicates the message that schoolwork is unpleasant (see textbook page 422).

7. The beating (or the pain associated with it) was an unconditioned stimulus (UCS) that elicited an unconditioned response (UCR) of fear or anxiety. School was associated with the beating, so it has become a conditioned stimulus (CS) that elicits fear as well. Miriam's fear of school is therefore a conditioned response (CR). See the section on "Classical Conditioning" that begins on textbook page 398.

8. a. The desired end result is catching a baseball regularly. You should describe this terminal behavior in specific, concrete, and observable terms (see textbook pages 410-411). For example, you might say that Leonard will catch 90 percent of the pitches thrown to him from a distance of 20 feet.
    b. The reinforcer should be something that is definitely reinforcing for Leon (see textbook page 411). If Leon truly wants to learn how to play baseball, his success at catching the ball should be reinforcement enough. Otherwise, you might use positive feedback, praise, points that are accumulated and eventually exchanged for a small prize, etc. You need to identify only one reinforcer here, but be sure to explain why you think it will be effective in this situation.
    c. Shaping is a process of reinforcing closer and closer approximations to the desired terminal behavior (see textbook page 412). There are several possible approaches that you might take to shape Leon's "catching" behavior. For example, you might begin with a very large ball and then gradually reduce the size of the ball Leon must catch. Or you might first pitch the ball to Leon from only a few feet away, gradually increasing your distance as he shows greater success. Your approach might even use a combination of decreasing ball size and increasing distance. Whatever you do, you should change the nature of the response you reinforce over time, and you should make sure that Leon demonstrates mastery of each new behavior before you proceed to the next one.

Chapter 11

SOCIAL COGNITIVE VIEWS OF LEARNING

Chapter Overview

This chapter describes concepts and principles that have emerged from social cognitive theory—a theory that focuses on how and what people learn by observing those around them. As you will see, social cognitive theorists' beliefs about how reinforcement influences learning and behavior are quite different from those of behaviorists. You will learn about the powerful effects of *modeling,* a process through which people acquire new behaviors and skills by watching the things that other people do and the consequences that they experience. As you read about *self-efficacy,* you will identify strategies for enhancing students' self-confidence about achieving goals and performing classroom tasks. Later in the chapter, as you explore the topic of *self-regulation,* you will learn how you can help your students become less susceptible to the influences of specific environmental stimuli and increasingly capable of controlling their own behavior. Many of the strategies that social cognitive theorists recommend are especially useful for helping students with diverse backgrounds and needs achieve success not only in the classroom but also in the outside world.

Common Student Beliefs and Misconceptions Related to Chapter Content

Below are two ideas that sometimes interfere with college students' ability to understand the things that they read about social cognitive theory. As you read Chapter 11, be on the lookout for evidence that contradicts these ideas:

1. Some students think that modeling always involves an actual person demonstrating a behavior. (See the textbook's discussion of *symbolic models*.)

2. In Chapter 10's discussion of operant conditioning, you learned about the concept of *extinction,* whereby a response decreases in frequency when it is no longer being reinforced. Social cognitive theorists have a very different view of what happens when reinforcement no longer occurs—a view that involves *expectations*.

CHAPTER OUTLINE	FOCUS QUESTIONS
BASIC ASSUMPTIONS OF SOCIAL COGNITIVE THEORY	• What general assumptions underlie social cognitive theory?

THE SOCIAL COGNITIVE VIEW OF REINFORCEMENT AND PUNISHMENT
 	
    Expectations
    Vicarious Experiences
    Cognitive Processing
    Choice of Behavior
    Nonoccurrence of Expected Consequences
	• From a social cognitive perspective, in what ways do reinforcement and punishment affect learning and behavior?
	
	• What are *vicarious reinforcement* and *vicarious punishment*? Think of examples of these phenomena in your own life.
	
	• What is an *incentive*? Why is it not necessarily the same as a reinforcer?
	
	• What happens when the expected consequences of behavior (either reinforcement or punishment) don't occur?

MODELING
 	
    How Modeling Affects Behavior
    Characteristics of Effective Models
    Helping Students Learn from Models
	• What's the difference between a *live model* and a *symbolic model*?
	
	• Describe the four effects of modeling—observational learning, response facilitation, response inhibition, and response disinhibition—in your own words.
	
	• What characteristics do effective models often have? Why do students model some behaviors yet not model others?
	
	• What four conditions are essential for learning from models? What implications do these conditions have for teachers?

SELF-EFFICACY
 	
    How Self-Efficacy Affects Behavior
    Factors in the Development of Self-Efficacy
	• What is *self-efficacy*? How is it different from self-esteem? What effects does it have on behavior and learning?
	
	• What experiences contribute to either high or low self-efficacy? What strategies can teachers use to enhance students' self-efficacy?

CHAPTER OUTLINE	FOCUS QUESTIONS

SELF-REGULATION
 	
    Components of Self-regulated Behavior
    Self-regulated Learning
    Self-regulated Problem Solving
	• What do social cognitive theorists mean by the term *self-regulation*? What role do standards and goals play in the process? What roles do self-monitoring, self-instructions, self-evaluation, and self-imposed contingencies play?
	
	• What does *self-regulated learning* involve? Why is it so important, and how can teachers foster it?
	
	• How can teachers promote more appropriate social behaviors through *self-regulated problem solving*?

RECIPROCAL CAUSATION	• Describe *reciprocal causation* in your own words. Identify several ways in which each of the three factors in reciprocal causation—environment, behavior, and person—affects the other two.

CONSIDERING DIVERSITY FROM A SOCIAL COGNITIVE PERSPECTIVE
 	
    Using Diverse Models to Promote Success and Self-Efficacy
    Promoting Self-Regulation in Students with Special Needs
	• Why do students benefit from observing models who are similar to themselves?
	
	• What concepts and principles from social cognitive theory are especially useful in understanding and helping students with special needs?

THE BIG PICTURE: COMPARING THE THREE PERSPECTIVES OF LEARNING	• How are cognitive psychology, behaviorism, and social cognitive theory similar? How are they different?

Chapter Glossary

Incentive. A hoped-for, but not certain, consequence of behavior.

Intrinsic motivation. The internal desire to perform a particular task.

Live model. An individual whose behavior is observed "in the flesh."

Mediation training. Training that involves teaching students how to mediate conflicts among classmates by asking opposing sides to express their differing viewpoints and then working together to devise a reasonable resolution.

Reciprocal causation. The interdependence of environment, behavior, and personal variables as these three factors influence learning.

Resilient self-efficacy. The belief that one can perform a task successfully even after experiencing setbacks; includes the belief that effort and perseverance are essential for success.

Self-efficacy. The belief that one is capable of executing certain behaviors or reaching certain goals.

Self-evaluation. The process of evaluating one's own performance or behavior.

Self-imposed contingencies. Contingencies that students impose on themselves; the self-reinforcements and self-punishments that follow various behaviors.

Self-instructions. Instructions that students give themselves as they perform a complex behavior.

Self-monitoring. The process of observing and recording one's own behavior.

Self-regulated learning. Regulating one's own cognitive processes to learn successfully; includes goal setting, planning, attention control, use of effective learning strategies, self-monitoring, and self-evaluation.

Self-regulated problem-solving strategy. A strategy that helps students solve their own interpersonal problems.

Self-regulation. The process of setting standards and goals for oneself and engaging in behaviors that lead to the accomplishment of those standards and goals.

Social cognitive theory. A theoretical perspective in which learning by observing others is the focus of study.

Symbolic model. A real or fictional character portrayed in various media.

Vicarious punishment. A phenomenon whereby a response decreases in frequency when another (observed) person is punished for that response.

Vicarious reinforcement. A phenomenon whereby a response increases in frequency when another (observed) person is reinforced for that response.

Application Exercise #18: Applying Principles of Social Cognitive Theory

Using social cognitive theory, explain what is happening in each of the following situations.

1. During the first week of his French I class, Mr. Rizzo says, "Repeat after me—*Le crayon rouge est sur la table vert.*" His students are all motivated to do well in French; however, they have trouble repeating the sentence because they can't remember what he said.

2. Max is making a sketch of a sports car. He stops to scrutinize his work and discovers that the front hood is the wrong shape. He erases the front end of his car and draws it again.

3. Erin is working extremely hard in her science class in the hopes that she will get an A from Mr. Richards—someone who has a reputation for being a tough grader.

4. Sylvia is trying to teach Wendy how to do a cartwheel. Sylvia performs several cartwheels in slow motion so that Wendy can see all the steps involved. Then she says, "You can do it, I know you can!" Wendy makes at least 20 unsuccessful attempts and eventually gives up. "I don't think I'll ever be able to do a cartwheel," she says dejectedly.

5. Rhea completes her research paper exactly as Mr. O'Brien has said it should be done. Yet Mr. O'Brien does not give Rhea full credit for the assignment because all the references in her bibliography are more than ten years old. Rhea is angry and frustrated because Mr. O'Brien never mentioned that the bibliography had to include things published within the last ten years.

6. Mickey thinks that if he can get elected as president of the student council, he will have a better shot at getting into a good college.

7. Ms. Wing wants the girls in her high school physical education class to develop better muscle tone. She invites Jim Davidson, a weight trainer at the local conditioning center, to come demonstrate appropriate use of the school's weight machines. The girls pay little attention to what he is doing, thinking that weight training is mostly for men, not women.

8. Gina notices that a girl who makes the cheerleading squad immediately becomes more "popular" at school. Gina wants to be popular, too, so she tries out for cheerleading the following year.

9. Martin frequently inserts inappropriate four-letter words into the comments that he makes in Ms. Zimmerman's class. Jason learned never to say such words in his previous classes, but apparently they're OK in Ms. Zimmerman's room. Jason begins to use them liberally whenever he speaks in class.

10. In Ms. Reese's math class, Melissa quickly gives up on problems she cannot immediately solve. When Ms. Reese expresses her concern, Melissa's response is, "I'm just no good at math, so why even try?"

11. Serena has always been a straight-A student. When she gets her first B *ever* in the second semester of her senior year, she bursts into tears. Her friends don't understand it; after all, Serena has already been accepted at the college of her choice, and a single B certainly won't change that fact.

12. Ms. Smith ridicules Jerry for asking a "stupid" question in class. After this, no one in class has the nerve to ask questions when something is confusing or unclear.

Answers to Application Exercise #18

1. <u>Modeling</u> is unlikely to occur unless four conditions—attention, retention, motor reproduction, and motivation—are all present. In this situation, <u>retention</u> is missing: Students can't remember the modeled behavior.

2. <u>Self-regulation</u> includes both <u>self-monitoring</u> (e.g., looking at the product one has created) and <u>self-evaluation</u> (e.g., determining whether the product meets one's standards).

3. Erin is working for an <u>incentive</u>—a hoped-for, but not guaranteed, reinforcer for her efforts.

4. Sylvia is <u>modeling</u> a cartwheel for Wendy. Wendy's self-efficacy is temporarily enhanced by Sylvia's message, but that self-efficacy soon decreases when Wendy's efforts repeatedly result in failure.

5. Here we see the <u>nonoccurrence of expected reinforcement</u>—in social cognitive theory, a form of punishment.

6. Mickey has an <u>expectation</u> that a particular behavior will be reinforced.

7. The girls are unlikely to model the behavior because they do not believe it is "<u>gender-appropriate" behavior</u> for females.

8. When Gina sees someone else be reinforced by "popularity," she experiences <u>vicarious reinforcement</u> for becoming a cheerleader.

9. The <u>nonoccurrence of expected punishment</u> is reinforcing to Jason. Here we see <u>response disinhibition</u>: A behavior that has previously been forbidden is being exhibited by a model (Martin) without adverse consequences.

10. People with low <u>self-efficacy</u> exert little effort and give up quickly when they experience failure.

11. As people become increasingly self-regulated, they begin to set <u>standards</u> for their own behavior and judge themselves unfavorably when they don't meet those standards.

12. When they see their classmate being ridiculed for asking a question, the students experience <u>vicarious punishment</u>.

Application Exercise #19: Identifying Effective Classroom Practices

From the perspective of social cognitive theory, which of the following teaching behaviors are likely to be effective, and which are not? Defend your choices.

1. Mr. Warner tells Brad, "I know you've never wrestled before, but with practice you can become a successful wrestler. Come on, let's see what you're made of." Mr. Warner pairs Brad with a stronger, more experienced wrestler who consistently pins him to the mat as the two boys practice over the next hour and a half.

2. It is December 20th, the day before school closes for a two-week vacation. Mr. Reagan's junior high school science students are restless, as their minds are on the upcoming holiday season. Nevertheless, Mr. Reagan is already three weeks behind in the schedule he has planned for the school year and believes he must make good use of this last day. In preparation for the day's lesson, he tells his class, "Today I will demonstrate how to use a microscope correctly. You will all be using microscopes in your lab session the first day you get back from vacation."

3. During a unit on tennis, Ms. Sommarstrom sees Marcy execute an especially good serve. "Excellent form on that serve," she tells Marcy in earshot of her classmates.

4. Mr. Tuttle tells his high school students many tales about the things he did as a teenager—driving recklessly on city streets, playing practical jokes on local merchants, drinking heavily, and experimenting with marijuana. "I regret it all," he says. "Looking back, I wish I'd taken my high school education more seriously than I did."

5. Belinda often cracks her knuckles in class, and her classmates find the behavior very annoying. Mr. Chi takes Belinda aside and explains the problem, but she responds, "Oh, Mr. Chi, I don't crack my knuckles *that* much." Because Belinda clearly has little awareness of how frequently she exhibits the distracting behavior, Mr. Chi asks her to record each instance of knuckle cracking on a piece of graph paper for the next five days.

6. As Ms. Etsitty shows her third graders how to write a lowercase cursive *b,* she says the words, "Up, down, around, and out."

7. During a cooperative learning activity, Mr. Sanchez reminds his students, "Remember, you will each be individually tested on the things you are learning as a group, so you should make sure that each and every one of you is learning the material. As an extra bonus, if any group gets an average of 90 percent on the test, all group members will get an additional three percentage points."

8. The day after Halloween, Ms. Levensohn's first graders are all a bit hyperactive. After an exasperating morning, Ms. Levensohn warns them, "If anybody in this room makes so much as a single peep in the next five minutes, the entire class will stay in during recess and work on the math assignment we didn't finish today." Jared immediately burps, and several students around him laugh. Ms. Levensohn thinks that her class might settle down after everyone has had a chance to run around outside for a while, so when the recess bell rings, she tells them to get on their jackets and line up by the outside door.

9. Ms. Struthers wants to promote self-regulation in her third graders, so she asks them to set their own goals regarding the number of spelling words they will each learn every week. Some students are saying that they will learn only one new word each week, even though they are clearly capable of learning many more than that on a weekly basis. Nevertheless, Ms. Struthers allows them to work toward these simple, easily achievable goals as a way of enhancing their self-efficacy about spelling.

10. In her classroom of white, middle-class eighth graders, Ms. Orlando is concerned when she hears some of her students make racist remarks about a community of Native Americans who live nearby. She decides to incorporate a unit on Native American culture into next month's class schedule—one in which students will encounter exemplary Native Americans through such novels as *Bury My Heart at Wounded Knee* and such films as *Dances with Wolves*.

11. Mr. Masterson is concerned about Sheri, a girl in his sophomore English class who is quite capable of doing challenging academic assignments but prefers to spend all her time attending social functions rather than doing her homework. Mr. Masterson wants to provide a good role model for Sheri, so he develops a homework assignment that students should do in groups of three. He includes Sheri in a group with two extremely conscientious, although relatively unpopular, students. Sheri expresses her dismay that she will be working with "geeks." Nevertheless, Mr. Masterson hopes that Sheri will begin to imitate some of the academic behaviors that the other two group members exhibit.

12. Scott tells Ms. Robinson, "I know I'm not reading my history book each night the way I'm supposed to, but I turn the television on as soon as I get home from school every day, and somehow I can never tear myself away from it except to eat dinner. I feel so guilty not doing my homework, but I don't seem to have any willpower." Ms. Robinson suggests to him, "Your reading assignments are usually only about ten pages apiece. When you get home from school every day, read the first five pages of your assignment *first*, then reward yourself by letting yourself watch TV. After dinner, read the last five pages, and reward yourself again. Think of your favorite television shows as a reward for a job well done. That way, you won't have that guilt trip when you watch them."

Answers to Application Exercise #19

1. Not effective. The effects of <u>others' messages</u> on self-efficacy are short-lived unless a student's efforts eventually lead to success. Brad is achieving no success in this situation.

2. Not effective. Mr. Reagan is unlikely to have all four conditions essential for successful <u>modeling</u> to occur. At a minimum, he probably won't have his students' <u>attention</u>. Furthermore, they may have little <u>motivation</u> to learn, and they will probably have difficulty with <u>retention</u> of the things he shows them.

3. Effective, provided that public praise is reinforcing for Marcy. Marcy is being directly reinforced, and other students are experiencing <u>vicarious reinforcement</u> for such a serve.

4. Not effective. Through the stories of his wild teenage years, Mr. Tuttle—as a teacher, a potentially very powerful model—is modeling very inappropriate behavior indeed.

5. Effective. Mr. Chi is helping Belinda engage in <u>self-observation</u>—an important step on the road to self-regulation.

6. Effective. By teaching students instructions that they can give themselves as they perform a new task, Ms. Etsitty is facilitating the <u>retention</u> component of modeling.

7. Effective. Mr. Sanchez is making the contingency between behavior and consequences clear. Furthermore, he is providing an <u>incentive</u> (bonus points) for students to help one another learn.

8. Not effective. The <u>nonoccurrence of threatened punishment</u> reinforces the noisy behavior. Ms. Levensohn should identify a consequence she can realistically carry out when undesirable behavior occurs. Having students miss recess is probably *not* a good idea at the first grade level (see Chapter 10).

9. Not effective. Although encouraging students to set their own goals promotes <u>self-regulation</u>, such goals should be challenging ones rather than ones that can be achieved easily. Accomplishing easy tasks does little, if anything, to enhance self-efficacy.

10. Effective. Ms. Orlando is exposing her students to positive role models—in particular, to <u>symbolic models</u>.

11. Not effective. The other two members of Sheri's group do not possess two important characteristics of effective models: They have little prestige in Sheri's eyes, and they are exhibiting behaviors that Sheri will probably think are irrelevant to her own situation.

12. Effective. Ms. Robinson is encouraging Scott to reinforce himself for appropriate behavior. Self-reinforcement is often effective when students are motivated to change their own behavior.

Answers to Selected Margin Notes

- Page 445: *Why is this called the disinhibition effect?*

  A response that was previously inhibited (because it was punished) is no longer being inhibited.

- Page 445: *How are the response facilitation and response disinhibition effects similar? How are they different?*

  Both involve an increase in behavior. But only the response disinhibition effect involves a *previously forbidden* behavior.

- Page 451: *What factors in Nathan's situation may have contributed to his low self-efficacy for learning French?*

  At least two factors—the failure of his friends and his belief that learning a foreign language is a "girl" thing—are definitely contributing to his low self-efficacy. In addition, Nathan may have had previous failures in learning a language that have led him to conclude that he is "no good" at this kind of thing.

- Page 455: *Students from low-income families typically set low goals for themselves in terms of career aspirations. Can you explain this fact in light of the discussion here?*

  The standards and goals that people adopt for themselves are often modeled after those of the people around them. Students from low-income families are probably exposed to more people with low expectations for themselves than to people with high self-expectations.

- Page 457: *Can you relate steps 3, 4, and 5 to Vygotsky's notions of self-talk and inner speech (Chapter 2)?*

  Vygotsky proposed that children guide themselves through a new task by talking themselves through the task, doing so first out loud (*self-talk*) and eventually in an internal, mental fashion (*inner speech*).

- Page 457: *How might you use this technique to help a student with sloppy work habits? to help a student who responds with uncontrolled anger in frustrating situations?*

  Depending on the particular way in which a student is "sloppy," self-instructions might include self-reminders to write more neatly or to make sure all the necessary parts of a task are completed. For a student who gets overly angry when frustrated, something as simple as counting to ten in a slow, controlled manner might be a good start.

Sample Test Questions

Items marked with a "**1**)" on the left-hand side are lower-level questions that assess your general knowledge and understanding of the material. Items marked with a "**2**)" on the left-hand side are higher-level questions that assess your ability to apply what you have learned to a new situation.

Multiple-Choice

1) 1. Three of the following are assumptions that underlie social cognitive theory. Which one is *not* an assumption that social cognitive theorists make?
   a. As people develop, they begin to take control of their own behavior, rather than be influenced solely by environmental events.
   b. People will learn something only if reinforcing or punishing consequences follow their behavior.
   c. People set goals for themselves and strive to achieve their goals.
   d. Learning doesn't always result in an immediate behavior change.

2) 2. Which one of the following is an example of *vicarious reinforcement*?
   a. Abigail sees the flash of a knife blade in Wade's pocket and is angry that Wade would violate school policy by bringing a weapon to class.
   b. Bernice does an excellent job on her science fair project, but she doesn't get feedback about her performance until several days after the science fair is over.
   c. Chad sees Jason cheat on a test and then later get an A on that test, whereas Chad himself receives only a C. Chad starts cheating on exams after that.
   d. Douglas reads as much as he can about life under the sea because he wants to be a marine biologist someday.

2) 3. Janice sees Mark drinking a soft drink in Ms. Murray's class. "Geez, Mark," she whispers to him after class, "taking drinks to class is against school rules. Aren't you afraid that you'll get caught?" Mark replies that he's been bringing drinks to class all year and Ms. Murray has never told him to stop; usually she doesn't even notice what he's doing. Janice begins bringing her own drink to class after that. Which one of the following effects of modeling does this situation illustrate?
   a. Response retention
   b. Response facilitation
   c. Response inhibition
   d. Response disinhibition

2) 4. Which one of the following students is most clearly demonstrating *self-regulation* as social cognitive theorists define the term?
   a. Antonio can type all 26 letters without looking at the keyboard.
   b. Bonnie behaves herself in class so that she can get the free time her teacher has promised for good behavior.
   c. Claude gets around the school building all by himself even though he is blind.
   d. Dana is quite proud of herself when she can finally do a handstand.

1) 5. *Mediation training* involves teaching students to:
    a. Give themselves instructions as they perform difficult tasks
    b. Help their classmates solve interpersonal conflicts
    c. Anticipate the consequences of their behaviors
    d. Remember the behaviors that their teachers demonstrate

1) 6. Which one of the following statements best reflects social cognitive theorists' concept of *reciprocal causation*?
    a. Not only are students' behaviors influenced by environmental circumstances, but those behaviors also change the environment that students later experience.
    b. Students are more likely to engage in a particular behavior when they see others being reinforced for that behavior.
    c. Students can learn only when they are paying attention to the things that happen around them.
    d. Students are more likely to engage in a particular activity when they believe that they can be successful at that activity.

Essay

2) 7. Imagine that, as a high school teacher, you want students to learn how to conduct themselves during a job interview. You decide to *model* the behaviors you want your students to learn (looking the interviewer in the eye, describing one's job-related experience and capabilities with confidence, etc.). Explain how, as you model effective interviewing techniques, you would take into account the four essential processes involved in *modeling*.

1) 8. Explain what psychologists mean by the term *self-efficacy*. Then describe three different strategies that social cognitive theorists believe can enhance students' self-efficacy about classroom tasks.

Answers to Sample Test Questions

1. b—Reinforcement and punishment have several indirect effects on learning. However, learning can also occur in their absence. (See the last bulleted item on page 438 in the section "Basic Assumptions of Social Cognitive Theory.")

2. c—Chad's cheating behavior increases as a result of seeing Jason reinforced for cheating. Vicarious reinforcement is described on textbook page 439.

3. d—Janice begins to engage in a previously forbidden behavior when she sees Mark engage in that behavior without adverse consequences. (See the description of response disinhibition on textbook page 445.)

4. d—As social cognitive theorists define the term, self-regulation involves a number of processes, including goal setting, self-observation, self-instructions, self-evaluation, and self-imposed contingencies. Of the four alternatives, only d clearly reflects one of these processes. More specifically, Dana's pride in her accomplishment is an example of a self-imposed contingency—in this case, self-reinforcement. See the discussion of self-imposed contingencies on textbook pages 458-459.

5. b—In mediation training, students learn to help one another resolve interpersonal problems (see textbook page 461).

6. a—Reciprocal causation is the belief that three factors—environment, behavior, and personal characteristics—all influence one another (see textbook pages 462-465). Alternative a describes the influence that two of these factors—environment and behavior—have on each other. The other three alternatives describe effects that are one-way rather than reciprocal (e.g., alternative b describes the effect of an environmental event on behavior).

7. Your response should include one or more strategies for:
   - Capturing and maintaining students' attention
   - Helping students remember the behaviors you model (retention)
   - Making sure your students are physically capable of the behaviors you model (motor reproduction)
   - Promoting students' motivation for learning the interviewing skills you are teaching them

   Relevant strategies are presented in the section "Helping Students Learn from Models" on textbook pages 447-449.

8. Self-efficacy is a person's belief that he or she is capable of executing certain behaviors or reaching certain goals. Social cognitive theorists propose that one's own prior successes, messages from others, and others' successes (especially the successes of peers) can all enhance self-efficacy (see textbook pages 451-453). The strategies you describe should reflect at least two of these three factors.

Chapter 12

MOTIVATING STUDENTS TO LEARN

Chapter Overview

In the last few chapters, you've learned a great deal about how to help students learn effectively. As you read about motivation in this chapter, you'll learn about how to help students *want* to learn. You will find that students who are *intrinsically* motivated to master classroom material are more likely to engage in productive learning processes and behaviors than students who are *extrinsically* motivated. You will discover, too, that learning and memory are often facilitated when material is emotionally charged—a phenomenon sometimes called *hot cognition*—but that anxiety may or may not enhance students' classroom performance, depending on the circumstances. In the latter part of the chapter, you will find that students' interpretations of the things that happen to them (the *attributions* that they make) have definite effects on how they behave in future situations.

Recommendations for motivating students to learn and achieve appear throughout the chapter. For example, you'll find strategies for fostering intrinsic motivation, addressing students' social needs, and keeping students' anxiety at a reasonable and productive level. Later on, you'll find suggestions for promoting a *mastery orientation*—an "I can do it" attitude about classroom objectives and activities. Near the end of the chapter, you'll discover teaching strategies that may be especially appropriate for students of particular ages, cultural groups, genders, and socioeconomic backgrounds, as well as strategies that are likely to facilitate the classroom success of students with special educational needs.

Common Student Beliefs and Misconceptions Related to Chapter Content

Below are two misconceptions that college students often have before studying the topic of human motivation—misconceptions that may interfere with an accurate understanding of what they read. As you read Chapter 12, be on the lookout for evidence that contradicts these common misconceptions:

1. Some people think of *achievement motivation* as a general characteristic that applies to all aspects of a student's life, rather than as a characteristic that is somewhat specific to a particular task or situation.
2. Many people believe that even small amounts of anxiety are detrimental to learning and classroom performance.

CHAPTER OUTLINE	FOCUS QUESTIONS
THE NATURE OF MOTIVATION How Motivation Affects Learning and Behavior	• What do psychologists mean by the term *motivation*? • What effects does motivation have on learning and behavior?

INTRINSIC VERSUS EXTRINSIC MOTIVATION
 	
    Maslow's Hierarchy of Needs
    Self-Efficacy and Self-Determination
	• What's the difference between intrinsic motivation and extrinsic motivation? Why is it more desirable to have students who are *in*trinsically motivated?
	
	• What five groups of needs does Maslow's hierarchy include? What implications does Maslow's hierarchy have for classroom practice?
	
	• What two conditions do many theorists believe are essential for intrinsic motivation? What teaching strategies can promote each of these conditions?

MOTIVATION TO LEARN
 	
    Learning Versus Performance Goals
    Fostering the Motivation to Learn
	• What do psychologists mean by the term *motivation to learn*?
	
	• How are *learning goals* and *performance goals* different? What characteristics are associated with each type of goal?
	
	• What strategies can teachers use to promote the motivation to learn?

SOCIAL NEEDS
 	
    Need for Affiliation
    Need for Approval
	• What is the *need for affiliation*? What behaviors do students with a high need for affiliation exhibit?
	
	• What is the *need for approval*? What behaviors do students with a high need for approval exhibit?
	
	• What strategies can teachers use to accommodate students' needs for affiliation and approval?

ROLE OF AFFECT
 	
    Hot Cognition
    Anxiety
	• What is *hot cognition*? How does it affect learning and memory?
	
	• What is *anxiety*? How are *state anxiety* and *trait anxiety* different? How are facilitating anxiety and debilitating anxiety different? What particular effects does debilitating anxiety have?
	
	• What are some possible sources of anxiety for students? With these sources in mind, identify ways of keeping students' anxiety at a productive level.

CHAPTER OUTLINE	FOCUS QUESTIONS

ATTRIBUTIONS: PERCEIVED CAUSES OF SUCCESS AND FAILURE
 	
   Dimensions Underlying Students' Attributions
   How Attributions Influence Cognition and Behavior
   Factors Influencing the Development of Attributions
   Mastery Orientation Versus Learned Helplessness
	• What is an *attribution*? Along what dimensions do students' attributions differ?
	
	• To what factors do students tend to attribute their successes, and why? To what factors do they tend to attribute their failures, and why?
	
	• In what ways do attributions affect behavior and cognition? What specific effects do different kinds of attributions have?
	
	• What gender differences are observed in boys' and girls' attributions for success and failure? How do boys' and girls' attributions influence the expectations they have for future success?
	
	• What factors influence the development of attributions? What implications do these factors have for classroom practice?
	
	• Under what circumstances do attributions to effort backfire? To what should a teacher attribute students' failures when students are already exerting considerable effort?
	
	• What is a *mastery orientation*? What is *learned helplessness*? What characteristics are associated with each of these? What strategies can teachers use to foster a mastery orientation?

CONSIDERING DIVERSITY IN STUDENT MOTIVATION
 	
   Age Differences
   Ethnic Differences
   Gender Differences
   Socioeconomic Differences
   Accommodating Students with Special Needs
	• What differences in students' motivation are associated with age? with cultural background? with gender? with socioeconomic status? with special educational needs? What implications do such differences have for classroom practice?

THE BIG PICTURE: MOTIVATION AND LEARNING	• What general principles emerge from the chapter's discussion of motivation? • In what ways does the chapter's discussion of motivation draw from cognitive psychology, behaviorism, and social cognitive theory?

Chapter Glossary

Affect. The feelings and emotions that an individual brings to bear on a task.

Anxiety. A feeling of uneasiness and apprehension concerning a situation with an uncertain outcome.

Attribution. A causal explanation for success or failure.

Attribution theory. A theoretical perspective that focuses on people's attributions concerning the causes of events that befall them, as well as on the behaviors that result from such attributions.

Challenge. A situation in which a person believes that he or she can succeed with effort.

Debilitating anxiety. Anxiety that interferes with performance. A great deal of anxiety is likely to be debilitating.

Deficiency need. In Maslow's hierarchy, a need that results from something a person lacks.

Extrinsic motivation. Motivation promoted by factors external to the individual and unrelated to the task being performed.

Facilitating anxiety. Anxiety that enhances performance. Relatively low levels of anxiety are usually facilitating.

Growth need. In Maslow's hierarchy, a need that serves to enhance a person's growth and development and is never completely satisfied.

Hot cognition. Learning or cognitive processing that is emotionally charged.

Intrinsic motivation. The internal desire to perform a particular task.

Learned helplessness. A general belief that one is incapable of accomplishing tasks and has little or no control of the environment.

Learned industriousness. The recognition that one can succeed at some tasks only with effort, persistence, and well-chosen strategies.

Learning goal. A desire to acquire additional knowledge or master new skills.

Mastery orientation. A general belief that one is capable of accomplishing challenging tasks.

Motivation. A state that energizes, directs, and sustains behavior.

Motivation to learn. The tendency to find school-related activities meaningful and worthwhile and therefore to try to get the maximum benefit from them.

Need for affiliation. The tendency to seek out friendly relationships with others.

Need for approval. A desire to gain the approval and acceptance of others.

Performance goal. A desire either to look good and receive favorable judgments from others, or else *not* to look bad and receive unfavorable judgments.

Self-actualization. The tendency for human beings to enhance themselves and fulfill their potential—to strive toward becoming everything that they are capable of becoming.

Self-determination. A sense that one has some choice and control regarding the future course of one's life.

Self-efficacy. The belief that one is capable of executing certain behaviors or reaching certain goals.

Situated motivation. A phenomenon whereby aspects of one's immediate environment enhance one's motivation to learn particular things or behave in particular ways.

State anxiety. A temporary feeling of anxiety elicited by a threatening situation.

Threat. A situation in which individuals believe that they have little or no chance of success.

Trait anxiety. A pattern of responding with anxiety even in nonthreatening situations.

Application Exercise #20: Considering Maslow's Hierarchy

Maslow proposed that learners are unlikely to strive for self-actualization until their deficiency needs are met. Which deficiency need is the teacher addressing in each of the following situations?

1. Mr. O'Malley provides a sufficient variety of tasks and activities so that virtually all students can find an area in which they can be exceptional.

2. Mr. Siegler acknowledges each student's birthday, congratulates students with special personal accomplishments during the year, and sends a card or personal note in times of illness or family tragedy.

3. Ms. Markstrom has regular and predictable procedures for how materials are handed out and collected, how assignments are to be completed, and how discipline problems are handled.

4. At the high school where Mr. Knobles teaches, classes are scheduled in a "block" format in which each class meets for two hours every other day. Mr. Knobles incorporates at least one activity into each class session that allows students to get up, move around, and release any pent-up energy.

5. Ms. Iwata gives awards to recognize special contributions or activities that might otherwise go unnoticed—for example, an award for a student who frequently serves as peacemaker on the playground and an award for a student who has helped her classmates improve skills or grades.

6. When Ms. Bidell sees Luke threatening his classmates during a class session, she puts him in a time-out situation until it is clear that his inappropriate behavior will stop.

Answers to Application Exercise #20

1. Mr. O'Malley is addressing students' <u>esteem needs</u>.

2. Mr. Siegler is addressing students' <u>love and belonging needs</u>.

3. Ms. Markstrom is addressing students' <u>safety needs</u>.

4. Mr. Knobles is addressing students' <u>physiological needs</u>.

5. Ms. Iwata is addressing students' <u>esteem needs</u>.

6. As a strategy for changing Luke's behavior, time-out is consistent with behaviorist principles rather than with Maslow's hierarchy. At the same time, however, Ms. Bidell is addressing the <u>safety needs</u> of the other students in her class.

Application Exercise #21: Promoting Intrinsic Motivation

Of the teaching strategies described below, which are likely to promote *intrinsic* motivation to learn or perform, and which are not? Defend your decisions.

1. Ms. McFalls looks at Jake's watercolor painting and tells him, "You've composed a well-balanced painting, and you have a fine eye for color. But it looks to me as if the different colors are bleeding together more than you want them to. Let me show you a strategy for keeping the bleeding to a minimum."

2. Mr. Welch tells his students, "Let's see which one of you can run fastest."

3. In a unit on percussion, Mr. Wyatt lets his second graders experiment with several different percussion instruments.

4. Mr. Chan gives students ten minutes of free time at the end of the day if they complete their seatwork assignments.

5. Ms. Jaworski reminds her fourth graders how proud their parents will be if they bring home good report cards.

6. Mr. Scudder shows Joel how to do a lay-up shot in basketball. As Joel practices the shot, he finds that he gets more baskets than he had previously.

7. Ms. Ramirez has her high school students set their own deadlines for turning in the five small papers due during the semester, with the stipulation that they set the five deadlines at least one week apart from one another.

8. As her second graders line up to go to lunch, Ms. Woerner reminds them, "Remember, I shouldn't hear any of you talking on the way to the cafeteria."

9. Ms. Kauffman finds the colonial period of American history absolutely fascinating; her enthusiasm about this period is obvious to her students as she describes the people, places, and events of the times.

Answers to Application Exercise #21

1. Likely. Ms. McFalls is giving competence-promoting feedback, which should enhance self-efficacy.

2. Not likely. Mr. Welch is encouraging his students to compare themselves with others, rather than to focus on their own improvement.

3. Likely. One way to promote interest in school subject matter is to get students actively involved.

4. Not likely. Extrinsic reinforcement promotes extrinsic motivation rather than intrinsic motivation.

5. Not likely. Ms. Jaworski is focusing students' attention on a performance goal (looking good to others), rather than on a learning goal.

6. Likely. Success enhances self-efficacy, and self-efficacy enhances intrinsic motivation.

7. Likely. By giving students control over an aspect of classroom life, Mr. Ramirez is promoting a sense of self-determination, which should enhance intrinsic motivation.

8. Not likely. Ms. Woerner is presenting the instruction in a controlling, rather than informational, manner. This strategy may promote extrinsic motivation, but it won't promote intrinsic motivation.

9. Likely. One way teachers can promote intrinsic motivation is to model their own interest in and enthusiasm for the subject matter.

Application Exercise #22: Identifying Effective Classroom Practices

Of the teaching strategies described below, which are consistent with guidelines presented in Chapter 12 for promoting students' motivation (either intrinsic or extrinsic), and which are not? Defend your decisions.

1. Ms. Proctor announces, "Vinnie's essay was by far the best essay in the class."

2. Mr. Murphy says, "The next lesson is not especially interesting, but it's important for you to learn. Let's see if we can all struggle through it together."

3. A mathematics teacher tells students, "Mathematics is important for many careers, including science, accounting, computer programming, business, nursing, construction, and sales."

4. An art teacher tells her students, "Here are the criteria I will be applying when I grade the sculptures you are working on now."

5. On Monday, the coach of a cross-country team tells her students, "Each day this week we'll run the same five-mile course we ran last Friday. Try to cut down your running time a little bit each day. See if you can cut sixty seconds off last Friday's time by the end of the week."

6. Peggy has spent several hours each night working on assignments for her chemistry class, but she still doesn't understand the material. "Maybe you just need to try a little harder, Peggy," her teacher suggests.

7. Ms. Smith says, "I know you don't want to learn this stuff, but it's important to know."

8. David is frustrated that he is having more difficulty learning to read than most of his classmates. His teacher reminds him, "Many students have trouble learning to read at first, but with practice it gets easier and easier. Let's look at some of the books you were reading last September. See how simple they are compared to what you are reading now?"

9. Mr. Jakes likes to keep students challenged all day long. As soon as it's clear to him that they have mastered one task, he introduces a more difficult one.

10. In a unit on softball, Ms. Ralston tells Tim, "When you hit the ball, it always seems to go too far to the right, so it becomes a foul ball rather than a base hit. I think I can explain why it's always going in that direction."

11. When José attains the status of "first chair" in the trumpet section, his music teacher tells him, "You're a good musician, José. You seem to have some natural musical talent, and you have obviously been practicing very hard."

12. Mr. Simpson allows unlimited retakes on each of his weekly quizzes so that students won't have any anxiety when they take them.

13. During a discussion of developing countries, a fifth-grade teacher describes how, in some countries, children as young as nine or ten work long days in factories to support their families. "Sometimes these children must get up at five o'clock in the morning, ride their bicycles an hour or more to work, put in a ten- or twelve-hour day, and then ride their bikes home in the dark. Many of them work in toy factories making toys for children in wealthier countries, but they could never afford to buy such toys themselves. Can you imagine how you might feel if you were one of those children?"

Answers to Application Exercise #22

1. Not consistent. For one thing, teachers should keep a student's successes private and confidential unless they have the student's permission to do otherwise. Second, teachers should keep competition among students to a minimum. By telling the class that Vinnie has done better than everyone else, this teacher is creating a competitive atmosphere.

2. Not consistent. Teachers are more likely to motivate students when they model interest in the subject matter.

3. Consistent. One effective motivational strategy is to relate school subject matter to students' future needs.

4. Consistent. The teacher is making her expectations for student performance clear.

5. Consistent. The coach is encouraging students to strive for challenging yet achievable goals. She is also promoting self-comparison rather than comparison with others.

6. Not consistent. Attributing failure to insufficient effort is effective only when a student clearly *hasn't* exerted much effort. Peggy has already been trying very hard to succeed in chemistry.

7. Not consistent. Teachers should communicate their belief that students want to learn school subject matter.

8. Consistent. The teacher is defining success in terms of the progress David has made. She is also defining it as eventual rather than immediate mastery.

9. Not consistent. Ideally, challenging tasks should be balanced with easier ones. This way, students' occasional mistakes occur within the context of an overall pattern of success.

10. Consistent. The teacher is evaluating Tim's performance in a way that will help him improve.

11. Consistent. The teacher is attributing José's success to both high ability and a lot of effort.

12. Not consistent. For most students, a small amount of anxiety facilitates performance. Students who are a little bit anxious about their performance will achieve at a higher level than students who have no anxiety whatsoever. (As you will discover in Chapter 13, an occasional retake of a classroom assessment may be appropriate in a mastery learning approach to instruction. Furthermore, as you will discover when you read Chapter 16, students should have some leeway to make mistakes without penalty. Nevertheless, *unlimited* retakes serve little purpose.)

13. Consistent. By evoking students' feelings about the subject matter, the teacher is promoting hot cognition—something that should help them remember the subject matter better.

Answers to Selected Margin Notes

- Page 472: *How is situated motivation similar to situated cognition, a concept discussed in Chapter 8?*

  Both situated motivation and situated cognition occur only in a particular environmental context.

- Page 473: *Can you find each of these effects in the case study of Anya?*

  Each effect is reflected in the case study as follows:
  - <u>Goal-directed behavior</u>: Anya wants to become a professional artist.
  - <u>Effort and energy</u>: Anya draws at every available opportunity.
  - <u>Initiation and persistence</u>: At her own initiative, Anya adds drawings to notebooks, essays, and spelling quizzes, and she buries herself in each new drawing assignment.
  - <u>Cognitive processing</u>: Anya pays close attention in art class.
  - <u>Reinforcement</u>: Drawing is an intrinsically reinforcing activity for Anya.
  - <u>Improved performance</u>: Her teacher comments on her improvement over the course of the school year.

- Page 475: *How might Maslow's hierarchy come into play in an economically diverse classroom?*

  Students from low socioeconomic backgrounds may be at the bottom of the hierarchy, with some of their physiological needs unmet (they may be hungry or cold, or they may have health needs unattended to).

- Page 476: *How is <u>self-efficacy</u> similar to Maslow's <u>need for self-esteem</u>? How are the two concepts different?*

  Both concepts relate to one's beliefs about one's competence. Self-efficacy is somewhat task- or domain-specific; that is, people may have high self-efficacy regarding one task yet have low self-efficacy regarding another. Maslow's need for self-esteem refers to a more general sense of competence and self-worth that transcends any particular task or domain.

- Page 483: *Consider Sheryl and Shannon (our trigonometry students) and Anya from our "Quick Draw" case study. For which girl(s) do we see a learning goal? For which girl(s) do we see a performance goal?*

  Both Shannon and Anya have learning goals—either to learn trigonometry or to acquire new drawing techniques. Sheryl has a performance goal—to get a C in trigonometry.

- Page 486: *Can you explain the value of inconsistent or discrepant information using Piaget's concept of <u>disequilibrium</u> (see Chapter 2)?*

  According to Piaget, when people cannot explain new information in terms of existing schemes, they experience disequilibrium, a sort of mental "discomfort." Such a state encourages them to revise their understanding of the world (e.g., by replacing, reorganizing, or better integrating schemes related to the topic at hand). When their existing schemes are sufficiently revised to account for the initially inconsistent information, they return to a state of equilibrium.

- Page 490: *Which of Maslow's needs does the concept <u>need for affiliation</u> most resemble?*

  It is most similar to Maslow's need for love and belonging.

- Page 492: *How is the concept of <u>threat</u> different from the concept of <u>challenge</u>?*

  In a threatening situation, people believe that they have little or no chance of succeeding. In a challenging situation, they believe that, with effort and perseverance, they *can* succeed.

- Page 499: *Older students and those with a history of learning problems are more likely to attribute their failures to lack of innate ability. Why might this be so?*
  Students with a history of learning problems are more likely to have experienced academic failure even when they have exerted considerable effort. Older students are more likely to compare their own performance to that of their peers (see Chapter 3); if they find that, despite significant effort, their performance is lower than the performance of others, they may understandably chalk up their failures to something that they can't control.

- Page 500: *How might learned industriousness be related to students' epistemological beliefs?*
  Students who believe that learning is a relatively rapid process give up quickly when they have to struggle to understand classroom material (see the description of epistemological beliefs in Chapter 8).

- Page 503: *How are teacher expectations and teacher attributions likely to be related? For example, if a teacher expects a student to fail, how is he or she likely to interpret a successful performance? How is a teacher who expects a student to succeed likely to interpret a failure?*
  A teacher who expects a student to fail (perhaps because he/she thinks that the student has low ability) may interpret a success as a "fluke"—something that resulted from chance or outside influences—rather than as the result of the student's effort or ability. In contrast, a teacher who expects a student to succeed (and presumably thinks that the student has high ability) will probably attribute a failure to low effort, poor strategies, or some other temporary condition that can be easily remedied.

Sample Test Questions

Items marked with a "**1)**" on the left-hand side are lower-level questions that assess your general knowledge and understanding of the material. Items marked with a "**2)**" on the left-hand side are higher-level questions that assess your ability to apply what you have learned to a new situation.

Multiple-Choice

1)　1.　Which one of the following teaching practices is consistent with Maslow's notion of a *safety need*?
　　　a.　Encouraging learning goals rather than performance goals
　　　b.　Making sure students don't bring weapons to school
　　　c.　Encouraging students to "try, try again" when they run into difficulty on challenging tasks
　　　d.　Giving students special privileges whenever they do something well

2)　2.　Which one of these students clearly has a *learning goal* rather than a performance goal?
　　　a.　Amanda wants to keep her 4.0 average so that she can get an academic scholarship at a good college.
　　　b.　Barney knows how proud his parents will be if he is accepted into the National Honor Society.
　　　c.　Candace is fascinated by the chapter about Ellis Island in her history book, because her grandparents were immigrants in the 1930s.
　　　d.　Dave is hoping he'll play exceptionally well in tonight's basketball game so that he can get the admiration of a girl he has a crush on.

2)　3.　Rita plans to visit Ecuador some day because that's where her cousins live. When she gets to junior high school, she finally has a chance to take Spanish—a language she will need when she travels to South America. But she decides to enroll in French instead so that she can be with her best friend. From this information, we can guess that Rita has a high need for:
　　　a.　Affiliation
　　　b.　Safety
　　　c.　Self-actualization
　　　d.　Approval

2)　4.　Given what we know about the effects of anxiety on learning and performance, which one of the following boys is likely to learn most effectively from his biology teacher's lecture on insects and arachnids?
　　　a.　Albert is very nervous because he has to give an oral report at the end of the class period.
　　　b.　Ben would like to do well in this class, but it won't be the end of the world if he doesn't.
　　　c.　Clark doesn't really care how he does in the class; he's a senior and has already been accepted by the college of his choice.
　　　d.　Dwight is very worried that his teacher will give a pop quiz at the end of class, and he didn't do the reading last night.

2) 5. Sharon studied very hard for a physics test but has gotten a D– on the test. Her teacher tells her that she probably would have done better if she'd just studied more. Given what we know from attribution theory, we can guess that Sharon will:

    a. Attribute her failure to a lack of effort

    b. Begin to use more effective study strategies

    c. Believe that performance on physics tests is all a matter of luck, so that she might do better next time even if she doesn't study

    d. Conclude that she doesn't have the ability to do well in physics

Essay

1) 6. Psychologists often make a distinction between *intrinsic motivation* and *extrinsic motivation*.

    a. Describe the nature of each of these two forms of motivation, and give a concrete example of each one in action.

    b. Explain why intrinsic motivation is more desirable in the classroom.

    c. Describe three different strategies that teachers can use to promote intrinsic motivation in their students.

2) 7. Explain each of the following student behaviors in terms of *attribution theory*.

    a. Edie gets a low score on a history test and is angry at her teacher for writing such "unfair" questions. She overlooks the fact that most of her classmates have done quite well on the test.

    b. Wilbur thinks of himself as being good at math. In fact, he notes, high math ability runs in the family: His father is an accountant and his mother is a statistician. So he is confident that he will do well in the accelerated calculus course he is taking next year.

Answers to Sample Test Questions

1. b—Keeping weapons out of school addresses students' need for safety. The other three alternatives may indeed be effective motivational strategies, but they do not relate directly to Maslow's safety need. (See "Maslow's Hierarchy of Needs" beginning on textbook page 474.)

2. c—Candace's fascination with Ellis Island reflects her desire to acquire additional knowledge about the topic. The other three students are striving to look good and receive favorable judgments from others; in other words, they are striving for performance goals. (See the section "Learning Versus Performance Goals" beginning on textbook page 482.)

3. a—Rita wants to be with her best friend as often as possible—behavior indicative of a strong need for affiliation. (See the section "Need for Affiliation" on textbook pages 489-490.)

4. b—A little anxiety is often facilitating, but a great deal is likely to be debilitating. Albert and Dwight appear to be overly anxious; Clark appears to have no anxiety at all. (See "How Anxiety Affects Classroom Performance" on textbook page 493.)

5. d—When students fail at a task at which they have expended a great deal of effort and are then told that they didn't try hard enough, they are apt to conclude that they don't have the ability to be successful at the task. (See "When attributions to effort can backfire" beginning on textbook page 503.)

6. a. Intrinsic motivation is an internal desire to perform a particular task; it is due to factors within the individual or inherent in the task being performed. Extrinsic motivation is promoted by factors external to the individual and unrelated to the task being performed. Your response should include a concrete example of each of these concepts. (To illustrate, interest in a topic is a form of intrinsic motivation, and working on an assignment for the good grade one might receive is a form of extrinsic motivation.)
    b. Students are most likely to show the beneficial effects of motivation (persistence, effective cognitive processing, etc.) when they are intrinsically motivated to engage in classroom activities (see textbook page 474).
    c. Numerous strategies for promoting intrinsic motivation appear on textbook pages 475-488. Your response should describe at least three of these strategies in specific, concrete terms.

7. a. Students have a tendency to attribute their failures to such external causes as luck or the behavior of others. (See the section "Dimensions Underlying Students' Attributions" beginning on textbook page 497.)
    b. When students attribute their success on a task to a stable factor such as high ability, they will anticipate continued success at that task. (See "How Attributions Influence Cognition and Behavior" beginning on textbook page 498.)

Chapter 13

CHOOSING INSTRUCTIONAL STRATEGIES

Chapter Overview

The last four chapters of the book apply principles of learning, motivation, development, and diversity to several critical aspects of teaching: planning, instruction, creating a productive classroom environment, and assessment. This chapter focuses on planning and instruction. As you read the section "Planning for Instruction," you will find guidelines for identifying instructional objectives, conducting task analyses, and developing lesson plans. Then, as you begin your exploration of instructional strategies, you will acquire many specific techniques for promoting student learning and academic achievement. Some of these techniques—those in the sections on expository instruction, discovery learning, mastery learning, direct instruction, and computer-based instruction—may be especially suitable for introducing new material. Others— those in the sections on teacher questions, in-class activities, computer applications, homework, and authentic activities—may be more useful for fostering elaboration and transfer. As you read the chapter, keep in mind one very important point: There is probably no single "best" approach to instruction.

Common Student Beliefs and Misconceptions Related to Chapter Content

Below are several misconceptions that future teachers often have about teaching. As you read Chapter 13, be on the lookout for evidence that contradicts these common beliefs:

1. Many future teachers think of planning, instruction, classroom management, and assessment as relatively separate aspects of teaching, rather than as the interdependent activities that they really are.

2. Some people think that there must be a single "best" approach to instruction. In reality, different instructional strategies are appropriate in different situations.

3. Some people believe that lecturing is a relatively ineffective teaching strategy.

4. Other people believe that one lecture is as good as another—that students can learn equally well regardless of how information is presented.

CHAPTER OUTLINE	FOCUS QUESTIONS

PLANNING FOR INSTRUCTION
    Identifying the Goals of Instruction
    Conducting a Task Analysis
    Developing Lesson Plans
	• What are the advantages of instructional objectives from a teacher's perspective? What are the advantages from a student's perspective?
	
	• How are *standards* and *taxonomies* helpful in developing objectives? What kinds of behaviors are included in the cognitive, psychomotor, and affective domains?
	
	• What guidelines should teachers keep in mind as they develop instructional objectives?
	
	• What is the difference between short-term and long-term objectives? In what situations is each type of objective appropriate?
	
	• What are the advantages of a *task analysis*? In your own words, describe behavioral analysis, subject matter analysis, and information processing analysis.
	
	• What components does a lesson plan typically have?

OVERVIEW OF INSTRUCTIONAL STRATEGIES	• What instructional strategies are especially useful for introducing new material? What strategies may be more useful for promoting elaboration and transfer?

INTRODUCING NEW MATERIAL
    Expository Instruction
    Discovery Learning
    Mastery Learning
    Direct Instruction
    Computer-based Instruction
	• What is *expository instruction*? What factors contribute to its effectiveness, and what implications do these factors have for classroom practice?
	
	• Explain how advance organizers, prior knowledge activation, analogies, concept maps, signals, and visual aids facilitate learning during expository instruction.
	
	• What is *discovery learning*? In what situations is it most useful and effective? What specific strategies should maximize the effectiveness of a discovery learning activity?
	
	• On what assumptions is *mastery learning* based? What are the typical elements of this approach, and in what situations is it most appropriate?
	
	• What is *direct instruction*? What activities does it typically include, and when is it most useful?
	
	• What forms does *computer-based instruction* take? What are its potential benefits?

CHAPTER OUTLINE	FOCUS QUESTIONS

PROMOTING ELABORATION OF CLASSROOM MATERIAL
 	
    Teacher Questions
    In-Class Activities
    Computer Applications
    Homework
    Authentic Activities
	• What functions can teacher questions serve? What strategies can enhance their effectiveness?
	
	• How can teachers use in-class activities, computer applications, and homework to promote elaboration and transfer? What guidelines should teachers keep in mind when assigning homework?
	
	• What are *authentic activities*? What benefits might they have?

TAKING STUDENT DIVERSITY INTO ACCOUNT Accommodating Students with Special Needs	• What student characteristics should teachers consider when choosing instructional strategies? What strategies may be especially suitable for students with special educational needs?

Chapter Glossary

Advance organizer. An introduction to a lesson that provides an overall organizational scheme for the lesson.

Affective domain. The domain of learning tasks that includes attitudes and values about the things one learns.

Behavioral objective. An instructional objective that describes a specific, observable behavior.

Bloom's taxonomy. A taxonomy in which six learning tasks, varying in degrees of complexity, are identified for the cognitive domain: knowledge, comprehension, application, analysis, synthesis, and evaluation.

Branching program. A form of programmed instruction in which students responding incorrectly to a question proceed to one or more remedial frames for further clarification or practice before continuing on with new information.

Cognitive domain. The domain of learning tasks that includes knowledge of information, as well as ways of thinking about and using that information.

Computer-assisted instruction (CAI). Programmed instruction presented by means of a computer; it is one form of computer-based instruction.

Computer-based instruction (CBI). Instruction provided via computer technology.

Concept map. A diagram of concepts within an instructional unit and the interrelationships among them.

Direct instruction. An approach to instruction that uses a variety of techniques (brief explanations, teacher questioning, rapid pacing, guided and independent practice) to promote learning of basic skills.

Discovery learning. An approach to instruction whereby students develop an understanding of a topic in a hands-on fashion through their interaction with the physical or social environment.

Expository instruction. An approach to instruction whereby information is presented in more or less the same form in which students are expected to learn it.

Higher-level question. A question that requires students to do something new with information they have learned—for example, to apply, analyze, synthesize, or evaluate it.

Hypermedia. A collection of computer-based instructional material, including both verbal text and such other media as pictures, sound, and animations. It is interconnected in such a way that students can learn about one topic and then proceed to related topics of their own choosing.

Hypertext. A collection of computer-based verbal material that allows students to read about one topic and then proceed to related topics of their own choosing.

Instructional objective. A statement describing a final goal or outcome of instruction.

Linear program. A form of programmed instruction in which all students proceed through the same sequence of instructional frames.

Long-term objective. An objective that requires months or years of instruction and practice to be accomplished.

Lower-level question. A question that requires students to express what they have learned in essentially the same way they learned it—for example, by reciting a textbook's definition of a concept or describing an application that their teacher presented in class.

Mastery learning. An approach to instruction whereby students learn one topic thoroughly before moving to a more difficult one.

Prior knowledge activation. Reminding students of information they have already learned relative to a new topic.

Programmed instruction (PI). An approach to instruction whereby students independently study a topic that has been broken into small, carefully sequenced segments.

Psychomotor domain. The domain of learning tasks that includes simple and complex physical movements and actions.

Short-term objective. An objective that can typically be accomplished within the course of a single lesson or unit.

Signal. In expository instruction, a cue that lets students know that something is important to learn.

Standards. General statements regarding the knowledge and skills that students should achieve and the characteristics that their accomplishments should reflect.

Task analysis. A process of identifying the specific knowledge and/or behaviors necessary to master a particular subject area or skill.

Application Exercise #23: Applying Criteria Related to Instructional Objectives

Of the instructional objectives listed below, which ones are consistent with guidelines presented in the textbook, and which ones are not? Defend your choices.

1. "To provide an introduction to the Vietnam War."

2. "To have opportunities to practice multiplication skills in real-world settings."

3. "To spell correctly the 500 words on the district's spelling list for third graders."

4. "To teach the breast stroke."

5. "To change the oil and oil filter in an automobile engine correctly."

6. "To know correct grammar."

7. "To demonstrate library research skills; for example:
    - To locate books related to a particular topic
    - To find articles about current events in newspapers and news magazines
    - To use computer data bases to find books or articles written by a particular author"

8. "To investigate the life cycles of butterflies and moths."

9. "To run a mile in under eight minutes."

10. "To identify foods in each of the basic food groups."

Answers to Application Exercise #23

1. Not consistent. The objective focuses on what the teacher will do, not on what students will do.

2. Not consistent. No observable outcomes are identified.

3. Consistent. The objective describes the outcome of instruction in terms of an observable behavior.

4. Not consistent. The objective focuses on what the teacher will do, not on what students will do.

5. Consistent. The objective describes the outcome of instruction in terms of an observable behavior.

6. Not consistent. No observable outcomes are identified.

7. Consistent. Complex skills can be described in general, abstract terms and illustrated with examples of behaviors that reflect those skills.

8. Not consistent. No observable outcomes are identified.

9. Consistent. The objective describes the outcome of instruction in terms of an observable behavior.

10. Consistent. The objective describes the outcome of instruction in terms of an observable behavior.

Application Exercise #24: Identifying Effective Instructional Strategies

Which of the following instructional strategies are consistent with guidelines presented in Chapter 13, and which are not? Justify your decisions.

1. As Ms. Horton talks about the characteristics of an insect, she uses a diagram that shows its six legs, three body parts, and antennae.

2. Ms. Kruger urges her physics students to relate her lesson on *momentum* to their own personal experiences. She doesn't describe specific experiences that they might relate it to, however, because she knows that different students have different backgrounds.

3. Mr. Troyer has broken his sixth-grade mathematics curriculum into a sequence of small units. Students must show that they understand the material in each unit by getting a score of 90 percent or better on a unit test; at this point, they proceed to the next unit in the sequence. Mr. Troyer provides additional assistance and practice when students need it to attain a score of 90 percent.

4. When Ms. Kirkpatrick discovers that she has forgotten to bring the materials she needs for the class activity she has planned for the day, she quickly digs into her file cabinet and finds a lesson on another topic that can fill the same amount of time—a lesson that students in previous years have enjoyed very much.

5. To provide a challenge for her students, Ms. Iglesias assigns her algebra class several complex and difficult word problems. When she finds that even her brightest students are spending more time than she expected on the problems and still not arriving at any reasonable solutions, she says, "All right, then, let's make these problems your homework for tonight. The assignment will be worth the same as one of the tests I give you every Friday."

6. Mr. Kosmicki tells his students, "The growth of a glacier is like pancake batter being poured into a frying pan. As more and more substance is added to the middle, the edges spread farther and farther out."

7. Ms. Rogers tells her class, "Today we'll be studying the Industrial Revolution—why it occurred, what industries it involved, and what living conditions were like at the time."

8. Mr. Epstein has his students learn about the geography of various Asian countries by means of a computer program. The computer presents information about each country in a single frame; when a student has finished reading the information presented in each frame, he or she presses the space bar to proceed to the next frame. After everyone has completed the program, Mr. Epstein gives his students a quiz to find out what they've learned.

9. Before introducing students to the concepts *acid* and *base,* Ms. Trussler makes several acids and bases available in the laboratory and allows students to explore their properties freely.

10. To check for students' understanding of ideas being discussed in class, Ms. Bush asks frequent questions of her students. Hoping to encourage automaticity in students' responding, she always calls on the student who raises his or her hand first.

11. Ms. McGill teaches her fifth graders the fundamentals of journalism within the context of having the class "publish" monthly issues of a school newspaper throughout the school year. She makes sure that, at one time or another, each student has the opportunity to serve as reporter, writer, editor, and desktop publisher.

12. At the end of class, Mr. Kelley asks his students, "Who can give us a short summary of what I've talked about today?"

13. Knowing that the lectures in his high school world studies class are usually packed full of information, Mr. Pease stops every ten minutes or so and gives his students a couple of minutes to compare notes and ask one another questions.

14. In past years, Mr. Vickarelli has found that his students get the various events of the Vietnam War confused with one another. This year, he decides to spread out his lectures on the war over an entire semester so that students don't get material in these lectures mixed up. He will devote each Friday to a specific event in the war, and spend Monday through Thursday talking about other topics in history.

15. After the students in Mr. Maar's art class complete the sculptures on which they have been working for the past week or so, Mr. Maar asks them to evaluate their creations on the basis of several criteria.

16. Ms. Krump knows that the students in her high school world history class have probably not studied World War I before now. She begins her unit on WWI by having students spend a day exploring a hypermedia program about the war.

17. Mr. Marquis is teaching an advanced placement course—a course that may allow his high school seniors to earn college credit. To make the course as similar as possible to a "college experience," Mr. Marquis assigns 50 to 60 pages of reading each week. His students complain that they feel overwhelmed by the amount of reading material, and they ask for his guidance about the things they should focus on as they read. Mr. Marquis responds by saying, "I know your reading assignments are very challenging for you. But they will help you develop the study skills you will need for college next year."

18. Ms. Dees is teaching her students about *adverbs*. She begins the lesson by briefly reviewing the parts of speech the students have previously studied. She then says, "Today you'll learn what an adverb is. You'll also be able to find adverbs in a variety of sentences." She defines an adverb and gives several examples; after that, she presents some sentences on an overhead projector and asks students to identify the adverbs in the sentences. Once it is clear that the students have a good understanding of adverbs, she has them work independently at their desks to find adverbs in their storybooks and textbooks. As they do so, she circulates throughout the classroom to give guidance and feedback.

Answers to Application Exercise #24

1. Consistent. Visual aids used to supplement expository instruction promote learning, perhaps by providing an additional way for students to encode the information being presented.

2. Not consistent. Teachers need to describe specific relationships between new material and the things students already know. Ms. Kruger's students undoubtedly share common experiences that involve momentum. For example, all of them have probably been in a car that stopped suddenly and seen objects in the car continue to move forward. And many of them have probably been on roller skates and found it difficult to stop.

3. Consistent. Mr. Troyer's instruction has the basic elements of mastery learning—small and discrete units (presumably sequenced in a logical order), demonstration of mastery of one unit before proceeding to the next, and remedial activities for those who need them.

4. Not consistent. Ms. Kirkpatrick is choosing an activity without consideration of what her instructional objectives are.

5. Not consistent. Homework assignments should involve tasks that students can accomplish with little if any assistance from others, and they should contribute only a minimal amount to students' final grades.

6. Consistent. Analogies are one effective way of helping students relate new information to what they already know.

7. Consistent. Ms. Rogers is presenting a brief advance organizer, something that should give students an overall structure for organizing the material she presents.

8. Not consistent. There is no advantage in presenting information on a computer screen when it could just as easily be presented through a textbook. Good educational computer programs provide numerous opportunities for students to make active responses—something that is often not possible through using textbooks alone.

9. Not consistent. Discovery learning is most effective when students already have some knowledge of the topic and are given some guidance and structure about how to proceed. (An additional problem here is that some of the chemicals, if improperly handled, might cause physiological damage, such as skin burns.)

10. Not consistent. If only students who raise their hands quickly are called on, there are probably many students who never have the opportunity to respond to the questions. Instead, Ms. Bush should provide sufficient wait time for most or all students to develop answers to her questions, and she should either call on different students each time *or* devise a means (e.g., "voting") through which all students can answer her questions simultaneously.

11. Consistent. Ms. McGill is teaching journalism through an authentic activity.

12. Consistent. In expository instruction, summaries facilitate learning. By asking a student to provide the summary, Mr. Kelley is checking for students' understanding of the material. If the student summarizes the material inappropriately, Mr. Kelley might either call on another student or give his own summary of what he has discussed.

13. Consistent. Mr. Pease is giving students time to process the information he presents.

14. Not consistent. By presenting different aspects of the war in little pieces spread out over the semester, Mr. Vickarelli is making it difficult for his students to see the interrelationships among those pieces. In other words, his students will have trouble organizing the information into a cohesive whole.

15. Consistent. One recommended strategy for in-class activities is to encourage students to reflect on and evaluate their own work.

16. Not consistent. The students have little if any prior knowledge about the war. As a result, they will probably not be able to make informed decisions about appropriate topics to pursue, nor will they be able to organize what they learn.

17. Not consistent. Whenever teachers must present a great deal of information through expository instruction, they should provide signals regarding what material is most important to study and learn.

18. Consistent. Ms. Dees's procedure includes many recommended components of direct instruction, including review of previously learned material, statement of the goals of a lesson, guided practice, and independent practice.

Answers to Selected Margin Notes

- Page 520: *Why is the third domain called affective?*
  Psychologists use the term *affect* to refer to feelings and emotions (see Chapter 12).

- Page 533: *Field trips can also be a form of expository instruction. What particular benefits might field trips have?*
  Field trips provide concrete experiences to which students can relate classroom material. They may also enable students to encode information in multiple forms—perhaps verbally, visually, and auditorially. (You may have identified other benefits as well.)

- Page 540: *Consider once again Reggie's "math problem" at the beginning of the chapter. What expository instruction techniques might the teacher use to help Reggie learn?*
  Several strategies that might be especially useful in teaching mathematics are these:
  - Connections to prior knowledge: Helping Reggie relate new mathematical concepts to concepts he has learned in previous math lessons and also to his own experiences with the physical world.
  - Visual aids: Helping Reggie encode information visually as well as verbally by using such visual aids as the number line, pictures depicting fractions (e.g., five pieces left in a pie that originally had eight pieces equals 5/8), and drawings that illustrate word problems (e.g., see the treehouse in Figure 8-1 on textbook p. 308).
  - Processing time: Pacing instruction slowly enough that Reggie and other students have time to process each new concept, procedure, example, and so on in a meaningful fashion.

- Page 541: *How might you make the concepts <u>negative number</u> and <u>improper fraction</u> concrete for students?*
  Doing so requires considerable creativity. Here are a couple of possibilities:
  - Think of zero as ground level, a negative number as a hole dug into the ground, and a positive number as a hill above the ground. If you add a positive number to a negative number, you must fill in the hole with dirt before you can start forming a hill above it.
  - Have two pizzas, each cut into 8 equal pieces. An improper fraction would be 9 or more pieces, such that their total forms more than one pizza.

- Page 553: *In what ways might CBI benefit Reggie in our opening case study?*
  A computer-based instructional program would allow the individualized instruction that Reggie needs. He could proceed at his own pace, and if a branching program were used, he could also get as much instruction as he needs for each new concept. Additional advantages are multiple opportunities to practice what he is learning and the immediate feedback he can receive for his responses.

- Page 555: *Look at the teacher questions in the lesson plan in Figure 13-3. What purposes do the questions serve?*
  Some of the questions (e.g., "What is *culture*?" and "What are some ways in which cultures are different from one another?") should help the teacher identify students' prior knowledge and misconceptions about the subject. Others (e.g., "What are some examples of how the cultures of other countries have become a part of our way of life?" and "If your parents or grandparents migrated to Colorado from another state or country, do you know *why* they did?") should help the students relate material from the lesson to things that they already know. Still others (e.g., "What patterns do you see in this table?" and "Why do you think the pattern of migration has changed over time?") are higher-level questions that encourage elaboration. Many of the questions should also help the teacher assess students' comprehension as the lesson proceeds.

Sample Test Questions

Items marked with a "**1)**" on the left-hand side are lower-level questions that assess your general knowledge and understanding of the material. Items marked with a "**2)**" on the left-hand side are higher-level questions that assess your ability to apply what you have learned to a new situation.

Multiple-Choice

2)   1.   "Describe what a democracy is in your own words." This objective can best be classified as being at the _____ level of Bloom's taxonomy for the cognitive domain.
   a. synthesis
   b. knowledge
   c. comprehension
   d. application

2)   2.   Which one of the following teachers is conducting a *subject matter* task analysis?
   a. Ms. Archibeque divides an upcoming unit on meteorology into five smaller topics—fronts, wind, temperature, clouds, and precipitation—and arranges them in a logical sequence.
   b. Mr. Barnett wants his students to become better writers and stops to consider the things that he himself thinks about as he writes.
   c. Ms. Coopersmith identifies the specific skills that a student must learn to use a video camera correctly.
   d. Mr. Delaney considers what his students must do to become better note takers—skills such as organizing, elaborating, and identifying main ideas.

1)   3.   Which one of the following best illustrates a *signal* in expository instruction?
   a. Mr. Anders pauses every few minutes to give students a chance to ask questions.
   b. Ms. Beck reminds students that they need to read Chapter 5 before Friday.
   c. Ms. Carson begins a lesson on gravity by asking, "What happens to a ball when we throw it in the air?"
   d. Mr. Drew writes important concepts on the chalkboard.

1)   4.   Which one of the following strategies is most consistent with guidelines presented in the textbook regarding *discovery learning*?
   a. Allowing at least 90 minutes for the activity
   b. Giving students some guidelines about how they should proceed
   c. Reinforcing desired "discoveries"
   d. Conducting the activity before students have acquired any information about the topic under investigation

1)   5.   Three of the following are characteristic of a mastery learning approach to instruction. Which one is *not necessarily* a component of mastery learning?
   a. Students must master both lower-level and higher-level skills.
   b. Students proceed through a sequence of units arranged in a logical order.
   c. Students must demonstrate mastery of one topic before proceeding to the next.
   d. Students receive extra help when they need it.

2)   6.   Three of the following teachers are assigning homework in ways consistent with the textbook's guidelines. Which one is *not*?

     a. Mr. Andrew gives homework assignments for which his students will need little or no assistance from anyone else.

     b. Ms. Blair has her students read a few pages in their social studies textbook each night.

     c. Ms. Crawford tells students that their performance on homework will be worth 60 percent of their final grades.

     d. Mr. Delgado occasionally gives his students a voluntary homework assignment—one that they can either do or not do, as they prefer.

Essay

1)   7.   Whether you use regular classroom lectures or shorter and less formal descriptions and explanations, expository instruction will almost certainly be a teaching strategy that you use regularly. With research on expository instruction in mind, describe four *specific* strategies that you can use to help your students learn the information that you present through expository instruction.

1)   8.   Describe the essential ingredients of *programmed instruction*. Explain how at least two principles of operant conditioning are incorporated into this approach to instruction.

Answers to Sample Test Questions

1. c—One indication of comprehension is the ability to translate an idea into one's own words (see Table 13-1 on textbook page 521).

2. a—A subject matter task analysis involves breaking the material to be taught into the specific topics and ideas that it includes (see textbook page 526). Alternatives b and d are examples of an information processing analysis, and alternative c is an example of a behavioral analysis.

3. d—Signals are the various techniques teachers use to let students know what things are most important for them to learn (see textbook page 538).

4. b—Students are most likely to benefit from a discovery learning session when the activity is structured to some extent (see textbook page 542).

5. a—Mastery learning does not necessarily need to include both lower-level and higher-level skills. The typical components of a mastery learning approach are described on textbook pages 545-546.

6. c—The textbook suggests that teachers minimize the degree to which they use homework assignments to determine final class grades (see textbook page 558).

7. The four strategies you describe should be based on factors that have been shown to facilitate learning during expository instruction. A number of possibilities are presented on textbook pages 534-540.

8. Programmed instruction consists of a series of frames that present tiny pieces of information in a logically sequenced fashion. Generally speaking, each frame includes (a) the correct answer to a previous question, (b) a small amount of new information, and (c) a new question for the student to respond to. Your response should identify at least two of these three operant conditioning principles: active responding, shaping, and immediate reinforcement (see textbook pages 551-552 for an explanation of the role that each of these principles plays in programmed instruction).

Chapter 14

PROMOTING LEARNING THROUGH STUDENT INTERACTIONS

Chapter Overview

This chapter focuses on instructional strategies that involve considerable interaction among students; in particular, it examines class discussions, reciprocal teaching, cooperative learning, and peer tutoring. The chapter also describes how you might create a *community of learners* in which you and your students work collaboratively toward common goals. Near the end of the chapter, you will discover that the specific instructional methods you use should depend on your instructional objectives, the nature of the subject matter, and student characteristics.

Throughout the chapter, you will find suggestions for maximizing the extent to which your students learn through their discussions with one another. For instance, you will discover that the success of cooperative learning depends on several key ingredients (e.g., interdependence among group members, individual accountability) that may have been missing from your own experiences with cooperative learning. And you will learn that, in general, interactive approaches to instruction are often more effective when students have some degree of structure that guides their interactions.

Common Student Beliefs and Misconceptions Related to Chapter Content

Below are two beliefs that future teachers often have before studying specific approaches to instruction—beliefs that may interfere with an accurate understanding of what they read. As you read Chapter 14, be on the lookout for evidence that contradicts these common misconceptions:

1. Some people have had bad experiences with cooperative learning and so are skeptical about its effectiveness.
2. Many people think that when one student tutors another, only the student being tutored benefits from the session.

CHAPTER OUTLINE	FOCUS QUESTIONS
BENEFITS OF STUDENT INTERACTION	• In what ways does student dialogue promote learning?

PROMOTING ELABORATION THROUGH STUDENT INTERACTION
 	
    Class Discussions
    Reciprocal Teaching
    Cooperative Learning
    Peer Tutoring
	• What strategies can enhance the effectiveness of class discussions?
	
	• What is *reciprocal teaching*? What learning strategies is it designed to promote? How can teachers scaffold a reciprocal teaching session?
	
	• What is *cooperative learning*? What strategies are important for its success?
	
	• What is the *jigsaw* technique? What is *scripted cooperation*? What are *base groups*? What functions might base groups serve in a classroom?
	
	• In what situations is peer tutoring useful? What are its potential benefits? How can teachers enhance the effectiveness of peer tutoring?

CREATING A COMMUNITY OF LEARNERS	• What is a *community of learners*? What advantages might it have for students?
TAKING STUDENT DIVERSITY INTO ACCOUNT Accommodating Students with Special Needs	• For what students might interactive and cooperative approaches to instruction be especially valuable? • Under what circumstances are interactive approaches helpful for students with special educational needs? How can teachers maximize the effectiveness of these approaches for students with disabilities?
THE BIG PICTURE: CHOOSING INSTRUCTIONAL STRATEGIES	• For what types of objectives, lessons, and students are different instructional strategies most useful?

Chapter Glossary

Base group. A cooperative learning group that lasts an entire semester or school year and provides a means through which students can be mutually supportive of one another's academic efforts and activities.

Community of learners. A classroom in which teacher and students actively and cooperatively work to help one another learn.

Cooperative learning. An approach to instruction whereby students work with their classmates to achieve group goals and help one another learn.

Distributed cognition. A process whereby people think about an issue or problem together, sharing ideas and working to draw conclusions or develop solutions.

Jigsaw technique. An instructional technique in which instructional materials are divided among members of a cooperative learning group, with individual students being responsible for learning different material and then teaching that material to other group members.

Peer tutoring. An approach to instruction whereby students who have mastered a topic teach those who have not.

Reciprocal teaching. An approach to teaching reading and listening comprehension whereby students take turns asking teacherlike questions of their classmates.

Scripted cooperation. In cooperative learning, a technique in which cooperative groups follow a set of steps, or "script," that guides members' verbal interactions.

Application Exercise #25: Identifying Effective Instructional Strategies

Which of the instructional strategies below are consistent with guidelines presented in Chapter 14, and which are not? Justify your decisions.

1. After her class reads several poems by Edgar Allan Poe, Ms. Marzano asks students to identify themes that underlie all of the poems. In the ensuing class discussion, it quickly becomes clear that her students are not likely to reach consensus about the poems. Therefore, she brings the discussion to a close after only a few minutes and turns to another topic.

2. Ms. Fornier divides her class into groups of four students apiece; each group will research the customs of a particular South American country. She instructs them, "In two weeks, your group must present a 15-minute report about its country to the rest of the class. Your best strategy as a group is to choose one person to give the report and then have the rest of the group help that student find and organize the information he or she needs to present."

3. Mr. Clooney is using a reciprocal teaching approach as he has his students read a chapter on bird migration. At one point, he asks Marie to pose a question about the information the group has just read.

4. As Mr. Paige's class studies the topic of weather, different groups of students conduct research on different topics (cloud formation, hurricanes, the effects of high- and low-pressure systems, the effects of the Gulf Stream, the meanings of meteorological symbols, etc.). Mr. Paige gives the groups guidance about how to proceed in their research but makes it clear that he does not know everything there is to know about the topics they are studying. After a couple weeks of research, students in each group teach their classmates the things they have learned.

5. When Mr. Young discovers that some of his students can use the Pythagorean theorem to solve geometry problems but others cannot yet use the theorem appropriately, he asks students who have achieved mastery to work with those who have not.

6. Ms. Shaklee conducts a cooperative learning exercise in which students meet in groups of three to learn about the three branches of the federal government—executive, legislative, and judicial. Each student in a group receives materials about a different branch of the government and must teach that information to the other two group members.

7. Mr. Goodsell's class often engages in lively debates about controversial topics. He notices that the same students tend to dominate every discussion and that other students speak rarely if at all. "Oh, well," he reasons, "we don't have time for *everyone* to speak."

8. Ms. Liu has her middle school students work in pairs to study a reading assignment in their science textbook. She teaches the students to query one another about the material using such questions as "Can you explain . . . in your own words?" and "What might happen if . . . ?"

9. After a cooperative learning activity, Mr. Meader gives each group a written evaluation of how cooperatively and effectively the group has functioned.

Answers to Application Exercise #25

1. Not consistent. Classroom discussions often help students process classroom material more effectively and are especially useful for helping students explore controversial topics.

2. Not consistent. There is no individual accountability for learning. Only the group member who actually presents the information needs to learn it.

3. Consistent. In reciprocal teaching, a teacher gradually turns the responsibility of asking questions over to students.

4. Consistent. Mr. Paige has created a community of learners in his classroom.

5. Consistent. Peer tutoring often enhances the academic achievement of both the students being tutored and the students doing the tutoring.

6. Consistent. Ms. Shaklee is using the jigsaw technique; in the process, she is creating a situation in which group members must depend on one another for their learning.

7. Not consistent. Students benefit more from class discussions when they participate actively in the discussions (see the section "Benefits of Student Interaction"). Mr. Goodsell might consider using small-group discussions as a way of encouraging all students to participate.

8. Consistent. Peer tutoring sessions are often more effective when students have a particular structure to follow.

9. Not consistent. Cooperative groups should evaluate their *own* effectiveness (although perhaps with their teacher's assistance).

Answers to Selected Margin Notes

- Page 573: *Can you explain the value of these four strategies by relating them to effective memory storage processes?*
    The four strategies have effects such as these:
    - Summarizing: Summarizing requires students to identify and organize (i.e., find interrelationships among) the main ideas.
    - Questioning: Depending on the types of questions being asked, questions can either facilitate comprehension monitoring or promote elaboration.
    - Clarifying: By clarifying things they don't fully understand, students are better able to learn them at a meaningful, rather than rote, level.
    - Predicting: By making predictions, students are drawing inferences from the things they have already learned (i.e., they are engaging in elaboration).

- Page 574: *Can you find at least one example each of summarizing, questioning, clarifying, and predicting in this dialogue? What strategies does the teacher use to elicit desired student responses?*
    Examples of each strategy are these:
    - Summarizing: Kam: The babies are born in the summer . . . The mother hides the babies in different places . . . To bring them food.
    - Questioning: Kam: How does she get the babies safe?
    - Clarifying: Milly: She needs to bring food. She probably leaves a twig or something.
    - Predicting: Milly: What she teaches her babies . . . like how to hop.
    The teacher models appropriate questions (e.g., "What would happen if the babies were born in the winter?"), guides the student "teacher" (e.g., "That's a good question to ask. Call on someone to answer that question."), and gives prompts (e.g., "And she visits them . . .").

- Page 575: *Why is this approach called reciprocal teaching?*
    The students take turns serving as "teacher" for their classmates.

- Page 593: *How might elements of cooperative learning and mastery learning be combined? In what way is computer-assisted instruction also expository instruction?*
    One way that cooperative learning and mastery learning might be combined is to include cooperative learning activities in an overall mastery learning approach. Computer-based instruction is expository instruction in the sense that computers often present new information for students to learn.

Sample Test Questions

Items marked with a "**1)**" on the left-hand side are lower-level questions that assess your general knowledge and understanding of the material. Items marked with a "**2)**" on the left-hand side are higher-level questions that assess your ability to apply what you have learned to a new situation.

Multiple-Choice

1) 1. Three of the following are benefits of student dialogue. Which one is *not* necessarily a benefit of student interaction in the classroom?
   a. From a motivational standpoint, it satisfies students' safety needs.
   b. Students model metacognitive processes for one another.
   c. Students may discover inconsistencies in their own thinking.
   d. Interaction may create disequilibrium that promotes cognitive development.

2) 2. In which one of the following situations would *reciprocal teaching* be most appropriate?
   a. Mr. Arias wants his students to remember the techniques they learn in woodworking class.
   b. Ms. Broughton wants her students to learn to interact more appropriately with their classmates.
   c. Mr. Conway is concerned that his students don't remember much of what they read in their history textbooks.
   d. Ms. Danforth wants her students to develop more effective problem-solving skills.

1) 3. Three of the following are accurate statements about cooperative learning. Which one is *not* accurate?
   a. Researchers find that it often promotes high academic achievement.
   b. Researchers find that it often promotes cross-cultural friendships.
   c. Researchers find that it is more effective when students are individually accountable for what they have learned.
   d. Researchers find that students work best when they can choose the other members of their group.

1) 4. Which one of the following best characterizes a *community of learners*?
   a. Students take turns lecturing to the rest of the class.
   b. At the beginning of each week, students vote on the topics they will study that week.
   c. Different students become "experts" on different topics and then share their expertise with their classmates.
   d. Students "buy" and "sell" what they have learned in much the same way that people in the outside world buy and sell goods they've grown or manufactured.

Essay

2) 5. Imagine that, as a teacher, you have three students in your class who have been identified as being gifted. Of the various instructional strategies described in Chapters 13 and 14, identify *four* that might be particularly valuable for helping these students achieve at levels commensurate with their abilities. In four short paragraphs, briefly describe how you would implement each strategy and justify why you believe it would be especially suitable for gifted students.

Answers to Sample Test Questions

1. a—Interaction with peers may help students meet their need for affiliation, but it will not necessarily address their safety needs (see the discussion of Maslow's theory in Chapter 12). The other three alternatives are listed in the section "Benefits of Student Interaction" on textbook pages 568-569.

2. c—Reciprocal teaching is used primarily as a method of enhancing students' reading comprehension skills (see textbook page 573).

3. d—Experts generally recommend that the teacher form the groups rather than let students form groups themselves (see textbook page 578).

4. c—In a community of learners, students serve as resources for one another, and they often become experts on particular topics (see textbook pages 586-587).

5. Possible responses to this question are presented in the bottom right-hand cells of Table 13-3 (textbook page 563) and Table 14-1 (textbook page 590). You might also consider the student characteristics described in Table 14-2 (textbook pages 592-593), Your answer need not be restricted to the tables, however. Each of your four paragraphs should include a concrete description of a strategy you intend to use and a rationale as to why it's appropriate for gifted learners. You may also want to draw on the discussion of giftedness in Chapter 5 when answering this question.

Chapter 15

CREATING AND MAINTAINING
A PRODUCTIVE CLASSROOM ENVIRONMENT

Chapter Overview

In this chapter, you will focus on *classroom management* — that is, on creating and maintaining a classroom environment conducive to students' learning. Here you will examine several general strategies (e.g., arranging the classroom to facilitate teacher-student interaction, creating a climate in which students feel they "belong," setting reasonable limits for student behavior) and many more specific ones for keeping your students engaged and on task throughout most or all of the school day. You will also explore various ways of dealing with student misbehaviors (e.g., cueing, promoting self-regulation, applying behaviorist principles) and discover that different kinds of behavior problems may warrant different responses on your part. Later in the chapter, you will identify student characteristics that you should take into account as you plan and carry out your classroom management strategies. Finally, you will consider how you might coordinate your efforts with colleagues, community agencies, and parents to maximize students' learning and development.

Common Student Beliefs and Misconceptions Related to Chapter Content

Below are two beliefs that future teachers sometimes have before learning about classroom management; such beliefs may interfere with an accurate understanding of what they read. As you read Chapter 15, be on the lookout for evidence that contradicts these commonly held beliefs:

1. Some future teachers think that a well-managed classroom must invariably be one that is quiet and orderly.

2. Some future teachers think of teaching as an activity that occurs in relative isolation from other adults, rather than as an activity that involves frequent coordination with other teachers, community agencies, and parents.

CHAPTER OUTLINE	FOCUS QUESTIONS
CREATING AN ENVIRONMENT CONDUCIVE TO LEARNING 　Arranging the Classroom 　Creating an Effective Classroom Climate 　Setting Limits 　Planning Activities That Keep Students on Task 　Monitoring What Students Are Doing 　Modifying Instructional Strategies When Necessary	• What is a well-managed classroom? • What strategies do effective classroom managers use in terms of: 　• Arranging the classroom? 　• Creating a classroom climate? 　• Setting limits? 　• Planning classroom activities? 　• Monitoring what students are doing? 　• Modifying instruction? • What rules and procedures might be appropriate for students at the grade level you will be teaching? • How can teachers strike a balance between giving students the easy tasks that are most likely to keep misbehaviors to a minimum and providing challenges that are most likely to promote cognitive growth? • How can teachers strike a balance between giving students enough structure that they know what is expected of them, yet not so much structure that higher-level thinking skills are stifled? • What is *withitness*? What purpose does it serve? • In what way do beginning teachers and expert teachers often think differently when their students engage in nonproductive classroom behavior?
DEALING WITH MISBEHAVIORS 　Ignoring the Behavior 　Cueing the Student 　Discussing the Problem Privately with the Student 　Promoting Self-Regulation 　Using Applied Behavior Analysis and Positive 　　Behavioral Support 　Conferring with Parents	• How does the textbook define *misbehavior*? • Why are some misbehaviors are best ignored? • What is *cueing*? When is it likely to be useful? • What are the advantages of discussing a problem behavior with a student? Why should such conversations be conducted in private? • What strategies can teachers use to promote self-regulation? In what situations are such strategies likely to be effective? • When are applied behavior analysis and positive behavioral support most useful? What specific strategies do these approaches include? • When is a conference with parents advisable?

CHAPTER OUTLINE	FOCUS QUESTIONS

TAKING STUDENT DIVERSITY INTO ACCOUNT
 	
  Creating a Supportive Climate
 	
  Defining and Responding to Misbehaviors
 	
  Accommodating Students with Special Needs
	• Why is a supportive classroom climate especially important when working with students from diverse ethnic backgrounds? Why is it important when working with students of low-SES families?
	
	• Why should students' cultural backgrounds be considered when addressing misbehaviors?
	
	• What classroom management strategies are particularly helpful when working with students with special needs?

THE BIG PICTURE: COORDINATING EFFORTS WITH OTHERS
 	
  Coordinating Efforts with Other Teachers
 	
  Working with the Community at Large
 	
  Working Effectively with Parents
	• What benefits result when teachers coordinate their efforts with one another?
	
	• What activities might "working with the community at large" involve?
	
	• What strategies can teachers use to communicate regularly with parents?
	
	• Why are some parents reluctant to become involved in their children's education? What strategies can teachers use to get them more involved?
	
	• What suggestions does the textbook offer for working successfully with parents?

Chapter Glossary

Classroom climate. The psychological atmosphere of the classroom.

Classroom management. Establishing and maintaining a classroom environment conducive to learning and achievement.

Cueing. A teacher's signal that a particular behavior is desired or that a particular behavior should stop.

Misbehavior. An action that has the potential to disrupt classroom learning and planned classroom activities.

Sense of community. In the classroom, a widely shared feeling that teacher and students have common goals, are mutually respectful and supportive of one another's efforts, and believe that everyone makes an important contribution to classroom learning.

Sense of school community. The sense that all faculty and students within a school are working together to help every student learn.

Withitness. The appearance that a teacher knows what all students are doing at all times.

Application Exercise #26: Identifying Effective Classroom Management Strategies

Which of the following teacher behaviors are effective classroom management strategies, and which are not? Justify your decisions.

1.   Mr. Dayton wants to make sure his fifth graders enjoy every minute of the school day, so he turns virtually all his lessons into games and other fun-filled activities. He also devotes the last 30 minutes of each school day to "fun time"—to nonacademic activities designed to leave students with a good feeling about school.

2.   Mr. Adams acknowledges his students' birthdays (or half-birthdays, for those who were born in the summer) with an "Adams Apple"—an apple with a birthday candle stuck in the top.

3.   Ms. Schutz describes the three major assignments that students in her literature class must complete during the semester, and together she and her students come to an agreement about a reasonable due date for each assignment.

4.   At the end of the third week of school, Ms. Jameson and her third graders discuss the procedures they have been using for daily activities—for starting the school day, going to lunch, getting ready to go home at the end of the day, etc. Several students say that the procedure they use for going to lunch isn't fair, and so together the class develops a procedure that might work better.

5.   Mr. Trenton knows that the first few months of junior high school are unsettling ones for many students, so he gives his classes free rein to do as they please during the first two weeks of school. After this, he sets rules for classroom behavior and begins to enforce them.

6.   Ms. Camareri lets her students sit wherever they want in the classroom. She figures that the occasional off-task behavior that results when friends sit by one another (whispering, passing notes, etc.) is counterbalanced by the fact that their affiliation needs are being met.

7.   Mr. Mireles has a specific procedure that he wants his third graders to follow when they need to use the restroom or get a drink of water. He has a sign-out sheet by the door; his students write their names on the sheet whenever they must leave the classroom, and they also enter the times that they leave and return. Mr. Mireles has a limit on the number of times a student can leave the classroom for such "errands": twice in the morning and twice in the afternoon.

8.   When Mr. Dembrowski must take a few minutes to help Stacey with a difficult math problem, he turns his chair so that he can simultaneously watch his other students working quietly at their desks.

9.   Ms. Piper has discovered that Raymond has a very short attention span. She puts him at the back of the classroom, where he won't disturb other students with his frequent off-task behaviors.

10. Mr. Keegan sends his students to the school library, telling them each to look up a particular kind of mammal.

11. When Mr. Fortuna gives his class a paper-pencil test, he works quietly at his desk but scans the room often to see what his students are doing.

12. Ms. McFadden tells her high school science students, "Always use a pen with black ink when you complete assignments for this class. I simply will not accept assignments written in pencil or in other colors of ink."

13. Ms. Sanguedolce's middle school social studies students know that when they first get to class, they should take out their journals and write about their reactions to an item described either in yesterday's newspaper or on last night's local television news program.

14. Mr. Burns gives his health class a general overview of a videotape that they are about to see. After he does so, he enlists the help of four students to help him get the video equipment from the end of the hall and set it up at the front of the class.

15. On the first day of her Algebra II class, Ms. Yocum gives her students several problems that they should be able to do based on what they learned in Algebra I last year. She knows that these problems are especially challenging ones that will require a great deal of thought.

16. Mr. Winfrey tells his students, "It's important to follow this format when you do your math assignments so that I can find your answers easily and give you credit when you've earned it."

Answers to Application Exercise #26

1. Not effective. The classroom should have a somewhat businesslike atmosphere. This is not to say that students cannot have fun in the classroom; however, it *is* to say that their energy should be focused on accomplishing instructional objectives.

2. Effective. The birthday apples show that Mr. Adams cares about his students as people.

3. Effective. This strategy gives students a sense of control over their classroom life and thereby promotes intrinsic motivation.

4. Effective. Ms. Jameson is getting students involved in decision making about classroom activities.

5. Not effective. The first few days of school are critical ones for communicating expectations for students' behavior. During the first two weeks of school, Mr. Trenton does not communicate any expectations for his students, nor does he create a businesslike atmosphere in his classroom.

6. Not effective. Students should be on task as much as possible; satisfying a need for affiliation is no substitute for classroom learning. A more effective strategy would be to allow friends to sit near one another only when they can stay on task as they do so.

7. Effective. Mr. Mireles's students don't have to ask permission every time they want to go to the restroom or drinking fountain. Therefore, they have a certain amount of control over an aspect of their school day.

8. Effective. Ideally, a teacher should be able to see what all students are doing at all times.

9. Not effective. It is better to seat inattentive students close to the teacher.

10. Not effective. Mr. Keegan has given his students very little structure for this task, and so they probably don't have a clear sense of what they are supposed to do.

11. Effective. Mr. Fortuna is demonstrating withitness.

12. Not effective. Ms. McFadden is presenting her requirement in a controlling manner. If she has a legitimate reason for requiring black ink from everyone, then she might instead say something like, "Black ink is easier for me to read. I can grade your work more consistently and fairly if you use black ink pens on all your assignments."

13. Effective. The procedure gives students something to do during a transition time.

14. Not effective. Mr. Burns is creating some "down time" in which students are not actively engaged in learning. He should have set up the equipment before class began.

15. Not effective. It is usually better to start out the year with relatively easy tasks and then introduce more challenging ones as the year goes on. Teachers are more likely to have behavior problems in their classrooms when the tasks that they assign are especially difficult ones for students.

16. Effective. Mr. Winfrey is describing a required procedure in an informational, rather than controlling, fashion.

Application Exercise #27: Dealing with Student Misbehaviors

For each of the following misbehaviors, decide which one of these strategies would probably be most appropriate, and defend your choices:
- Ignoring
- Cueing
- Private discussion with the student
- Self-regulation
- Applied behavior analysis or positive behavioral support (ABA/PBS)
- Parent conference

1. As her class takes a weekly quiz, Ms. Stewart notices Robert looking in the direction of Kevin's test paper. She suspects that he hasn't yet had a chance to decipher any of Kevin's responses.

2. Missy clicks her ballpoint pen constantly during class, to the point where the students around her are being distracted and annoyed. Over the past few weeks, Ms. Givens has repeatedly asked Missy to stop the behavior, but it continues unabated. Missy tells her teacher, "I know I should stop, Ms. Givens, but most of the time I don't even realize I'm doing it."

3. Although Jerri willingly completes tasks that she can do at her desk or in small cooperative groups, she consistently refuses when Mr. Baranski asks her to do anything that involves speaking in front of the entire class.

4. As he hurries past Melanie to get to his seat in French class, Lucas unintentionally knocks Melanie's looseleaf notebook out of her hands. The notebook falls to the floor, and some of the pages fall out. Lucas is obviously embarrassed and offers to help put the notebook back together again. As a result of the disturbance, Ms. Winston must wait a couple extra minutes before she can begin class.

5. Stanley throws the bat wildly whenever he hits the ball during baseball practice. Mr. Greene has repeatedly asked him to stop doing so because the flying bat poses a danger to other team members. Unfortunately, Stanley seems to have no interest in changing his behavior.

6. It's Halloween, and Mr. Ritchey's fourth graders have all brought their costumes to school so that they can dress up for the class Halloween party and school costume parade later in the day. The festivities don't start for another 30 minutes, so Mr. Ritchey has his students working in cooperative groups on a science project that is due next week. Unfortunately, the children are talking more about their costumes than about the science project, and their attention to the project disappears altogether when three of the children's parents come in with cookies and punch for the class party.

7. Heidi becomes physically aggressive with her classmates whenever things don't go her way. Mr. Elliott has talked with her about her behavior several times but has seen little improvement in her behavior. Heidi seems to have little interest in changing how she interacts with other students.

8. During independent seatwork time, Oliver often talks to himself, distracting those around him. He wants to stop because he knows that his classmates make fun of him for his incessant chattiness to no one in particular. Yet Ms. Young's frequent reminders to work more quietly haven't made a difference.

9. Ms. Schweck finds Andrew sleeping in her class two or three times a week. When she speaks with Andrew about the problem, he tells her that he really enjoys her class and wishes he could stay awake. He says that he often has trouble falling asleep at night and so is quite tired in school the following day.

10. Keith is not contributing constructively to his cooperative group. Furthermore, he's doing everything he can to distract the rest of the group from getting its assigned task accomplished. The other group members have complained to Ms. McMartin and requested that she take him out of their group. Ms. McMartin doesn't want to do this, because she suspects that Keith will be a distracting influence no matter which group he is in; furthermore, she wants him to learn to work effectively in a group setting. She has spoken with Keith after class about the situation, but he clearly is not interested in learning or in helping his classmates learn.

11. Mr. Nouri has his students working in pairs on "brain teaser" mathematics word problems. He overhears one pair of students gossiping about a classmate rather than doing the assignment, although he doubts that anyone else in the classroom can hear their conversation.

12. Mr. Marzetta notices that Janie is doodling in her notebook during his explanation of the water cycle. He is surprised to find her doing so, because she is a good student who always performs well on assignments and quizzes.

13. Mary, who has mild mental retardation, is a member of Mr. Caro's third-grade classroom for most of the school day. Mr. Caro finds that when Mary goes to the pencil sharpener to sharpen a pencil, she sometimes gets distracted by things that are happening elsewhere in the classroom and forgets to return to her seat. Mr. Caro knows that Mary wants desperately to please him and is frustrated about her own forgetfulness. But his occasional little admonishments haven't helped.

14. Midway through the school year, Michael's classroom performance, which has previously been quite good, suddenly deteriorates to a consistent "D" level.

15. At the end of art class, Eric is so busy talking to someone else that he has forgotten to clean his pottery wheel.

Answers to Application Exercise #27

1. Cueing. Cheating interferes with students' learning. A simple cue will let Robert know that Ms. Stewart is aware of the behavior and wants it to stop.

2. Self-regulation. Missy is motivated to change her behavior. Ms. Givens might have Missy begin with self-observation, recording each click she catches herself making.

3. Private discussion. Jerri seems motivated to do well in school, as evidenced by her willingness to complete other tasks. Yet repeated cueing has not produced a change with regard to public speaking tasks. By talking privately with Jerri, Mr. Baranski may be able to find out why she balks at such tasks.

4. Ignoring. Lucas didn't intend to knock the notebook to the floor, and the natural consequences of his action (feeling embarrassed and having to help Melanie pick things up) are probably sufficient to discourage him from being so careless in the future.

5. ABA/PBS. The behavior has continued over a period of time, and Stanley has little motivation to change his habits. Reinforcement for putting the bat down appropriately combined with mild punishment for throwing the bat might be effective.

6. Ignoring. The children's off-task behavior is due to special circumstances and will not necessarily occur after today.

7. ABA/PBS. Heidi's behavior is interfering with school activities and is potentially jeopardizing the safety of others. Cueing hasn't worked, and Heidi isn't motivated to change on her own. Mr. Elliott might try to extinguish or punish aggressive behavior (e.g., with time-out) and then teach and reinforce more appropriate behaviors.

8. Self-regulation. Oliver wants to change his behavior, yet cueing hasn't worked. Ms. Young might suggest self-observation along with self-reinforcement for working quietly.

9. Parent conference. A private discussion with the student has been ineffective, and the source of the problem appears to lie outside school walls.

10. ABA/PBS. Keith's behavior is interfering with his own learning and that of other group members. Cueing hasn't worked, and he's not interested in changing his behavior. Using applied behavior analysis, Ms. McMartin might identify an effective reinforcer to encourage more productive behavior in cooperative learning activities. Or, using positive behavioral support, she might try to determine the purpose(s) that Keith's inappropriate behaviors serve for him and then identify alternative behaviors that serve the same purpose(s) for Keith.

11. Cueing. The behavior is interfering with learning but may stop once the students know that Mr. Nouri is aware of what they are doing.

12. Ignoring. Janie's behavior does not appear to be interfering with her learning.

13. Self-regulation. Mary wants to change her behavior but doesn't know how. Mr. Caro might teach Mary some self-instructions (e.g., "Sharpen my pencil, then go back to my seat") that she can repeat to herself each time she goes to the pencil sharpener.

14. Private discussion. Michael's recent grades have presumably been sufficient to cue him that his performance is not what it should be, yet there has been no improvement. A sudden drop in motivation for no apparent reason warrants a private discussion to try to identify and remedy the problem.

15. Cueing. Eric simply needs a reminder about appropriate behavior.

Answers to Selected Margin Notes

- Page 599: *Is it possible to over-manage a classroom? If so, what might be the negative ramifications of doing so?*

  Teachers who present a lengthy list of rules and procedures for every imaginable situation and those who punish every conceivable misbehavior (no matter how minor) are probably over-managing their classrooms. Such approaches are likely to (a) create an uncaring, threatening atmosphere and (b) reduce students' sense of control about classroom tasks.

- Page 602: *In what sense do Eli, Jake, and Vanessa have a sense of control in Ms. Cornell's class? What might Ms. Cornell do to help them control their classroom lives in more productive ways?*

  They are "in control" in the sense that they can do almost anything they want to in Ms. Cornell's class. Strategies for promoting a sense of control while also maintaining some order in the classroom can be found in the sections "Giving Students a Sense of Control" (textbook p. 602) and "Promoting Self-Regulation" (textbook pp. 617-618), as well as in Chapter 12's discussion of self-determination.

- Page 606: *Do you see parallels between an authoritative home (described in Chapter 3) and the guidelines for setting limits described in this chapter?*

  Authoritative parents hold high expectations and standards for children's behavior, explain why some behaviors are acceptable and others are not, and include children in decision making. All of these characteristics are evident in the textbook's discussion of setting limits.

- Page 608: *With this point in mind, how might Ms. Cornell (in the opening case study) have gotten the year off to a better start?*

  Rather than begin a new curriculum on the first day of class, she might have begun with a few "get-to-know-one-another" activities and some academic tasks that involve only a review of last year's curriculum.

- Page 609: *Can you relate this strategy to behavioral momentum (Chapter 10)?*

  Behavioral momentum is a phenomenon whereby people are more likely to make desired responses if they are already making similar responses. Keeping students busy during transition times maintains students' "momentum" with regard to academic tasks.

- Page 614: *Can you relate ignoring to a specific concept in operant conditioning?*

  When a response is not reinforced in any way, *extinction* occurs.

- Page 614: *Why is ignoring not an effective strategy in Ms. Cornell's classroom?*

  Although Ms. Cornell is not reinforcing the misbehaviors of Eli, Jake, and Vanessa, classmates apparently *are* reinforcing the misbehaviors.

- Page 619: *What behaviorist techniques might Ms. Cornell use to help Eli, Jake, and Vanessa become more productive members of her classroom?*

  Reinforcing appropriate behaviors (if necessary, shaping such behaviors over a period of time), punishing inappropriate behaviors, and encouraging other students not to reinforce undesirable behaviors are three obvious strategies. Furthermore, Ms. Cornell should make response-consequence contingencies clear (e.g., she might use contingency contracts), and she should apply both reinforcement and punishment consistently. Using a positive behavioral support approach, Ms. Cornell might also determine the purpose that the students' misbehaviors serve (e.g., perhaps the three students crave attention) and identify alternative, more productive behaviors that can serve the same purpose.

- Page 619: *Social cognitive theorists also advocate following through with the consequences students are expecting. Do you recall their rationale?*

  According to social cognitive theorists, the nonoccurrence of expected reinforcement for appropriate behavior amounts to punishment of that behavior. Similarly, the nonoccurrence of expected punishment for inappropriate behavior has the effect of reinforcing the behavior.

- Page 628: *How might a chronically abusive parent react to the conversation with Ms. Johnson?*

  Unfortunately, some parents may overreact and administer severe, abusive punishment. Should you expect that a parent might react in such a manner to a poor report about his or her child's school performance, or should you suspect that one of your students is the victim of abuse, consult with your school principal or guidance counselor *immediately* for guidance about how to proceed.

Sample Test Questions

Items marked with a "1)" on the left-hand side are lower-level questions that assess your general knowledge and understanding of the material. Items marked with a "2)" on the left-hand side are higher-level questions that assess your ability to apply what you have learned to a new situation.

Multiple-Choice

1)   1. Consider the three teaching strategies described below:
    - Giving students an opportunity to plan ahead by letting them know about upcoming assignments well in advance
    - Giving students choices about how to do some of their assignments
    - Having regular procedures that students should always follow for routine activities

    What do all three of these classroom management strategies have in common?
    - a. They give students a sense of control about certain aspects of classroom life.
    - b. They are the three most effective ways of handling transition times.
    - c. They make it unnecessary for teachers to set limits.
    - d. They facilitate teacher-student interaction.

2)   2. Which one of the statements below is the best example of presenting a classroom rule or procedure in an *informational* manner?
    - a. "During the test, please keep your eyes on your own papers at all times."
    - b. "You'll get your group projects done more quickly if you decide immediately which group members will do which tasks."
    - c. "I will accept your papers only if you have typed them. Handwritten essays are unacceptable."
    - d. "You should always wear a T-shirt, loose-fitting shorts, wool socks, and tennis shoes to physical education class, and you should always shower before you go to your next class."

2)   3.   Which one of the following examples is most consistent with the textbook's definition of a *misbehavior*?
    a. Angela refuses to participate in the class volleyball lesson.
    b. Brad asks Wally how to spell the word *separate* during a creative writing assignment.
    c. Claudette sucks on a Life Saver during free time.
    d. Dustin does his homework on unlined paper when his teacher specifically asked that it be done on lined paper.

2)   4.   Which one of the following strategies is the best example of *cueing*?
    a. Establishing rules at the beginning of the school year
    b. Giving reinforcement for appropriate behavior
    c. Punishing unacceptable behavior
    d. Giving a student a stern look

2)   5.   Which one of the following examples best illustrates *self-monitoring* as a means of changing behavior?
    a. Anna wonders if her obnoxious behavior on the playground is costing her the friendships that she values.
    b. Bill is asked to list the kinds of jobs he will be able to get if, because of his chronic truancy, he never earns his high school diploma.
    c. Cullen keeps a running count of every time an inappropriate curse word slips into the things he says in the classroom.
    d. Dale thinks about how he feels when other people borrow school supplies without returning them and realizes that he should not have kept Monte's pencil sharpener as long as he did.

1)   6.   Three of the following are recommended strategies for conducting parent-teacher conferences. Which one is *not* recommended?
    a. Be as flexible as possible when scheduling a time to meet with each child's parents.
    b. Suggest ways in which parents might have caused the child's inappropriate behaviors.
    c. Plan an agenda for the conference.
    d. Avoid jargon that parents are unlikely to understand.

Essay

1)   7.   Describe six different strategies that you might use to establish and maintain a productive learning environment in your classroom. Your strategies should be based on the textbook's discussion of effective classroom management.

2)   8.   On several occasions, Olivia has been found vandalizing school property—spray-painting walls, breaking windows, damaging equipment, and so on. Describe how you might use applied behavior analysis and/or positive behavioral support to change Olivia's behavior.

Answers to Sample Test Questions

1. a—All three of the bulleted items are recommended strategies for giving students a sense of control (see "Giving Students a Sense of Control" on textbook page 602).

2. b—This statement presents a procedure (dividing up tasks at the beginning of the group session) as an item of information, whereas the other three clearly indicate that the teacher is in control. See "Presenting Rules and Procedures in an Informational Manner" on textbook pages 604-605.

3. a—Angela's behavior interferes with her learning (see the definition of *misbehavior* on textbook page 612).

4. d—Cueing sometimes takes the form of body language (see textbook page 615).

5. c—Having students engage in self-monitoring typically involves asking them to record the frequency with which certain behaviors occur (see textbook page 617).

6. b—The textbook suggests that the teacher create a *nonjudgmental* atmosphere and focus on constructive solutions (see Figure 15-3 on textbook page 626).

7. Numerous strategies are described in the section "Creating an Environment Conducive to Learning" on textbook pages 598-612; many of them are also presented as "apple" margin notes. Your response should include at least six of the strategies presented in the text.

8. Ideally, your response should draw from both Chapter 10 (the discussion of behaviorism) and Chapter 15. At a minimum, your response should include reinforcement for appropriate behavior—perhaps for behavior incompatible with vandalism (e.g., you might do something similar to what was done in the litterbug situation on page 419 of Chapter 10). Your response might also include punishment for further vandalism (e.g., you might use the logical consequence of having to repaint, repair, or replace whatever has been vandalized). And you might take a positive behavioral approach, whereby you determine the purpose(s) that the vandalism serves for Olivia and identify more constructive behaviors that accomplish the same end. Be specific about the responses you intend to reinforce and punish, as well as about the particular consequences that will follow those responses.

Chapter 16

ASSESSING STUDENT LEARNING

Chapter Overview

In this chapter, you will learn how you can most effectively determine what your students have achieved in your classroom. As you will discover, assessment doesn't always involve pencil and paper, and different assessment strategies are called for under different circumstances. An important point to keep in mind throughout the chapter is that classroom assessment practices not only help teachers ascertain what students have learned but also *influence* what students learn. Students study and mentally process classroom subject matter differently depending, in part, on how they expect their learning to be assessed.

Early in the chapter, you will examine four important "RSVP" characteristics of good assessment: reliability, standardization, validity, and practicality. You will then use these characteristics to evaluate a variety of informal and formal assessment strategies; as you do so, you will find that there is probably no "perfect" way of assessing student learning. You will also explore several strategies for summarizing what students have achieved, including test scores, class grades, and portfolios. Without a doubt, assessing student learning will be one of your most important tasks as a teacher, but it will also be one of the most challenging.

Common Student Beliefs and Misconceptions Related to Chapter Content

Below are several misconceptions that college students often have before studying the topic of classroom assessment; such misconceptions may interfere with an accurate understanding of effective assessment practice. As you read Chapter 16, be on the lookout for evidence that contradicts these commonly held beliefs:

1. Some college students think that classroom assessment (e.g., "tests") must always involve paper and pencil.
2. Many think of classroom assessment practices as being activities totally separate from the process of classroom learning.
3. Some think (and may even have heard elsewhere) that such innovative forms of assessment as performance tests and portfolios are *always* preferable to traditional paper-pencil assessment.
4. Many college students think of multiple-choice questions as invariably being "multiple-guess" items that can measure only rote memorization of trivial details.
5. Most think that informing children or adolescents of one another's assessment results (e.g., by announcing test scores in class or by having students grade one another's papers) is pedagogically and legally appropriate.

CHAPTER OUTLINE	FOCUS QUESTIONS

THE VARIOUS FORMS OF CLASSROOM ASSESSMENT
 	
   Standardized Tests Versus Teacher-developed Assessment
 	
   Paper-Pencil Versus Performance Assessment
 	
   Traditional Versus Authentic Assessment
 	
   Informal Versus Formal Assessment
	• What is *assessment*? What aspects of the textbook's definition are especially important to note?
	
	• What are the differences between:
	  • Standardized tests and teacher-developed assessment instruments?
	  • Paper-pencil and performance assessment?
	  • Traditional and authentic assessment?
	  • Informal and formal assessment?

USING ASSESSMENT FOR DIFFERENT PURPOSES
 	
   Using Assessment to Promote Learning
 	
   Using Assessment to Promote Self-Regulation
 	
   Assessing Achievement of Instructional Objectives
	• How are *formative evaluation* and *summative evaluation* different? In what situations is each one appropriate?
	
	• In what ways do classroom assessments influence student learning?
	
	• What strategies are helpful when teachers use assessment to facilitate learning? when they use it promote self-regulation?

IMPORTANT CHARACTERISTICS OF CLASSROOM ASSESSMENTS
 	
   Reliability
 	
   Standardization
 	
   Validity
 	
   Practicality
	• What is *reliability*? Why is it important? What can teachers do to enhance the reliability of their classroom assessment instruments?
	
	• What is *standardization*? Why is it important?
	
	• What is *validity*? How are *construct validity*, *predictive validity*, and *content validity* different? In what situations is each one important?
	
	• What is *practicality*? Why is there sometimes a trade-off between practicality, on the one hand, and reliability and validity, on the other?

INFORMAL ASSESSMENT RSVP Characteristics of Informal Assessment	• What different forms can informal assessment take? • What are the potential strengths and weaknesses of informal assessment with respect to the RSVP characteristics?

CHAPTER OUTLINE	FOCUS QUESTIONS

PLANNING A FORMAL ASSESSMENT
   Identifying the Domain to Be Assessed
   Selecting Appropriate Tasks
   Obtaining a Representative Sample
	• What are the trade-offs between testing very broad areas of achievement versus testing very narrow, specific areas?
	
	• What issues should teachers consider when choosing the questions and tasks they will use to assess students' learning?
	
	• Why is it important that an assessment instrument be a representative sample of the content domain being assessed?
	
	• What is a *table of specifications*? For what purpose is such a table used?

PAPER-PENCIL ASSESSMENT
   Choosing Appropriate Tasks and Questions
   Constructing and Administering the Assessment
   Scoring Students' Responses
   RSVP Characteristics of Paper-Pencil Assessment
	• What kinds of paper-pencil items can be used to assess higher-level thinking skills?
	
	• How are *recognition tasks* and *recall tasks* different? What are the advantages and disadvantages of each?
	
	• When is it appropriate to give students access to reference materials during an assessment?
	
	• What guidelines does the textbook offer for constructing and administering paper-pencil assessment instruments?
	
	• How can teachers keep students' test anxiety at a facilitative level?
	
	• How can teachers maximize the reliability of their paper-pencil assessment instruments?
	
	• What are the potential strengths and weaknesses of different kinds of paper-pencil instruments with respect to the RSVP characteristics?

CHAPTER OUTLINE	FOCUS QUESTIONS

PERFORMANCE ASSESSMENT
 	
    Choosing Appropriate Performance Tasks
 	
    Constructing and Administering the Assessment
 	
    Scoring Students' Responses
 	
    RSVP Characteristics of Performance Assessment
	• On what occasions is performance assessment preferable to paper-pencil assessment?
	
	• When might *dynamic assessment* be useful? When might it be appropriate to assess *extended performance*?
	
	• What guidelines does the textbook offer for developing and administering performance assessments? Why is each one important?
	
	• What difficulties are teachers likely to encounter when they score students' responses on a performance assessment? What strategies can teachers use to minimize such difficulties?
	
	• What are the potential strengths and weaknesses of performance assessment with respect to the RSVP characteristics?

TAKING STUDENT DIVERSITY INTO ACCOUNT
 	
    Cultural Bias
 	
    Language Differences
 	
    Testwiseness
 	
    Accommodating Students with Special Needs
	• When is an assessment instrument *culturally biased*? How can teachers minimize such bias?
	
	• What implication do language differences among students have for classroom assessment practices?
	
	• What is *testwiseness*? What skills does it encompass? How can teachers help students become more "testwise"?
	
	• What characteristics must teachers keep in mind when they assess the achievement of students with special needs?

CHAPTER OUTLINE	FOCUS QUESTIONS

SUMMARIZING STUDENTS' ACHIEVEMENT
 	
    Assigning Test Scores
    Determining Final Class Grades
    Using Portfolios
    Keeping Assessment Results Confidential
	• What are *raw scores, criterion-referenced scores,* and *norm-referenced scores*? Why are raw scores often less useful than other scores? In what situations are criterion-referenced scores appropriate? In what situations are norm-referenced scores appropriate?
	
	• Why are traditional grading practices controversial? Why do these practices continue despite the controversy?
	
	• What guidelines does the textbook offer with respect to assigning final grades?
	
	• Why should teachers base grades on hard data, rather than on subjective impressions?
	
	• What problems are associated with grading effort or improvement? What problems are associated with giving students extra credit for special projects?
	
	• What rationale does the textbook offer to support using criterion-referenced grades in most circumstances?
	
	• What is a *portfolio*? What guidelines does the textbook offer regarding the use of portfolios? What are the strengths and weaknesses of portfolios in comparison with traditional class grades?
	
	• Why should teachers keep students' assessment results confidential?

THE BIG PICTURE: KEEPING CLASSROOM ASSESSMENT IN PERSPECTIVE	• In what ways is assessment interrelated with both planning and instruction?

Supplementary Readings

Your instructor may assign one or more of these supplementary readings:

- Appendix A, "The Seven Themes of the Book," in the textbook.
- Appendix B, "Describing Relationships with Correlation Coefficients," in the textbook.
- Appendix C, "Interpreting Standardized Test Scores," in the textbook.
- Supplementary Reading #1, "Standardized Tests," near the end of this study guide.
- Supplementary Reading #2, "Constructing Paper-Pencil Tests," near the end of this study guide.
- Supplementary Reading #3, "Calculating Standard Deviations," near the end of this study guide.

Chapter Glossary

Assessment. The process of observing a sample of students' behavior and drawing inferences about students' knowledge and abilities.

Authentic assessment. Assessment of students' knowledge and skills in an authentic, "real-life" context; in many cases, an integral part of instruction rather than a separate testing experience.

Checklist. An assessment mechanism that enables a teacher to evaluate students' performance in terms of specific qualities that the performance either does or does not have.

Construct validity. The extent to which an assessment accurately measures an unobservable educational or psychological characteristic.

Content validity. The extent to which an assessment includes a representative sample of tasks within the content domain being assessed.

Criterion-referenced score. A test score that specifically indicates what students know and can do.

Cultural bias. The extent to which the items or tasks of an assessment instrument either offend or unfairly penalize some students because of their ethnicity, gender, or socioeconomic status.

Dynamic assessment. Examining how a student's knowledge or reasoning may change over the course of performing a specific task.

Formal assessment. A systematic attempt to ascertain what students have learned. It is typically planned in advance and used for a specific purpose.

Formative evaluation. Evaluation conducted during instruction to facilitate students' learning.

Halo effect. A phenomenon whereby people are more likely to perceive positive behaviors in a person they like or admire.

Informal assessment. Assessment that results from teachers' spontaneous, day-to-day observations of how students behave and perform in class.

Norm-referenced score. A score that indicates how a student's performance on an assessment compares with the average performance of other students (i.e., with the performance of a norm group).

Norms. Data regarding the typical performance of various groups of students on a standardized test or other norm-referenced assessment.

Paper-pencil assessment. Assessment in which students respond to written items in a written fashion.

Performance assessment. Assessment in which students demonstrate their knowledge and skills in a nonwritten fashion.

Portfolio. A systematic collection of a student's work over a lengthy period of time.

Practicality. The extent to which an assessment instrument or procedure is relatively easy to use.

Predictive validity. The extent to which the results of an assessment predict future behavior.

Rating scale. An assessment tool that enables one to evaluate students' performance in terms of one or more continua that reflect desired characteristics of the performance.

Raw score. A test score based solely on the number or point value of correctly answered items.

Recall task. A memory task in which one must retrieve information in its entirety from long-term memory.

Recognition task. A memory task in which one must recognize correct information among irrelevant information or incorrect statements.

Reliability. The extent to which an assessment instrument yields consistent information about the knowledge, skills, or abilities one is trying to measure.

Standardization. The extent to which assessment instruments and procedures involve similar content and format and are administered and scored in the same way for everyone.

Standardized test. A test developed by test construction experts and published for use in many different schools and classrooms.

Summative evaluation. An evaluation conducted after instruction is completed and used to assess students' final achievement.

Table of specifications. A two-way grid that indicates both the topics to be covered in an assessment and the things that students should be able to do with each topic.

Teacher-developed assessment instrument. An assessment tool developed by an individual teacher for use in his or her own classroom.

Test anxiety. Excessive anxiety about a particular test or about tests in general.

Testwiseness. Test-taking know-how that enhances test performance.

Traditional assessment. Assessment that focuses on measuring basic knowledge and skills in relative isolation from tasks more typical of the outside world.

Validity. The extent to which an assessment instrument measures what it is supposed to measure.

Here is an additional glossary item if your instructor has assigned Appendix B:

Correlation coefficient. A statistic that indicates the nature of the relationship between two variables.

Here are additional glossary items if your instructor has assigned Appendix C:

Age equivalent score. A test score that indicates the age level of students to whom a student's test performance is most similar.

ETS score. A standard score with a mean of 500 and a standard deviation of 100.

Grade equivalent score. A test score that indicates the grade level of students to whom a student's test performance is most similar.

IQ score. A standard score with a mean of 100 and (for most tests) a standard deviation of 15.

Mean. The arithmetic average of a set of scores. It is calculated by adding all the scores and then dividing by the total number of people.

Normal distribution (normal curve). A theoretical pattern of educational and psychological characteristics in which most individuals lie somewhere in the middle range and only a few lie at either extreme.

Percentile rank (percentile). A test score that indicates the percentage of people in the norm group getting a raw score less than or equal to a particular student's raw score.

Standard deviation (SD). A statistic that reflects how close together or far apart a set of scores are and thereby indicates the variability of the scores.

Standard score. A test score that indicates how far a student's performance is from the mean in terms of standard deviation units.

Stanine. A standard score with a mean of 5 and a standard deviation of 2; it is always reported as a whole number.

z-score. A standard score with a mean of 0 and a standard deviation of 1.

Application Exercise #28: Considering RSVP Characteristics

In each of the situations below, a teacher has failed to address one or more of the RSVP characteristics of good classroom assessment. Identify the problem(s) in each case.

1. Mr. Marshall gives an essay test when three students are absent from class. He worries that the three absent students might learn what the questions are from their classmates and therefore would have an unfair advantage over everyone else. He makes up a test of true-false items for the three students to take instead.

2. Mr. Ermer uses a standardized achievement test as a final exam in his science class. He knows that this test has been carefully developed by its publisher, and he follows the test manual's administration instructions to the letter.

3. Ms. Martino believes she can get a better sense of what students in her advanced literature class have learned when she gives them an oral exam rather than a paper-pencil test. Therefore, she meets with each of her 25 students individually for 30 to 45 minutes apiece to discuss some of the novels they have read. She finds that the individualized format allows her to ask questions specially tailored to each student's interests; she can also ask for more information whenever she doesn't understand what a student is saying.

4. Mr. Thomas has a student teacher in his classroom this semester. Whenever the students do in-class assignments, the two teachers split the stack of papers they take home to grade. This way, they have to grade only fifteen assignments apiece—something they can easily do in a single evening—and the students can get feedback about their performance the following day. Although the two have agreed on their scoring criteria ahead of time, Mr. Thomas always grades students' responses more leniently than his student teacher does.

5. Mr. Whitman, the football coach, has learned that more than 100 boys are planning to go out for the football team; this is far too many boys for him to handle at practice. To cut down on the number of potential players, Mr. Whitman gives everyone a multiple-choice test that assesses knowledge of the basic rules of football. He then eliminates 30 boys from the team on the basis of their low test scores.

6. On the day of a big geography test, several students are home sick with a 24-hour virus. Their teacher, Ms. Leighton, gives them an equivalent test the following day—a day when the school heating system has broken down and the building is exceptionally chilly. Ms. Leighton notices that the students who took the test late have done more poorly than their classmates, and she wonders if the cold temperature interfered with their concentration.

7. Austin is taking the final exam in Ms. Lundberg's world history class. He has an hour to write two essays on these topics: "Identify two similarities between the government of ancient Rome and the current democratic government of our own country," and "Describe three major turning points of World War II, explaining how each one affected the final outcome of the war." If Austin can successfully answer both questions, he will get an A in the course.

8. Ms. Underwood uses more stringent scoring criteria when she scores the performance of her brightest students so that they will be challenged to do their very best.

Answers to Application Exercise #28

1. The nature of the assessment is not <u>standardized</u> for all students. As a result, the <u>reliability</u> of the test results is also affected.

2. Mr. Ermer has not determined whether the test has <u>content validity</u> for his own class.

3. The assessment does not have <u>practicality</u>: It requires a minimum of twelve and a half hours of Ms. Martino's time. Furthermore, it is not <u>standardized</u> in terms of either time or nature of the questions asked.

4. Because one teacher scores responses more leniently than the other, students' scores are affected by the particular individual who takes their assignments home to grade. This is a source of error in students' scores that lowers the <u>reliability</u> of those scores.

5. Mr. Whitman has failed to show that his test has <u>predictive validity</u> for identifying boys who are most likely to become successful football players.

6. Conditions under which students are taking the test are not <u>standardized</u>. The possible effects of room temperature are a source of error that contributes to lower <u>reliability</u>.

7. Students' responses to two essay questions are unlikely to provide a representative sample of what they have learned in an entire world history course. Hence, the exam has poor <u>content validity</u> in the sense that it is not a good reflection of students' overall achievement in the course.

8. Ms. Underwood's scoring criteria are not <u>standardized</u> for all students.

Application Exercise #29: Evaluating Assessment Practices

Which of the following assessment practices are consistent with guidelines presented in Chapter 16, and which are not? Defend your choices.

1. At the beginning of his final exam in basic accounting, Mr. Wagner reminds his students, "I want to emphasize once again how important it is to do well on this test. Remember, the score you get is worth one-third of your final grade."

2. Ms. Hovak is planning a homework assignment for students in her middle school literature class. She thinks about asking her students to write an essay comparing a particularly absentminded character in a novel they've read to the personality of Winnie the Pooh. Although she thinks the question is a good one, she eventually decides *not* to assign it because she suspects that some of her students never read Winnie the Pooh books when they were young.

3. After all of her students have finished a quiz over a recent unit on reptiles and amphibians, Ms. Rosenbloom has them exchange test papers across the aisle and grade one another's work.

4. Ms. Jensen has three students who have recently moved to this country from Nigeria. These students have been raised speaking English, but Ms. Jensen is worried that they may have had little experience with multiple-choice tests and that, as a result, they will do poorly on an upcoming standardized achievement test. She develops a short "practice test" similar to the standardized test the class will be taking so that she can show the three students what a multiple-choice test is like. She also gives the students practice in filling out computer-scorable answer sheets.

5. Mr. Romero tells his students, "Most of you did a pretty mediocre job on yesterday's assignment. Let's see if you can do better today."

6. To meet a school district objective, Mr. Silvestri's sixth graders must know basic history facts about their hometown and their state. A fellow teacher suggests that Mr. Silvestri use a performance test to assess students' knowledge, but Mr. Silvestri instead uses a paper-pencil test made up primarily of short-answer questions.

7. Ms. George's class has just finished a unit on World War II. Because she wants her students to be able to synthesize what they have learned, she thinks that an essay test will be more appropriate than a true-false or multiple-choice test would be. Therefore, she asks her students to respond to a single essay question: "What important roles did Winston Churchill play during the war?" She gives her students the entire class period to answer the question.

8. Mr. O'Hara must give a make-up test to two students who had the flu on the day of his last government exam. He constructs a special test for these students, making sure that the items are similar to those on the original test and being careful to give the students the same instructions and time limits their classmates had.

9. At the end of a unit on gymnastics, Mr. Valentine administers a performance assessment in which each student must perform a forward roll and a backward roll on the mat, as well as a vault over the horse and a dismount from the parallel bars. He has developed specific criteria for grading student's performance of each skill. Rather than having each student execute all four skills in a row, he first has all of his students, one at a time, do the forward roll. He then has all of his students do a backward roll. Following this, each student does a vault, and then each one executes a dismount from the bars.

10. Mr. Hiratska wants his chemistry students to master the symbols for the basic elements (*O* is oxygen, *C* is carbon, *Ag* is silver, etc.). He constructs a quiz that includes symbols for 20 of the elements, assuming that the elements he has included on the quiz are a representative sample of all the elements. Students who don't get a score of 100% on the quiz the first time must continue to take it until they get all 20 items correct.

11. Ms. Romano has been teaching her students to sew in her junior high school "life skills" class. There are several techniques she wants them to know: how to sew a hem, finish a seam, attach a button, and so on. All of these skills are fairly cut-and-dried: Either students can do them correctly or they can't. To assess what students have learned about sewing, Ms. Romano gives a multiple-choice test on which they choose the correct procedure for each task from among four possibilities.

12. Mr. Newton instructs his fourth graders to "Write a paragraph describing the solar system we live in. Write the very best paragraph that you can."

13. Ms. Orlando looks at the instructional objectives she has established for the unit on microorganisms. She believes that some objectives can be easily assessed by multiple-choice questions, others are better assessed by short-answer questions, and still others can really be assessed only by asking students to perform certain tasks in the lab. She therefore constructs an assessment instrument that includes both performance items and two different kinds of paper-pencil items.

14. Ms. Willis discourages students from asking questions during a test because such questions might be distracting to others.

15. Mr. Norwood has a chart on the wall that lists his students' names in alphabetical order. Every time a student gets 100% on a weekly spelling test, he pastes another gold star next to the student's name.

16. Mr. Quackenbush wants to assess his students' ability to apply the things they have learned in mathematics to real-life situations, so he gives them problems related to three real-world tasks—throwing a football, building a treehouse, and riding a skateboard.

17. Ms. Katkowski asks her students to write a short story using the writing techniques she has taught them over the past three weeks. Because her students are writing their stories on the computer, she allows them to use the thesaurus and spell-check functions included in the word processing program. She also lets them use a dictionary to check on the meanings of words they might want to use.

18. When grading essay exams, Ms. Urquhart always makes sure she knows whose paper she is grading at any one time. She believes it is important to take students' prior achievement into account when she grades their current performance.

19. Mr. Wilkewicz asks his high school English students to analyze a short story in terms of its underlying themes and the techniques (symbolism, etc.) that the author uses to communicate those themes. The very nature of the task is such that different students are likely to respond in a wide variety of ways. Although Mr. Wilkewicz is able to identify some general criteria to use as he evaluates what students have written, he is also finding that his evaluation of each student's response is somewhat dependent on how it compares with the quality of other students' responses.

20. The students in Ms. Slobojan's advanced high school math class really enjoy the things they are studying; in fact, many of them are planning careers in mathematics or in such related fields as science and engineering. Ms. Slobojan repeatedly reminds her students how important it is to do well on weekly quizzes, pointing out that their final grades in the class will influence the decisions that college admissions officers make.

21. Ms. Duran wants to boost her students' self-esteem, so she constructs a test on which everyone can do well, regardless of how well they have learned the material.

22. Ms. Enriquez gives spelling tests in the traditional manner, asking students to spell each word that she dictates on a lined piece of paper. She finds that she sometimes has trouble grading students' spelling tests accurately because their handwriting is difficult to decipher (an *e* might look like an *i*, an *r* might look like an *n*, etc.). She is worried about the reliability of her tests and wonders if she should instead use a multiple-choice format to test her students' spelling. She eventually decides to continue testing spelling as she has before (i.e., by dictating the words to her students) but to insist that students write more legibly.

23. Mr. Nguyen wants his students to be able to apply the things they learn in physics to new situations. After a unit on simple machines (levers, wedges, inclined planes, and pulleys), he asks students to explain how they might use these devices to solve everyday problems (lifting heavy objects, cutting objects in half, etc.). The particular problems that he asks his students to solve are ones that they have never actually discussed in class.

Answers to Application Exercise #29

1. Not consistent. Increasing students' anxiety at this point is unlikely to be helpful. For one thing, it's too late for students to study any more than they already have. Second, Mr. Wagner's statement is likely to raise students' anxiety to a debilitating level.

2. Consistent. Ms. Hovak is attempting to eliminate cultural bias in her assignment.

3. Not consistent. This practice violates the confidentiality of students' test scores.

4. Consistent. A test may be culturally biased if some students are unfamiliar with its format. By giving the Nigerian students experience with a multiple-choice test, Ms. Jensen increases the likelihood that their test scores will be valid indicators of what they have learned.

5. Not consistent. Mr. Romero's feedback does not provide concrete, constructive information about how students can improve their performance.

6. Consistent. Paper-pencil assessment is often quite appropriate for assessing students' knowledge of basic facts, and it is far more practical than performance assessment.

7. Not consistent. First, the single essay question is not a representative sample of what students presumably have studied about WWII. Second, essay tests tend to have lower reliability than objective tests do, and a single essay question would have low reliability indeed; for example, a student who knows the material well but misinterprets the question might get an F rather than the A that he or she should actually get. Third, the question provides insufficient structure regarding how students should respond—a factor that will lead to difficulty scoring the test consistently from one student to the next and therefore will decrease reliability even further. If Ms. George wants to assess students' ability to synthesize what they have learned, she might combine two or three short essay questions with some objective, quick-response items (multiple-choice, short-answer, etc.); this way, she can get a representative sample of what students have learned about WWII.

8. Consistent. By keeping the items on both tests similar, and by giving the same instructions and time limits, Mr. O'Hara is keeping the test standardized for all students.

9. Consistent. Teachers can score students' performance more consistently when they evaluate it task by task, rather than student by student. If Mr. Valentine had each student perform all four tasks in a row, his judgments of a student's performance on one task might influence his judgments of that student's performance on other tasks.

10. Not consistent. The assessments that students expect influence what and how they study. When students are allowed to retake the same quiz, they may master the specific items on the quiz without necessarily mastering the larger content domain that it represents. A better strategy would be to ask about different symbols on each retake, so that students can do well on the quiz only if they know the symbols of *all* the elements.

11. Not consistent. Having students actually demonstrate their skills with needle and thread would have greater content validity than simply identifying the correct procedures on a paper-pencil test. Ms. Romano doesn't need to watch every student as he or she performs the skills; she needs to look only at the products that students have created. Therefore, a performance assessment can be as easily administered and scored as a paper-pencil test (i.e., it can be just as practical), and it is undoubtedly a more authentic assessment of whether students have achieved the objectives.

12. Not consistent. The task is not clearly defined. Thus, students' responses are likely to vary widely in content and scope, and so they will be difficult to score consistently and reliably.

13. Consistent. It's perfectly acceptable to mix item types on the same instrument, especially if different types are better suited to assessing different objectives.

14. Not consistent. Students can perform well on a test only when they know how they are supposed to respond. Teachers cannot always anticipate the difficulties students will have interpreting test items; they must therefore encourage students to seek clarification whenever they don't understand an item. To minimize distractions, Ms. Willis might have students approach her desk when they have a question; she can then confer with them without distracting others.

15. Not consistent. This practice violates the confidentiality of students' test scores.

16. Not consistent. Males are more likely to have experience in these areas than females, so the test is culturally biased.

17. Consistent. By allowing students to use a thesaurus, spellchecker, and dictionary, Ms. Katkowski is essentially giving them access to certain reference materials. The point of the assignment is to assess students' ability to write a story; it is *not* meant to assess vocabulary or spelling. Therefore, the use of the three resources is appropriate in this situation.

18. Not consistent. Scoring criteria should be consistently applied from one student to another. Generally speaking, it is *not* appropriate to hold some students to higher performance standards than others. A better strategy would be to help all students achieve the standards Ms. Urquhart believes are truly important.

19. Consistent. Many experts believe that when criteria for a complex skill are difficult to pin down, assigning norm-referenced scores may be the only alternative.

20. Not consistent. Although tests can be used as motivators, these students are already intrinsically motivated to learn mathematics. Ms. Slobojan's statements may raise students' anxiety to a debilitative level. Furthermore, tests tend to be *extrinsically* rather than intrinsically motivating; if we consider principles of intrinsic motivation (Chapter 12), we should expect such statements to undermine the students' intrinsic motivation for learning mathematics. Ms. Slobojan might instead point out the value of the weekly quizzes for giving students feedback about how well they understand the material.

21. Not consistent. The difficulty level of a test should reflect the level of performance a teacher wants students to achieve. A more effective way to enhance students' self-esteem would be to help them master the material.

22. Consistent. In this situation, a recall test has higher content validity than a recognition test because it more closely resembles what the students must eventually be able to do in real life: remember word spellings without benefit of four or five possible spellings to choose from.

23. Consistent. Mr. Nguyen's objective is for students to apply principles of physics to new situations, and the test asks them to do exactly that. If he were to limit his test only to problems the class had already discussed, the test would be measuring knowledge rather than application. Not only does the test have high content validity for Mr. Nguyen's objective, but it also provides a new learning experience for his students.

Application Exercise #30: Interpreting Test Scores

For each of the situations below, determine whether the teachers are interpreting test scores appropriately. Justify your decision in each case. *Note: You should complete this exercise only if your instructor has assigned Appendix C ("Interpreting Standardized Test Scores") in addition to Chapter 16.*

1. Mr. Croot receives the test scores from the standardized achievement tests that his fourth graders took last month. One of his students, Jennifer, has gotten grade equivalents of 6 or 7 on tests in every area—in reading, spelling, math, science, history, and geography. He recommends that Jennifer be placed in sixth grade rather than fifth grade next year.

2. When Mr. Doherty learns that all of his math students have gotten scores at the 90th percentile rank or above on a standardized high school mathematics test, he concludes that they have definitely achieved his instructional objectives in trigonometry.

3. When assessing performance in her driver education class, Ms. Crandall gives her students a separate score for each one of a number of important driving skills: using different gears at appropriate speeds, coming to a complete stop at stop signs, parking successfully in a parallel parking space, and so on. When students have a check mark next to each of these behaviors, Ms. Crandall tells them they are ready to take the state test for a driver's license.

4. Earnest, a high school senior, gets a percentile rank of 48 on a physical fitness test. His teacher concludes that he has performed about as well as the average high school senior.

5. Ms. Thurrell learns that Jason recently got a score of 110 on an IQ test that the school psychologist administered. She concludes that Jason is capable of much more challenging work than the average student and so plans to recommend that Jason be placed in several advanced classes next year.

6. When Ms. Wooten finds that all of her sixth graders have gotten at least 75% of the items correct on a standardized mathematics achievement test, she concludes that they have attained mastery of the school district's instructional objectives for sixth-grade math.

7. Ms. Simons enters her students' scores on yesterday's history test into a computer program that will compute the test's mean and standard deviation. Although she wasn't specifically interested in the students' z-scores, the computer calculates and prints out these scores just the same. She notices that Frieda has a z-score of 3 on the test and concludes that Frieda did exceptionally well on the test compared to her classmates.

8. When Mr. Bedinger gives his fourth graders a test of the week's 20 spelling words, they all get 100% correct. He concludes that they have mastered these words and are ready to move on to next week's list.

9. Mr. Almajbari learns that students in his advanced science class have all gotten stanines of 7, 8, or 9 on a standardized science achievement test. He concludes that his students have done well on the test compared to other students across the nation.

10. Ms. Katz is concerned when she learns that a few students in her eighth-grade social studies class have scored at a sixth-grade level on the reading comprehension subtest of a standardized achievement test. She wonders if her eighth-grade-level textbook might be too difficult for them.

Answers to Application Exercise #30

1. Not appropriate. Although Jennifer has performed as well as the average sixth grader on the tests, this does not necessarily mean that she is capable of sixth-grade work. In any classroom, students are likely to show considerable variability in the grade-equivalent scores they obtain on a standardized test.

2. Not appropriate. Mr. Doherty needs criterion-referenced scores to draw such a conclusion. This test has yielded norm-referenced scores.

3. Appropriate. Ms. Crandall is using criterion-referenced scores to decide whether students have attained mastery of essential driving skills.

4. Appropriate. The test is obviously norm-referenced; Earnest's performance has presumably been compared to a norm group of twelfth graders. The 50th percentile reflects average performance (in a normal distribution, it is the *mean* of the distribution), and the 48th percentile is very close to this average.

5. Not appropriate. An IQ score of 110 is within one standard deviation of the mean, so it is essentially an "average" score.

6. Not appropriate. A score of 75% is a raw score. Standardized achievement tests are designed to yield norm-referenced scores, and raw scores on these tests are relatively meaningless. Ms. Wooten needs a criterion-referenced score to determine whether her students have achieved mastery—a score that this particular test doesn't provide.

7. Appropriate. A *z*-score of 3 indicates that Frieda's performance was three standard deviations above the mean.

8. Appropriate. Mr. Bedinger's test is not assessing just a sample of what students have learned in spelling this week; it is a measure of the entire domain. A score of 100% therefore indicates that his students have mastered all 20 words.

9. Appropriate. His students have all performed between one and two standard deviations above the mean.

10. Not appropriate. In any classroom, students will get varying grade-equivalent scores on an achievement test; it is highly unlikely that all of Ms. Katz's eighth graders would get a grade equivalent of *exactly* 8. The low-scoring students will not necessarily have exceptional difficulty with the eighth-grade textbook, although Ms. Katz probably should monitor their academic progress carefully just to be sure.

Answers to Selected Margin Notes

- Page 638: *Students tend to study more for essay tests than for multiple-choice tests. Why might this be so?*
  Three likely explanations are these:
  - Multiple-choice tests are recognition tests, whereas essay tests are recall tests. Generally speaking, recognition tests provide more retrieval cues than recall tests, making it easier to remember correct answers.
  - Multiple-choice tests typically assess lower-level skills, whereas essays may test either lower-level or higher-level skills. Students must process information more thoroughly (they should engage in elaboration, organization, etc.) to do well on questions involving higher-level skills.
  - Because multiple-choice tests have many more items than essay tests do, students can more easily skip over items related to material they don't understand, knowing that the "holes" in their knowledge will probably not have a major impact on their overall test performance.

- Page 642: *A quick review: What do we call a memory aid such as RSVP?*
  RSVP is an example of a mnemonic—more specifically, a superimposed meaningful structure.

- Page 647: *Why do you think affective outcomes are usually assessed informally rather than formally?*
  Airasian (1994) has suggested two reasons. First, affect (e.g., students' feelings, attitudes, interests) is often difficult to assess formally. For example, students can "fake" the responses that they believe to be desirable, and issues of privacy often arise. Second, it is not always possible or appropriate to identify "desired" affective objectives. For example, although we might strive to help our students learn classroom material, it may be inappropriate to insist that they develop a certain set of attitudes or feelings with regard to it.

- Page 652: *What are ill-defined problems?*
  An ill-defined problem is one in which the desired goal is unclear, information needed to solve the problem is missing, or several possible solutions exist.

- Page 654: *As noted in Chapter 6, recognition tasks are typically easier than recall tasks. Can you explain why this is so using the concepts of <u>retrieval</u> and <u>retrieval cues</u>?*
  Recognition tasks provide more retrieval cues to assist one's search of long-term memory, thereby increasing the probability that the desired information will be retrieved.

- Page 657: *Look again at our opening case study, "Studying Europe." Which test can be scored more objectively—Ms. Peterson's or Ms. Montgomery's?*
  Ms. Peterson's test can be scored more objectively and, as a result, more reliably.

- Page 658: *Can you explain how each of these recommendations affects the reliability of the assessment instrument?*
  The following underlined phrases are the recommendations presented on pages 657-658:
  - <u>Specify scoring criteria in concrete terms</u>: Specific, concrete criteria should help us score students' responses more consistently.
  - <u>Score grammar and spelling separately from the *content* of students' responses</u>: By limiting the criteria that we use at any one time, we increase the likelihood that we apply those criteria consistently when scoring students' responses.
  - <u>Skim a sample of students' responses ahead of time, looking for responses we didn't anticipate and revising our criteria if necessary</u>: If our scoring criteria need to be changed

for reasons we didn't expect, we are more likely to score students' responses consistently, fairly, and reliably if we change those criteria *before* we begin scoring rather than midway through a stack of papers.

- Score all responses to a single task or question at once (scoring task by task, rather than student by student): We can evaluate students' performance more consistently when we score everyone's response to the same item at once.

- Score responses on a predefined continuum, rather than on an all-or-none basis, if responses are likely to have varying degrees of correctness: When we have only two choices—right or wrong—we may make varying, inconsistent judgments about responses that are partially correct. A continuum enables us to capture the partially correct nature of some responses in a way that is likely to be more consistent than strictly "right" or "wrong" judgments could be.

- Try not to let our expectations for students' performance influence our judgments of their *actual* performance. We all have a tendency to perceive a person's behaviors in a positive light—to see the best in someone—if we have a high regard for that person's competence and ability (the *halo effect*). Similarly, we often seem to find weaknesses and errors in the behaviors of an individual we don't like or respect. Strategies such as shuffling papers after grading one question and using a cover sheet where students' names appear help minimize the effects of such expectations and, as a result, reduce error in scoring.

- Score some or all responses a second time to check for consistency: If we find that we have been inconsistent, we can revise our scoring criteria and score students' responses again.

- Page 662: *Can you use the concept of <u>working memory</u> to explain the value of having only a half dozen criteria?*
  Working memory is the component of the memory system in which active "thinking" takes place. This component appears to have a limited capacity: It can hold only a small amount of information at any one time.

- Page 668: *Look back at the treehouse problem depicted in Figure 8-1. Is this problem culturally biased? Why or why not?*
  It is culturally biased. Students who have experience with carpentry (which is more likely to be true for boys, for instance) may have an advantage over those who do not. This advantage is unrelated to the ability being assessed.

- Page 674: *What are students likely to conclude about these two teachers?*
  They might reasonably conclude that the two teachers do not take the job of evaluating students seriously and/or that they do not have the students' best interests at heart.

- Page 676: *Have you ever known a student who did little work all semester but was able to pull off a passing grade by doing an extra-credit project? Would such a student "learn a lesson" and develop more regular study habits over the long run? Why or why not?*
  The student would not develop more regular study habits because procrastination and asking to do an extra-credit project have been reinforced.

Sample Test Questions

Items marked with a "**1)**" on the left-hand side are lower-level questions that assess your general knowledge and understanding of the material. Items marked with a "**2)**" on the left-hand side are higher-level questions that assess your ability to apply what you have learned to a new situation.

Multiple-Choice

1) 1. Three of the statements below accurately describe the effects that summative classroom assessments have on students' learning. Which statement is *not* accurate regarding summative assessments?

    a. They promote students' intrinsic motivation to learn.

    b. They can provide specific feedback about what students have and have not learned.

    c. They encourage meaningful learning of class material, but only if students expect that test items will require meaningful learning.

    d. They provide a mechanism through which students can review important material.

2) 2. Which one of the following assessment instruments is most likely to have high *reliability*?

    a. A paper-pencil instrument with five multiple-choice questions.

    b. A paper-pencil instrument with 50 true-false items.

    c. A single comprehensive essay question that requires students to synthesize their knowledge of several topics.

    d. Three complex performance tasks that are rated on a scale of 1 to 10.

2) 3. In which of the following situations should a teacher be most concerned about the *predictive validity* of an assessment instrument?

    a. An essay test is used as a final exam in a history class.

    b. A physical fitness test is used to assess the general fitness of students at Emerson Middle School.

    c. A series of mathematics word problems is used to determine whether students have mastered the processes of multiplication and division.

    d. A foreign language aptitude test is used to select students for an accelerated Spanish class.

1) 4. Three of the following practices are consistent with the textbook's guidelines for constructing classroom assessment instruments. Which one is *not* consistent with these guidelines?

    a. Assessing lower-level skills if instructional objectives focus on such skills.

    b. Combining paper-pencil and performance tasks if such a combination can better assess instructional objectives.

    c. Identifying scoring criteria at the same time that you develop the questions or tests you plan to administer.

    d. Occasionally asking ambiguous questions to see how students respond when they have little, if any, structure and guidance.

1)   5. Three of the strategies below should keep students' anxiety at a facilitative level during a classroom assessment task. Which one will *not*?

        a. Telling students that they will have as much time as they need to finish the task.

        b. Reminding students that their scores will be an important factor in determining final class grades.

        c. Allowing reference materials for things that don't necessarily need to be memorized.

        d. Explaining that the assessment can help students identify the things they know well and the things they still need to work on.

1)   6. The textbook recommends that students' grades always be based on hard data rather than on teachers' subjective judgments. What is the rationale behind this recommendation?

        a. Students will be more motivated to achieve when they are evaluated on the basis of such data.

        b. Actual numbers are more concrete and therefore easier for students to understand.

        c. Students want everything they do to be graded.

        d. Subjective judgments tend to be less accurate assessments of achievement.

Essay

1)   7. Explain what educational psychologists mean when they say that an assessment is *culturally biased*. Then, describe two different strategies you can use to minimize the cultural bias of the assessment instruments (either standardized tests or teacher-developed instruments) that you use in your classroom.

2)   8. As a German teacher, you want your students to carry on a simple conversation entirely in German. Describe an appropriate method you can use to assess your students' achievement of this objective, being sure to indicate whether your method should:

        a. Be paper-pencil or performance

        b. Assess recall or recognition

        c. Focus on lower-level or higher-level skills

        d. Be scored in a criterion-referenced or norm-referenced fashion

    Justify your decisions.

Answers to Sample Test Questions

1. a—Traditional classroom assessments promote extrinsic motivation, rather than intrinsic motivation (see textbook page 637).

2. b—An assessment instrument is more reliable when it has objective items, rather than subjective ones, and when it has many items rather than just a few (see the bulleted list of conditions affecting reliability on textbook pages 643-644).

3. d—Predictive validity is essential when a test is being used to predict students' future performance (see textbook page 646). The foreign language aptitude test is being used to predict how well students are likely to do in the accelerated Spanish class. (Content validity is more relevant in the other three situations.)

4. d—Ambiguous questions are usually *not* recommended. Regardless of whether students know the answers to the questions, they should at least know what the questions are asking them to do (see textbook page 655).

5. b—Teachers are more likely to keep students' anxiety at a facilitative level when they portray assessments as learning opportunities, rather than as evaluations of student performance (see Table 16-2 on textbook page 656).

6. d—Some teachers are better judges of student achievement than others. Furthermore, teachers often underestimate the achievement of low-ability students (see textbook page 674).

7. An assessment is culturally biased if any of its items either offend or unfairly penalize some students on the basis of their ethnicity, gender, or socioeconomic status (see textbook page 667). Strategies for minimizing cultural bias include these:
   - Scrutinize assessment instruments for items that may be offensive to certain groups or items that students may have trouble answering solely because of their cultural backgrounds (textbook page 667).
   - Explain the general nature of the assessments students will be taking when some of them have not had prior experience with such assessments (textbook page 669).
   - Give students practice with the assessment format (e.g., answering multiple-choice questions and filling out computer-scorable answer sheets) (textbook page 669).

   Your response should include at least two of the strategies listed above.

8. a. Teachers should assess the specific behaviors they want students to acquire (see textbook page 638). The best way to assess students' ability to carry on a conversation is to actually have them converse with someone else in German—a performance assessment.
   b. People seldom have the luxury of having several statements to choose from when they talk to someone else. They must instead recall the words and grammatical rules they need from their own long-term memories. Hence, recall tasks provide a more valid measure in this situation (see textbook page 654).
   c. You presumably want to assess your students' ability to apply what they have learned to a new conversation. Therefore, you should be testing higher-level skills. (See the discussion of transfer in Chapter 8.)
   d. Because you want to assess what your students can and cannot do rather than how they compare to one another, criterion-referenced scoring is appropriate (see textbook page 672).

Supplementary Readings

Supplementary Reading #1

STANDARDIZED TESTS

A wide variety of standardized tests—tests developed by test publishers for use in schools nationwide—are currently available on the market. Most of these tests are paper-pencil tests that are relatively easy to administer. Furthermore, most of them yield norm-referenced scores—scores that tell us how the performance of our own students compares to that of other students across the country. Appendix C in the textbook provides a description of the forms that such scores often take.

A standardized test typically comes with a test manual that provides:
- Specific instructions for administering and scoring the test
- Norms to which a particular student's performance can be compared
- Information about test reliability, as well as information from which we can draw inferences about test validity for our own purpose and situation

Here we will look at the three kinds of standardized tests that school districts use most frequently: tests of achievement, intelligence, and specific aptitude. Critical aspects of these tests are summarized in Table 1-1.

Achievement Tests

Standardized achievement tests are designed to assess how much students have learned from the things they have specifically been taught. Test items are, at least in theory, written to reflect the curriculum common to most schools; for example, a history test will focus on national or world history rather than the history of a particular state or community. And the overall test scores usually reflect achievement in a very broad sense: They tell us how much a student has learned about mathematics or language mechanics (compared to the norm group) but not necessarily whether that student knows how to multiply fractions or use commas appropriately.

Standardized achievement tests are useful in at least two important ways (Ansley, 1997). First, they provide us with a means of determining how well our students' performance compares with that of students elsewhere; this information may indirectly tell us something about the effectiveness of our instructional programs. Such tests also provide a means of tracking students' progress over time. For example, if Johnny has been getting average test scores over the years, then suddenly performs well below average in eighth grade (even though the test and norm group are the same as they have been in previous years), we have a signal that Johnny may possibly not be learning and performing at a level commensurate with his ability. At this point, we would want to ascertain whether Johnny's low performance was a fluke (perhaps due to illness on the testing day or to some other temporary condition) or whether Johnny's relative decline in performance is due to other, longer-term factors that need our attention.

Content validity is our main concern when we test achievement, and we need to determine each test's validity for our own situation. We can assess the content validity of a standardized achievement test by comparing a table of specifications (either one that the test manual provides

Table 1-1. Comparing Standardized Tests of Achievement, Intelligence, and Specific Aptitude

KIND OF TEST	PURPOSE	RELIABILITY AND VALIDITY	SPECIAL CONSIDERATIONS
Achievement Tests	To assess how much students have learned from what they have specifically been taught	• Reliability coefficients related to overall test scores are often .90 or higher; they are typically higher for secondary students than for elementary students. Reliability coefficients for subtest scores are considerably lower than those for overall test scores. • Content validity must be determined for each situation.	• These tests are usually more appropriate for assessing broad areas of achievement than for assessing specific knowledge and skills.
Intelligence Tests	To assess a general capability to learn; to predict general academic success over the short run	• Reliability coefficients are often .90 or higher; they are typically higher for secondary students than for elementary students. • Predictive validity for academic success ranges from .40 to .70, depending on the situation and student population.*	• Test scores should not be construed as an indication of learning potential over the long run. • Individually administered tests (in which the tester works one-on-one with a particular student) are preferable when students' verbal skills are limited or when significant exceptionality is suspected.
Specific Aptitude Tests	To predict how well students are likely to perform in a specific content domain	• Reliability coefficients are often .90 or higher. • Predictive validity for academic success often falls below .50.*	• Test scores should not be construed as an indication of learning potential over the long run.

*Predictive validity coefficients are correlation coefficients between the test scores and the behaviors being predicted.

or one that we construct ourselves) and compare it to our own curriculum. In addition to looking at topics covered by the test, we should also scrutinize the extent to which test items address lower- and higher-level thinking skills; many commonly used achievement tests focus more on lower-level skills (Alleman & Brophy, 1997; Marzano & Costa, 1988). A test has high content validity for our situation only if both the topics and thinking skills emphasized in test items match our own local objectives.

We should note here that standardized achievement tests have come under fire in recent years precisely because they don't always have validity for the situations in which they're used. For one thing, they may reflect only a small portion of our instructional objectives (Stiggins, 1997). Furthermore, the preponderance of multiple-choice and other objectively scorable items on standardized tests may limit the ability of the tests to assess higher-level thinking skills and performance on authentic, real-life tasks (Darling-Hammond, 1991; Hiebert & Raphael, 1996). Therefore, we must be *extremely* cautious about the conclusions we draw from standardized achievement tests regarding the achievement of our students and the effectiveness of our schools.

Intelligence Tests

Intelligence tests, rather than assessing what students have learned from school instruction, are designed to assess a general *capability* to learn. For this reason, they may also be called *general aptitude, scholastic aptitude,* or *general mental ability* tests. If you have read the discussion of intelligence in Chapter 4 of the textbook, then you already know that an IQ score is not a permanent characteristic and may, in some cases, change considerably over time.

Intelligence and other general scholastic aptitude tests are used mainly for prediction—that is, to estimate how well students are likely to learn and perform in a future academic situation. One way to predict how well students can learn in the future is to assess what they have learned already. But rather than focusing on what students have specifically been taught in school, intelligence tests typically assess how much students have learned and deduced from their general, everyday experiences. For example, many intelligence tests include items dealing with vocabulary, determining the extent to which students understand the meanings of the words they have presumably encountered over the years. They sometimes include analogies, looking at how well students can recognize similarities among well-known relationships. They may also ask students to analyze pictures or manipulate concrete objects. Most intelligence tests include measures of general knowledge, as well as tasks requiring deductive reasoning and problem solving.

Specific Aptitude Tests

Intelligence tests are useful when we want to predict general academic performance. But when we are interested in how well students are apt to perform in a particular area—perhaps in art, music, or auto mechanics—then specific aptitude tests may be more appropriate. Such tests focus on students' ability to learn and perform in very specific content domains. Some aptitude tests are designed to predict future performance in just one area, while others—called *multiple aptitude batteries*—yield subscores for a variety of areas simultaneously.

Aptitude tests are sometimes used by school personnel to select students for specific instructional programs—for example, to identify those students most likely to succeed in a particular course. They may also be used for counseling students about future educational plans and career choices. Aptitude tests are based on the notion that one's ability to learn in a specific area is fairly stable. In recent years, however, many educators have begun to argue that we should focus more on developing abilities in *all* students than on identifying the specific aptitudes that may be present in *some* students (Boykin, 1994; Nichols & Mittelholtz, 1997). Accordingly, specific aptitude tests now appear less frequently in wide-scale school testing programs than they once did.

Choosing the Most Suitable Standardized Test

So far, we have talked about achievement, intelligence, and aptitude tests as if they are all distinctly different entities, but in fact the differences among the three are not always so clear-cut. To some extent, all three kinds of tests assess what a student has already learned. And all three can be used to predict future performance; in many cases, achievement tests predict future scholastic performance as well as general intelligence and specific aptitude tests do (Jencks & Crouse, 1982; Sax, 1989; Stevens & Clauser, 1996). Our best bet is to choose the test that has the best validity for our particular purpose, regardless of what the test is called. And of course we want a test that has been shown to be highly reliable with students similar to our own.

Another consideration in choosing a standardized test is the norm group against which our own students will be compared. We should scrutinize the test manual's description of the norm group used with questions like this in mind:

- Is the norm group a representative sample of the population at large—that is, does it include students from the entire region (for example, the community, state, or country) with which we want to compare our own students?
- Does it include students of the same age, educational level, and cultural background as our own students?
- Does it include students of both genders?
- Is it large enough that its average performance is likely to be similar to that of the population it represents?
- Have the normative data been collected recently enough that they reflect how students typically perform at the present time?

When we determine norm-referenced test scores by comparing students with an inappropriate norm group, those scores are meaningless. For example, I once knew of a situation in which the performance of university students on a standardized achievement test was compared to norms for high school seniors—a practice that made no sense whatsoever.

Because different standardized tests almost always have different norm groups, we cannot really compare students' performance on one test with their performance on another. For example, if Susan takes the Basic Skills Test (BST), we can compare Susan's score on the BST Reading subtest with her score on the BST Mathematics subtest (perhaps concluding that she is better in math than in reading) because both scores are from the same test and have been derived from the same norms. But we cannot compare Susan's BST scores with her scores on a *different* standardized achievement test, because the two sets of scores are likely to be based on entirely different norm groups.

Pitfalls to Avoid When Using Standardized Tests

There are several common mistakes that teachers and other school personnel make when using standardized tests (Worthen & Spandel, 1991):

- They use tests that are inappropriate for the task at hand.
- They accept the claims that test publishers make about their tests without determining the validity of the tests for their own situations.

- They assume that the tests measure *all* of the content, skills, and/or behaviors related to particular abilities or content domains.
- They set arbitrary cutoffs for acceptable performance instead of gathering evidence in support of appropriate cutoffs.
- They use a single test score to make important decisions about students.

As teachers, we must be extremely careful that we don't make such mistakes as well.

Telling Parents About Standardized Test Results

In the United States, the *Family Educational Rights and Privacy Act* of 1974 (also known as the Buckley Amendment) gives parents the right to know their children's test scores. Furthermore, school personnel must present and interpret these test scores in a way that parents can understand. As teachers, how can we describe tests and test results to parents when most of those parents have never read a chapter on assessment in an educational psychology textbook? Here are some general guidelines that theorists offered many years ago yet still have relevance today (Durost, 1961; Ricks, 1959):

- <u>Make sure you understand the results yourself.</u> As teachers, we need to know something about a test's reliability and validity for the situation in which we have used it. We also need to know how the test scores have been derived. For example, we should know whether the scores are criterion-referenced or norm-referenced and, if norm-referenced, something about the norm group to which our students have been compared.

- <u>Remember that, in many cases, it is sufficient to describe the test and students' test performance in broad, general terms.</u> To illustrate, we might describe an achievement test as a general measure of how much a student has learned in mathematics compared to other students around the country, or we might describe an aptitude test as something that gives a rough idea about how well a student is likely to do in a particular instructional program. It's sometimes possible to describe a student's test performance without mentioning test scores at all. For example, we might say, "Your daughter scores like students who do well in college mathematics courses," or "Your son had more than average difficulty on the spelling portion of the achievement test; this is an area in which he may need extra help in the next few years." However, if parents want to know their child's specific test scores, the Buckley Amendment requires that we reveal those scores and provide sufficient information to help parents understand what the scores mean.

- <u>When reporting specific test scores, use percentile ranks and stanines rather than grade equivalents or IQs.</u> Many parents mistakenly think that a child's grade-equivalent score reflects the grade that the child should actually be in, so they may argue for advanced placement of their high-achieving children or feel distressed that their low-achieving children are in over their heads. And many parents interpret IQ scores as reflecting a permanent, unchangeable ability rather than as a mere estimate of a child's present cognitive functioning. By reporting test scores as percentile ranks or stanines instead, we are less likely to have parents jumping to such erroneous conclusions. Many parents are familiar with percentile ranks, and most others can easily grasp the notion of a percentile if it is explained to them. But because percentile ranks misrepresent actual differences between students (as noted in Appendix C, they overestimate differences in the middle range of a characteristic and underestimate differences at the extremes), we may also want to describe test performance in terms of stanine scores. Although most parents are unfamiliar with standard scores in general, we can often present stanines in a graphic and concrete fashion, such as I have done in Figure 1-1.

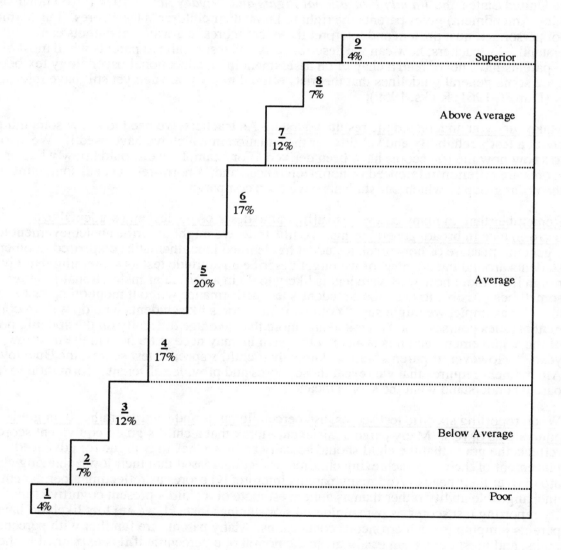

Figure 1-1. A graphic technique for explaining stanines to parents
(modeled After Durost, 1961)

CONSTRUCTING PAPER-PENCIL TESTS

There often are occasions when paper-pencil tests can provide a valid means of assessing students' achievement of instructional objectives. Yet constructing a good paper-pencil test takes considerable thought, planning, and work. In this supplementary reading, I offer some general guidelines for constructing paper-pencil tests that will provide valid assessments of what your students know and can do.

Determining the Length of the Test

Imagine that you come to class on the day a test is scheduled. Your teacher passes out the test sheets, and you discover that the entire test consists of only two true-false questions! You know the course material thoroughly, so you *should* get both questions correct. However, you misinterpret the second question and mark it false when it is actually true. Your test score is 50% instead of 100% because of a single misinterpretation—a big price to pay! But now imagine that the test consists, not of two items, but of twenty. You know the material so well that you should answer all twenty questions correctly, but once again you misinterpret the second question. This time, however, the single mistake affects your test score by only 5%.

Your misinterpretation of the second question is a source of error in your test score. When a test has only a few questions, a single error can have a major influence on overall test scores. When it has numerous questions, the same error will have much less impact, and various sources of error (for example, misinterpreting one question and guessing correctly on another) are more likely to balance one another out. In general, then, longer tests—those with a greater number of questions—have higher reliability.

Obviously, we want to make our tests as long as is reasonable and practical. Yet we must realize that "longer is better" only up to a point. Our students may get tired or bored after too long a test; once they do, their performance on further items may not accurately reflect their knowledge and skills. Furthermore, there is only so much time we can reasonably devote to testing before we begin to use up valuable instructional time.

However long we decide to make our test, we must make sure our students will have sufficient time to complete it. Students need time to write their responses. They also need time to think about those responses, especially when test items require higher-level thinking skills. Many beginning teachers underestimate how long students will need to take a test, so we should probably allow more time than we think our students need, at least until we learn how much time they actually *do* need.

Scrutinizing "Test Bank" Items Carefully

Many textbooks come with *test banks*—collections of test items related to the content that the books cover. Although it is certainly convenient to have items provided for us, we must note that such items have oftentimes *not* been field-tested for reliability or validity. In any case, we will need to determine their content validity for our own instructional objectives. My own experience has been that I am usually better off writing my own test items than using the ones that textbook publishers provide.

Constructing Recognition Test Items

Recognition test items ask students to identify correct answers within the context of incorrect statements or irrelevant information. The three most common examples are multiple-choice, true-false, and matching questions.

Recognition items have two main advantages. First, students can usually answer many items in a single test session. Hence, we can construct a test that adequately samples topics within the content domain we are testing (thus enhancing content validity) and is sufficiently long to ensure some degree of reliability. Second, we can score the items quickly and with little if any scoring error, thereby meeting our needs for practicality and further promoting test reliability.

However, recognition items have disadvantages as well. For one thing, scores on recognition tests are usually higher than they should be as a result of guessing. For example, students taking a true-false test can get about 50 percent of the questions correct without knowing anything at all simply by picking "true" or "false" at random. A second disadvantage of recognition items is their tendency to measure knowledge of discrete facts rather than higher-level thinking skills such as application, synthesis, or problem solving. Finally, the very nature of such items, which ask students only to recognize correct information that is directly in front of them, is different from most real-world situations, which typically require people to recall that information from their own long-term memories.

Of the various recognition items we might use, most testing experts recommend multiple choice questions for at least two reasons. First, the number of items that students get correct simply by guessing is relatively low, especially in comparison with true-false items; for example, when items have four alternative answers, students can get only about 25 percent of them correct through guessing alone. Second, of all the recognition item types, the multiple-choice format lends itself most readily to measuring higher-level thinking skills (examples are presented in Chapter 16 of the textbook).

Constructing True-False Items

A true-false item is one for which the student must indicate whether a particular statement is true or false. Although testing experts generally do not recommend its use, it may sometimes be suitable when we want to measure students' knowledge of discrete facts relatively quickly. If true-false items are appropriate for your purpose, here are several guidelines to consider.

☂ <u>Rephrase statements presented in class or the textbook; don't state ideas in the identical wording that students have previously heard or read.</u> Regardless of what your instructional objectives are, you probably want your students to learn instructional material as meaningfully as possible. To test for meaningful learning (as well as to encourage students to engage in meaningful learning in the future), you should rephrase the ideas students have been studying when you present those ideas in your test items. When students know that test items will be taken word for word from class material, they will tend to study that material in a rote, verbatim fashion. When they instead know that you will check for understanding by using different words and phrases to express the same idea, they will be more likely to learn with understanding in mind.

- **Make statements clearly true or clearly false.** A knowledgeable student should be able to recognize each item as being definitely true or definitely false. When you write items that are "sort of" true or "possibly" false, then even your best students will resort to trying to guess what you had in mind when you wrote the questions rather than taking those questions at face value. Such guessing games lead to a higher error factor in students' test scores and therefore contribute to lower test reliability.

- **Use words with precise meanings.** Stay away from words that may have different meanings to different people. For example, avoid using words like *sometimes, usually,* or *often.* The words you use should mean the same things to your students that they do to you.

- **Avoid excessive use of negatives, especially for false statements.** Consider these true-false items:

    The south poles of two magnets don't repel each other.

    In the history of human civilization, the beginning of animal domestication was unrelated to human settlement patterns.

  Were these questions difficult for you to answer? Did the negatives (the *don't* in the first item and the *un-* in the second one) confuse you? Negative words and prefixes in true-false items (e.g., *no, not, never, un-, mis-*) often make these items unnecessarily confusing, particularly if the statements themselves are false (the "falseness" is yet another negative to contend with). By the way, both of my items above *are* false.

- **Include the authors or sources of controversial ideas.** Consider these true-false items:

    From a scientific standpoint, cold fusion cannot possibly occur.

    The best way to finish the end of a machine-sewn seam so that it doesn't unravel is to tie the two threads together in a square knot.

  The answer to each of these items is probably—"it depends on whom you talk to." Reputed scientists disagree about the possibility of cold fusion, and competent seamstresses have different methods of finishing the end of a seam (e.g., some prefer tying the two threads together, whereas others prefer sewing a second time over the last inch or so of the seam). If you wish to measure students' knowledge of various opinions, begin your true-false statements with a qualifier such as this one:

    According to physicist Dr. Kevin Davis, cold fusion cannot possibly occur.

- **Make approximately half of the statements true and the other half false, and sequence the two types randomly.** Consider the experience of a former college student in one of his college classes:

    The instructor graded on a strict percentage basis (90% for an A, 80% for a B, and so on) and used only true-false items on weekly tests. It soon became apparent that about 85% of the items were true. Most of us went through the test rapidly, marking only the obvious false items F and all others T. By playing the probabilities, we obtained our B with no studying. The instructor—and unfortunately several students—never understood how we could complete the tests so rapidly, yet do so well (Brown, 1981, p. 50).

  To increase the chances that students' test scores reflect what they actually know, a true-false test shouldn't have any consistent pattern of *T*s and *F*s.

Constructing Matching Items

A matching item presents two columns of words, phrases, or data; students must match each item in the first column with an appropriate item in the second. Matching items lend themselves most readily to assessing knowledge of "pairs"—countries and their capitals, vocabulary words and their meanings, and so on. If matching items are appropriate for your purpose, here are two guidelines to consider as you develop test items.

🍎 <u>Keep the items in each column homogeneous.</u> Consider this matching question from a world history test:

> Match each item on the left with its description on the right:
> 1. George Patton
> 2. The *Graf Spee*
> 3. Poland
> 4. 1941
>
> a. German battleship that sank numerous British ships
> b. Year in which the Japanese attacked Pearl Harbor
> c. Country invaded by Germany in 1939
> d. General who led American troops into Italy

Even if you know nothing about World War II, you should be able to match the items easily. After all, the first item in the left-hand column is a person, and there is only one description of a person on the right. Similarly, there is only one country, one year, and one "name of something" (in italics), so the question gives itself away. Instead, the items in each column should be homogeneous: They should all be members of the same category, whether the category be dates, generals, capital cities, or word definitions. By keeping the items similar to one another, you avoid giving clues to help students answer questions correctly when they know very little about the material being assessed.

🍎 <u>Have a different number of items in one column than in the other.</u> Consider this matching test for the human digestive system:

> Match each function with the component of the digestive system where that function occurs. Items on the right can be used only once.
> 1. Production of enzyme secreted to the mouth
> 2. Mixing of food with digestive enzymes
> 3. Production of bile
> 4. Production of insulin
>
> a. Pancreas
> b. Liver
> c. Stomach
> d. Salivary glands

Even if you don't know much about human digestion, you can probably identify some of the correct answers here. If you can figure out three of the four items correctly, you know the last one by a simple process of elimination. But consider an alternative version of the same question:

> Match each function with the component of the digestive system where that function occurs. Items on the right can be used more than once.
> 1. Production of enzyme secreted to the mouth
> 2. Mixing of food with digestive enzymes
> 3. Production of bile
> 4. Production of insulin
> 5. Storage place for food
>
> a. Colon
> b. Gall bladder
> c. Stomach
> d. Salivary glands
> e. Liver
> f. Large intestine
> g. Pancreas

Here's a case where the process of elimination doesn't help very much. Items on the right can be used more than once (and in fact "stomach" is the correct choice for both 2 and 5), and there are several extra terms on the right that aren't correct responses at all.

Constructing Multiple-Choice Items

A multiple-choice item includes a question or incomplete statement (the *stem*) followed by a series of alternatives. In most cases, a multiple-choice item is written so that only one alternative correctly answers the question or completes the statement; the other (incorrect) alternatives are known as *distractors*. If a multiple-choice format is appropriate for the knowledge or skills you wish to assess—and especially if you want to assess higher-level skills—here are several guidelines to keep in mind.

⚫ <u>Write distractors that are clearly wrong to students who know the material but are plausible to students who don't.</u> Distractors should not be obviously incorrect. Instead, they should reflect common errors that students make or frequent misunderstandings that they have. To illustrate, consider these two multiple-choice questions for an educational psychology test:

1. Which one of the following illustrates the typical duration of information in short-term memory?
   a. Arla looks up a phone number in the telephone directory. She dials the number and gets a busy signal. When she tries to dial the number again about ten seconds later, she realizes she's already forgotten the number.
   b. Berta remembers a formula long enough to take a physics test of 40 questions. But an hour after the test is over, she can't remember the formula anymore.
   c. Carla learns how to spell *bicycle* on Monday morning and spells it correctly later that day. But on Wednesday's spelling test, she spells it incorrectly.
   d. Darla learns quite a bit about operant conditioning in her psychology class fall semester. But by the end of spring semester, she's forgotten what operant conditioning is.

2. John takes an achievement test and gets a percentile rank of 65. This score means that John has:
   a. Mastered course objectives
   b. Failed to master course objectives
   c. Performed better than 65 percent of the people who have taken the test
   d. Answered 65 percent of the questions correctly

The answer to the first question is *a*, because short-term memory (a.k.a. working memory) lasts less than a minute. The other three alternatives reflect students' common misconceptions about short-term memory—that it lasts a few minutes, a few hours, or a few weeks. The answer to the second question is *c*: John's score indicates that he has performed better than 65 percent of the people who have taken the test. Buried in the three distractors are two misconceptions that many students have—that a percentile rank reflects the number of items correctly answered, and that norm-referenced test scores can give us information about mastery and nonmastery. Students who do not completely understand course material often choose distractors that represent common errors and misconceptions.

⚫ <u>Avoid putting negatives in both the stem and the alternatives.</u> Having negatives such as *not* and *don't* in two places at once amounts to a double negative that students have trouble understanding. Consider this test question (modeled after one actually found in the test bank for an educational psychology textbook) as an example:

Which one of the following is *not* a characteristic of most gifted children (in comparison with their classmates)?
   a. They are not as old.
   b. They are physically uncoordinated.
   c. They do not feel uncomfortable in social situations.
   d. They do not perform poorly on standardized achievement tests.

Confused? It's difficult to sort through all the *not*s and *un*s in order to determine which statement is true and which three are false. The answer in this case is *b*: Contrary to a popular stereotype, students who are gifted are just as coordinated as their nongifted peers.

❖ Avoid using "all of the above" or "none of the above" as an alternative, especially as the correct alternative. My own experiences as a student test-taker have taught me that "all of the above" is the correct choice more frequently than we would expect by chance alone; it seems to provide a way for teachers to list several correct answers as alternatives without having to dream up some plausible incorrect answers. Similarly, my students frequently tell me that they have learned that, when in doubt, "all of the above" is usually correct.

"None of the above" is discouraged for a different reason. When we tell students to choose the "best" or "most accurate" answer and then give them the "none of the above" alternative, they may understandably become confused about their task. Should they choose the "best" of several imperfect possibilities, or can they default on the instructions by picking "none of the above"?

❖ Avoid giving logical clues about the correct answer. Do you remember the califractions quiz that you took in Chapter 16 (it appears in one of the "Experiencing Firsthand" exercises)? If you were shrewd, you were able to answer one question correctly simply by picking the only alternative that grammatically fit the stem. You could answer another question by eliminating three alternatives that all had the same meaning. Students who know little or nothing about the material being tested can sometimes answer multiple-choice questions by using such logical clues to the correct response (e.g., Petersen, Sudweeks, & Baird, 1990).

When students do well on a test even though they know little about the subject matter being assessed, their test scores have little validity. As a teacher, you will want to minimize the extent to which a multiple-choice question gives away its answer. Here are several ways you can avoid giving logical clues about the correct alternative:
- Make all alternatives grammatically consistent with the stem, so that each one, when combined with the stem, forms a complete sentence.
- Make all alternatives different in meaning from one another (don't present two or more alternatives that say essentially the same thing).
- Make all alternatives equally long and precise. (Teachers have a tendency to make the correct alternative longer and more specific than the others.)

Constructing Recall Test Items

Recall items require students to generate answers themselves; students must retrieve the information they need from their long-term memories with only minimal retrieval cues. Examples of recall items on a paper-pencil test are completion and short-answer questions, essays, and problems. Performance items—those asking students to demonstrate their knowledge and skills in a nonwritten manner—also qualify as recall items.

Some recall items have only one correct response; consider these short answer questions as examples:

Who was the prime minister of Great Britain during World War II (give both his first and last names)?

How many feet are in a mile?

We can score such items as objectively and reliably as true-false, matching, and multiple-choice questions. But other recall items may yield variability in the answers students give, such as the following questions are likely to do:

Why does Shakespeare's Lady MacBeth keep washing her hands?

What is an *amphibian*?

When we have open-ended questions that different students can answer somewhat differently, we have to make decisions about which responses are right and which are wrong; thus, we must inevitably score these items more subjectively.

Recall items have two main advantages. First, they allow us to assess higher-level skills more easily than recognition items do; if our instructional objectives include such skills, recall items will often be a better choice. Second, the "recall" nature of such items more closely matches real life: We rarely have the benefit of a multiple-choice format at home or in the workplace.

Yet we should also note two disadvantages to using recall items. First, because students will often require considerable time to respond to questions, we will be able to ask fewer questions in a single testing session (affecting reliability) and tap a more limited sample of the content domain (affecting content validity). Second, we will typically take longer to score such items (a practicality issue) and make more errors in scoring them (an additional reliability issue).

Constructing Short-Answer and Completion Items

A short-answer item is one that poses a question to be answered with a single word or number, a phrase, or a couple of sentences. A completion item is one that presents an incomplete sentence with a "blank" for a student to fill in. Both item types lend themselves most readily to measuring lower-level skills. There are two guidelines to keep in mind as you write such test items.

- ☛ Indicate the type of response required. For example, if you want students to include both the first and last names of Great Britain's prime minister during World War II—"*Winston Churchill*" rather than just "Churchill"—you should say so. If you want students to include the unit of measure in their answer to the question about a mile—"5280 *feet*" rather than just "5280"—you should tell them that as well.

- ☛ For completion items, include only one blank per item. Too many blanks in a completion item make it difficult to understand. To see what I mean, try filling in the blanks in this statement concerning material presented in Chapter 16 of the textbook:

    Constructing an assessment instrument with high _____ _____ for the instructional objectives of a lesson or unit can be accomplished by constructing a _____ that describes both the _____ and the _____ .

If you're having trouble filling in these blanks, you're not alone. There are too many blanks here to enable students to determine what information is being called for. (The answers that I had in mind for my somewhat ambiguous completion item are "content validity," "table of specifications," "topic to be covered," and "student behaviors related to each topic," or words to that effect.)

Constructing Essay Questions

An essay question requires a student to write a lengthy verbal response—at least a paragraph, and perhaps as much as several pages. Essays are especially useful when we want students to demonstrate higher-level skills in a written format—for example, when we want them to analyze a piece of literature, compare and contrast two points of view, or apply scientific principles in explaining a particular phenomenon. Following are several guidelines to keep in mind as you write essay questions.

🍎 <u>Have several essays requiring shorter responses rather than one essay requiring a lengthy response.</u> The more items a test includes, the more widely it can sample from the content domain it is designed to represent and the more reliable it is likely to be. In most situations, a test consisting of only one or two essay questions cannot cover the breadth of knowledge and skills that you expect your students to have acquired, and errors in your scoring may seriously impact the overall test scores. Unless you are confident that one or two essay questions *do* provide a representative sample of the domain being tested and, furthermore, that each question yields responses that can be scored consistently, you may want to consider one of two alternatives: (a) having several shorter essay questions or (b) combining one or two lengthy essays with other item types that can be answered quickly and easily.

🍎 <u>Give students a structure for responding.</u> You may remember essay tests you've taken that provided little information or structure about how to respond; for example, perhaps you had to respond to an item such as this one:

> List the causes of the American Civil War.

You may remember other tests that provided clear guidance about the nature of the responses required, such as this item does:

> Identify three policies or events between 1850 and 1860 that contributed to the outbreak of the American Civil War. For each of the three things you identify, explain in three to five sentences how it increased tension between the North and the South.

When you ask a totally unstructured question (such as my first question about the causes of the American Civil War), your students' responses may go in so many different directions that you will have difficulty scoring them consistently and reliably. Especially in situations where a great deal of material is potentially relevant to a question, you should give your students some guidance about the length and completeness of the desired response and about the things they should specifically address. My second essay question concerning the Civil War illustrates how you might guide students toward responding in particular ways without necessarily giving the answer away. When all students follow a similar structure in responding to a question, you can score their responses more objectively and reliably.

🍎 <u>Ask questions that can clearly be scored as correct or incorrect.</u> Consider these essay questions:

> How can the dilemma of the world's diminishing rain forests best be solved?

> Which one of these three artists—Renoir, Monet, or Degas—was the best French Impressionist, and why?

The problem with both questions is that they ask for opinions that are difficult to score as right or wrong. This is not to say that we must limit our essay items to those with only one correct answer. Consider these alternative versions of my "rain forest" and "artist" items:

> Develop and explain a possible solution to the problem of the world's diminishing rain forests. Show how your solution addresses at least two of the economic, social, or political factors contributing to rain forest devastation.

> Choose one of these three artists: Renoir, Monet, or Degas. Describe how the artist's works incorporated: (1) components common to many French Impressionists and (2) components unique to the particular artist.

A response to the question on rain forests can be judged on the basis of how well the proposed solution addresses contributing factors to deforestation (factors that were presumably described in class or the textbook). A response to the second question can be judged on the basis of how accurately a student compares the chosen artist's work with the works of other Impressionists.

 Determine your criteria for scoring responses. At the same time that you write an essay question, you should also determine your criteria for scoring students' responses to it. To maximize the likelihood of scoring the responses reliably, you should, at a minimum, list the components that a correct response must include. You might even develop an "ideal" response to the question—one you can eventually show students as you provide feedback about their test performance.

Constructing Problems

A problem test item requires students to manipulate or synthesize data and develop a solution to a new problem situation. We most typically see this item type as word problems in mathematics, but we can develop them for other subject areas as well; here are some examples for science:

> You have a four-liter container of hot water (60°C) and a one-liter container of cold water (10°C). If you mix the water in the two containers together, what temperature will the water be?

> Maria drops a small rubber ball from a second story window located 20 feet above the ground. Considering only gravity and ignoring other factors that might affect the ball's movement (such as air resistance), how long will the ball take to reach the ground?

If your instructional objectives include problem solving, you may wish to include problems in your classroom test, in which case you should keep two guidelines in mind.

 Use new examples and situations. When you present a problem that students have already seen in a textbook or solved in class, students may solve it correctly again without necessarily knowing how to apply the same procedures to situations they haven't seen before. In most cases, you will want your students to be able to apply procedures and principles to virtually *any* situation, so you should check for their ability to do so by giving them situations they haven't already encountered.

 Include irrelevant information as well as information necessary to solve the problem. What is the area of this parallelogram?

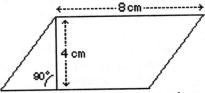

Even if you have completely forgotten how to compute the area of a parallelogram, you may be able to figure out how to solve the problem by virtue of the fact that only two pieces of information are given in the problem statement. Because areas are typically calculated through multiplication, you may have correctly obtained the solution of 32 square centimeters simply by multiplying the two numbers included in the figure.

But now imagine that you see this figure instead:

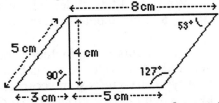

If you couldn't remember how to determine the area of a parallelogram, you would undoubtedly have a more difficult time with the problem in this form because of all the extra information provided.

Although we don't necessarily want to make problems more difficult for students to solve, we *do* want to make them as true to real life as possible. And the fact is, real life usually presents a great deal of information irrelevant to the solution of specific problems. Part of successful problem solving is knowing what information is necessary and what information *isn't,* and the problems we present to students on our tests should reflect this fact.

Arranging Test Items

Once we have written our test items, we need to put them together in a particular order. To put our students at ease, we may want to present easier items at the beginning of the test. When students begin a test with easy items—with items they can answer—they will probably approach the rest of the test with more self-confidence and less anxiety than would be true if they were to encounter an exceedingly difficult question right off the bat. Other things being equal, students perform better on tests when items are arranged in order from easy to difficult (Gronlund, 1993; Sax & Cromack, 1966).

In addition, we should probably place items that can be answered quickly (e.g., multiple-choice and matching) at the beginning of the test, leaving items requiring lengthy responses (e.g., essays and problems) for the end. Some students approach tests very strategically, answering quick and easy items first regardless of the order in which the items are sequenced. But other students answer items in the order they appear, sometimes spending so much time on one question (perhaps a lengthy essay) that they leave little time to tackle other, shorter items. By placing the quick-response items at the beginning, we increase the chances that *all* students will give us their best effort on the test.

Setting Parameters for Students' Responses

Students cannot always read our minds about what we expect them to do in response to the questions we ask on a paper-pencil test. So in addition to constructing test items, we should develop test directions (either included in written form on the test itself or described verbally in class) that describe how students should respond. Such directions should include several pieces of information:

- <u>Time limits</u>: We should tell students whether or not they have a limited amount of time to complete the test. And when some items require lengthy responses, we may want to give guidelines about how long to spend on each question.
- <u>Nature of desired responses</u>: There is often more than one way to respond to a test question, so we should specify exactly what we want students to do. For example, for each multiple-choice question, should students choose a single best answer or identify *all* correct alternatives? For matching questions, can students use each response only once or more than once? For essays, should students focus more on describing the things they have learned or on analyzing, synthesizing, and critiquing those things?
- <u>Method of recording responses</u>: We should tell students how and where to record their answers—whether on the test itself, a blank sheet of paper, or a specially prepared answer form.
- <u>Appropriateness of guessing</u>: A typical classroom includes some students who guess at test items they don't know and other students who leave items blank rather than guessing randomly. Because guessers will typically guess some correct answers, they will get higher test scores than nonguessers, even when the two groups of students know the same amount of material. To minimize differences in test scores due to guessing, we may want to encourage all students to guess on questions they don't know. If we want to *dis*courage students from

guessing, we should inform students about any penalties for incorrect answers (Brown, 1981; Popham, 1990; Ruggiero, 1988).

To get a representative sample of a broad content domain *and* to assess complex, higher-level skills within that domain, some teachers give a test with several lengthy items and allow students to choose the specific questions they will answer. For example, you have undoubtedly taken tests on which you were instructed to answer only one of two questions or to respond to three out of five items. Unfortunately, this practice of letting students answer some rather than all test questions creates several problems. First, we get different samples of behavior from different students (different students are in reality taking different tests), so the test scores we obtain are not comparable to one another. Second, some items will inevitably be more difficult than others, and students who have unwittingly chosen more difficult items will get lower test scores than those choosing the easier ones (another source of error affecting reliability). Finally, when students know in advance that they will be able to choose among test items, they will see less need to master all of the material being tested. Why struggle to understand the concept of convection or learn how to compute the area of a trapezoid if you know that you can avoid such things on a test simply by *not* choosing items that ask about them? Because of such problems, most testing experts advise us *not* to let students make choices about which test items they respond to.

Bww North
Grill & Bar
7 E. Woodruff Ave.
Columbus, OH 43201
614-291-2362

92943

CASHIER A Table **36**
Sat 11/15/03 10:52 AM Guests **1**

1	PATIO	0.00
1	[WAGNER]	0.00
1	6 WINGS	3.29
1	BSKT_CHP W/CHZ	3.99
1	CHEDDAR	0.00
1	20_OZ DRINK	1.49

SubTotal 8.77
Taxes... 0.59

Total 9 36

MASTERCRD Amount Applied 9.36

MASTERCRD Tendered 9.36

```
*********************************
*  Thank you for dining with us!  *
*  Any comments or suggestions,   *
*  please visit our website:      *
*                                 *
*  www.buffalowildwings.com       *
*                                 *
*       Or Write to us:           *
*                                 *
*   Buffalo Wild Wings, Inc.      *
*    1600 Utica Avenue South      *
*     Minneapolis, MN 55416       *
*                                 *
*********************************
```

Bww North

Grill & Bar
7 E. Woodruff Ave.
Columbus, OH 43201
614-291-2362

EMP: CASHIER A	MASTERCRD
Date 11/15/03	Time 10:52
Table 36	

Card Holder WAGNER/AILEEN J
Card Number XXXXXXXXXXXXX92124   XX/XX
Auth-Code.. 031115   Ctrl: 4015

Amount..   9.36

Tip....   _____

Total..   _____

X _____

Cardmember agrees to pay total in
accordance with agreement governing
use of such card.

*** Customer Copy ***

Supplementary Reading #3

CALCULATING STANDARD DEVIATIONS

The **standard deviation** (SD) of a set of test scores tells us how close together or far apart these scores are from one another; that is, it tells us the *variability* of the scores. Roughly speaking, the standard deviation tells us the *average distance* of scores from the mean. But more exactly, we take the following steps in order to calculate a standard deviation:

1. Calculate the *mean* for the scores. We calculate the mean by adding all the scores and then dividing by the total number of people involved. We'll use the symbol N for the total number of people and M for the mean.

2. Calculate the *difference* between each score and the mean. We'll use the symbol X for each score, so that $X - M$ equals the difference between each score and the mean.

3. Square each difference—in other words, multiply each difference by itself. This square is symbolized as $(X - M)^2$. Any negative numbers we obtained in Step 2 will become positive when we square them.

4. Add all the squared differences together. The symbol for adding things is Σ, so the total of the squared differences is $\Sigma(X - M)^2$.

5. Divide this total by the number of people (N).

6. Find the square root of the number obtained in Step 5 (most calculators have a square root function). We now have the standard deviation for our set of scores. We'll use the symbol *SD* for standard deviation.

The formula for calculating a standard deviation, which incorporates the steps I've just listed, is this:

$$SD = \sqrt{\frac{\Sigma(X - M)^2}{N}}$$

Let's look at how we can calculate the standard deviation for the heights of the 25 students in Ms. Oppenheimer's third-grade class (these are the same heights presented in Appendix C of the textbook), following the same six steps.

Step 1.   We divide the sum of all the heights (1250) by the number of people (25), so the mean height for Ms. Oppenheimer's class is 50.

Steps 2 & 3.   Following are the 25 third graders, their heights, the difference between each height and the mean (Step 2), and the square of that difference (Step 3).

Child	Height	**Step 2** Diff. from Mean $X - M$	**Step 3** Square of Difference $(X - M)^2$
Amy	47	3	9
Ben	50	0	0
Cal	52	2	4
Don	48	2	4
Eve	51	1	1
Fay	50	0	0
Gil	49	1	1
Hal	53	3	9
Ivy	49	1	1
Jan	55	5	25
Ken	51	1	1
Les	50	0	0
Max	48	2	4
Nan	49	1	1
Oly	49	1	1
Pat	46	4	16
Roy	53	3	9
Sal	51	1	1
Tom	50	0	0
Una	50	0	0
Val	52	2	4
Wil	47	3	9
Xan	50	0	0
Yul	51	1	1
Zek	49	1	1

Step 4.   We add all the squared differences together. When we add all the numbers in the right-hand column above, we get:

$$\Sigma(X - M)^2 = 102$$

Step 5.   We divide the total obtained in Step 4 by the number of people (or scores), like this:

$$\frac{\Sigma(X - M)^2}{N} = \frac{102}{25} = 4.08$$

Step 6.   We find the square root of the number we calculated in Step 5, like this:

$$\sqrt{4.08} = 2.02$$

We can summarize Steps 4 through 6 this way:

$$SD = \sqrt{\frac{\Sigma(X - M)^2}{N}} = \sqrt{\frac{102}{25}} = \sqrt{4.08} = 2.02$$

As you may have learned if you have read Appendix C in your textbook, you can interpret *standard scores*—IQs, ETS scores (e.g., SAT scores), stanines, and *z*-scores—only when you know both the mean and standard deviation of those scores. But you will encounter standard deviations in other contexts as well. For example, when educational researchers describe their research in professional journals, they typically provide information about the variability of students' performance—variability that is often summarized as a standard deviation. So as you continue to read the educational research literature in your field, you will undoubtedly see reference to this statistic time and time again.

Practice Exercises

Here are two problems in which you can practice the procedure for calculating standard deviations.

1. Fifteen students get the scores below on a geography quiz. What is the standard deviation of these scores?

9	10	4
4	6	8
6	6	9
8	7	8
5	10	5

2. Ms. White's class and Mr. Black's class both take a test over the same 20 spelling words on Friday. Which class has greater variability in its test performance? Answer this question by calculating standard deviations for each class.

Ms. White's Class	Mr. Black's Class
14	16
16	18
20	20
15	17
13	16
10	17
17	14
18	15
12	18
13	16
15	17
17	18
	19
	17

Answers to Practice Exercises

1. There are 15 scores, so $N = 15$. The total of all the scores is 105. Therefore, the mean of the scores is 105/15, or <u>7</u>. Here are $X - M$ and $(X - M)^2$ for each score:

Score	$X - M$	$(X - M)^2$
9	2	4
4	−3	9
6	−1	1
8	1	1
5	−2	4
10	3	9
6	−1	1
6	−1	1
7	0	0

10	3	9
4	−3	9
8	1	1
9	2	4
8	1	1
5	−2	4

The sum of the right-hand column, $\sum(X - M)^2$, is 58. Entering this value and N into the equation, we find that the standard deviation is the square root of 58/15, or <u>1.97</u>. The standard deviation for the 15 scores, then, is approximately 2.

2.   In Ms. White's class, there are 12 scores, so $N = 12$. The total of all the scores is 108. Therefore, the mean of the scores is 180/12, or <u>15</u>. Here are $X - M$ and $(X - M)^2$ for each score:

Score	$X - M$	$(X - M)^2$
14	−1	1
16	1	1
20	5	25
15	0	0
13	−2	4
10	−5	25
17	2	4
18	3	9
12	−3	9
13	−2	4
15	0	0
17	2	4

The sum of the right-hand column, $\sum(X - M)^2$, is 86. Entering this value and N into the equation, we find that the standard deviation is the square root of 86/12, or <u>2.68</u>.

In Mr. Black's class, there are 14 scores, so $N = 14$. The total of all the scores is 238, so the mean of the scores is 238/14, or <u>17</u>. Here are $X - M$ and $(X - M)^2$ for each score:

Score	$X - M$	$(X - M)^2$
16	−1	1
18	1	1
20	3	9
17	0	0
16	−1	1
17	0	0
14	−3	9
15	−2	4
18	1	1
16	−1	1
17	0	0
18	1	1
19	2	4
17	0	0

The sum of the right-hand column, $\sum(X - M)^2$, is 32. Entering this value and N into the equation, we find that the standard deviation is the square root of 32/14, or <u>1.51</u>.

When we compare the standard deviations of the two classes, we find that Ms. White's class has greater variability.

REFERENCES

Airasian, P. W. (1994). *Classroom assessment* (2nd ed.). New York: McGraw-Hill.

Alleman, J., & Brophy, J. (1997). Elementary social studies: Instruments, activities, and standards. In G. D. Phye (Ed.), *Handbook of classroom assessment: Learning, achievement, and adjustment*. San Diego: Academic Press.

Ansley, T. (1997). The role of standardized achievement tests in grades K-12. In G. D. Phye (Ed.), *Handbook of classroom assessment: Learning, achievement, and adjustment*. San Diego: Academic Press.

Boykin, A. W. (1994). Harvesting talent and culture: African-American children and educational reform. In R. J. Rossi (Ed.), *Schools and students at risk: Context and framework for positive change*. New York: Teachers College Press.

Brown, F. G. (1981). *Measuring classroom achievement*. New York: Holt, Rinehart & Winston.

Buckhout, R. (1974). Eyewitness testimony. *Scientific American*, *231*(6), 23-31.

Darling-Hammond, L. (1991). The implications of testing policy for quality and equality. *Phi Delta Kappan*, *73*, 220-225.

Durost, W. N. (1961). How to tell parents about standardized test results. *Test Service Notebook*, No. 26. New York: Harcourt, Brace, & World.

Gronlund, N. E. (1993). *How to make achievement tests and assessments* (5th ed.). Boston: Allyn & Bacon.

Hiebert, E. H., & Raphael, T. E. (1996). Psychological perspectives on literacy and extensions to educational practice. In D. C. Berliner & R. C. Calfee (Eds.), *Handbook of educational psychology*. New York: Macmillan.

Jencks, C., & Crouse, J. (1982). Should we relabel the SAT ... or replace it? In W. Shrader (Ed.), *New directions for testing and measurement: Measurement, guidance, and program improvement*, No. 13. San Francisco: Jossey-Bass.

Lindsay, D. S. (1993). Eyewitness suggestibility. *Current Directions in Psychological Science*, *2*, 86-89.

Loftus, E. F. (1991). Made in memory: Distortions in recollection after misleading information. In G. H. Bower (Ed.), *The psychology of learning and motivation: Advances in research and theory*, Vol. 27. San Diego: Academic Press.

Loftus, E. F. (1992). When a lie becomes memory's truth: Memory distortion after exposure to misinformation. *Current Directions in Psychological Science*, *1*, 121-123.

Marzano, R. J., & Costa, A. L. (1988). Question: Do standardized tests measure general cognitive skills? Answer: No. *Educational Leadership*, *45* (8), 66-71.

Nelson, T. O., & Dunlosky, J. (1991). When people's judgments of learning (JOLs) are extremely accurate at predicting subsequent recall: The "delayed-JOL effect." *Psychological Science*, *2*, 267-270.

Nichols, P. D., & Mittelholtz, D. J. (1997). Constructing the concept of aptitude: Implications for the assessment of analogical reasoning. In G. D. Phye (Ed.), *Handbook of academic learning: Construction of knowledge*. San Diego: Academic Press.

Ormrod, J. E. (1989). *Using your head: An owner's manual*. Englewood Cliffs, NJ: Educational Technology Publications.

Petersen, G. A., Sudweeks, R. R., & Baird, J. H. (1990, April). *Test-wise responses of third-, fifth-, and sixth-grade students to clued and unclued multiple-choice science items*. Paper presented at the American Educational Research Association, Boston, MA.

Popham, W. J. (1990). *Modern educational measurement: A practitioner's perspective* (2nd ed.). Englewood Cliffs, NJ: Prentice Hall.

Ricks, J. H. (1959). On telling parents about test results. *Test Service Bulletin*, No. 59. New York: Psychological Corporation.

Ruggiero, V. R. (1988). *Teaching thinking across the curriculum*. New York: Harper & Row.

Sax, G. (1989). *Principles of educational and psychological measurement and evaluation* (3rd ed.). Belmont, CA: Wadsworth.

References

Sax, G., & Cromack, T. R. (1966). The effects of various forms of item arrangements on test performance. *Journal of Educational Measurement, 3*, 309-311.

Stevens. J. J., & Clauser, P. (1996, April). *Longitudinal examination of a writing portfolio and the ITBS*. Paper presented at the annual meeting of the American Educational Research Association, New York.

Stiggins, R. J. (1997). *Student-centered classroom assessment* (2nd ed.). Upper Saddle River, NJ: Merrill/Prentice Hall.

Weaver, C. A., III, & Kelemen, W. L. (1997). Judgments of learning at delays: Shifts in response patterns or increased metamemory accuracy? *Psychological Science, 8*, 318-321.

Worthen, B. R., & Spandel, V. (1991). Putting the standardized test debate in perspective. *Educational Leadership, 48*(5), 65-69.